MW00713199

THE BLUE ENAMEL CUP

An MK's China Legacy

Rosalie Hall Hunt (signature)

ROSALIE HALL HUNT

The Blue Enamel Cup: An MK's China Legacy

Copyright © 2022 Rosalie Hall Hunt

All Rights Reserved

Cover Photo:
The blue enamel cup is held by the author's great-grandson Bobby, against a background of Yangzhou, China, her first home.

Cover Design: Eric J. Hudiburg, Justusproductions.org

ISBN 978-1-955295-08-6

Greenville, South Carolina

PUBLISHED IN THE UNITED STATES OF AMERICA

Endorsements for *The Blue Enamel Cup*

Rosalie and Bob Hunt have inspired me throughout my adult life. *The Blue Enamel Cup* continues the story of their love of Christ, missions and the Chinese people. The story is exhilarating, inspiring and deeply touching. I cried as I read sections of it; perhaps you will, too.

Taylor Field, Send Relief Missionary, NAMB
Founder and Director Emeritus, Graffiti, New York City
Author of Relentless: The Path of Holding On

With each new book, Rosalie Hunt pulls back the curtain and invites you into the intimate details of living a missionary life. *The Blue Enamel Cup: An MK's China Legacy* is especially intriguing as Rosalie takes us back home to China. Your heart will be overwhelmed at the reunions and the reminder of the importance of our missionaries' tasks.

Candace McIntosh, Executive Director
Alabama Woman's Missionary Union

Every time I read one of Rosalie Hunt's books, I find myself knowing more, understanding more, loving more — more history and legacy, purpose and commitment of the foremothers of missions, my own passion.

But, with *Six Yellow Balloons,* my heart was touched and stirred by Rosalie's own story as a missionary kid and then as a young woman in love, preparing to go as a missionary herself. And now comes *The Blue Enamel Cup,* the rest of the story. You will laugh, you will cry, you will again "fall in love" with Rosalie's writing.

Ruby Fulbright, Missionary 1974-1986, Zambia, Africa
Executive Director Emeritus, North Carolina Woman's Missionary Union

While this is the story of one missionary family, it is also a story about *all* missionary families. If you have served on the field or supported a family member who has, you will relate, understand and reminisce about your own experiences as you read this excellent book. Or, if like me, you have supported God's mission through His missionaries all your life, you need to read this book to better understand the call, the commitment and the courage of every missionary who has followed God's leadership, whether across the ocean or just across the street. Perhaps through this book, we can more easily grasp the sacrifices and joys of living on mission with God.

David George, President
Woman's Missionary Union Foundation, SBC

With a monumental missions inheritance as a foundation, and an unshakable pursuit of personal faith, the Hunt family set out on an adventure that unleashed the power of God across thousands of miles and touched countless lives for His kingdom. This book confirms what I have always known: Rosalie Hall Hunt has a tenacious conviction to run toward God with all her heart. You will be inspired by these stories of living vibrantly through radical obedience to His call.

Sandy Wisdom-Martin, Executive Director-Treasurer
Woman's Missionary Union, SBC

Rosalie has done it again. Her storytelling ability takes you on a journey, *her* journey. You can see the places she describes, smell the fragrances, hear the beautiful languages, feel the fear of experiencing an earthquake, and enjoy the excitement of going to a new country.

Connie Dixon, President
Woman's Missionary Union, SBC

Rosalie Hall Hunt is a gifted storyteller. I eagerly await each book she writes, both for the history she shares and for the lessons I take away from each story. It is no different with *The Blue Enamel Cup: An MK's China Legacy*. I invite you to read, to learn, and to be challenged by this MK's story.

Laurie Register, Executive Director-Treasurer
South Carolina Woman's Missionary Union

DEDICATION

To Bobby, and all the great-grands who will follow:
This is a portion of your legacy. The rest will be yours to write.

TABLE OF CONTENTS

FOREWORD

It was the late 1990s and my ability to grasp the opportunities in front of me seemed inadequate. The who, what, when and where made sense, but the why and how shied away from the foreground, preferring to remain a bit blurry.

The nearly two and a half years I had spent serving on the mission field truly changed me. God opened my eyes to the condition of the world and expanded my ability to love and care beyond what I thought could be possible. Career missionaries, fellow short-term missionaries, my home church family, family and friends back in Alabama, the new friends I met on the field and the local faith family who adopted me all poured into my life.

With a keen awareness of the importance of missions, a confirmed sense of calling and an "only God could do this" next step, I should have tackled the transition from the field to my next assignment with complete confidence. I struggled to find my footing, however.

Then Rosalie Hall Hunt entered the scene. A treasure trove of stories about life on the mission field and a mesmerizing style of storytelling, she almost didn't seem real. How could one person pack all she has experienced into one lifetime — and bring even the most routine of moments to vivid, high-def impact? To be honest, I'm still working to figure her out, but it is Rosalie's ability to transport us inside every story she shares that captivated my attention and drew me to her.

The more I listened, read and observed, the more I realized Rosalie's storytelling ability takes us on a journey beyond the scenes she shares. She helps us see ourselves and what God is doing in the world around us. Her words surface the importance of passing our stories on to ensure we all understand our worth and the value of others — that we all belong and have a role. Rosalie also helps us see how God is at work, even when we don't understand.

In an almost seamless shift soon after my first encounter with Rosalie, the why and how of my journey came into focus. She has remained among my most encouraging of mentors for more than twenty-five years now. Let her become the same for you through *The Blue Enamel Cup: An MK's China Legacy* and its counterpart, *Six Yellow Balloons: An MK's China Story*.

Jennifer Davis Rash
President and Editor-in-Chief
TAB Media Group
(The Alabama Baptist and The Baptist Paper)

Preface

Whatever made me think I could encompass a century and a quarter of family history and living in a simple one-volume work? Somehow, it just didn't happen. *Six Yellow Balloons: An MK's China Story,* was the beginning, as I explored the early years of my parents' lives and that of my Aunt Grace Wells, how they ended up in China and how God used their lives there. It became an odyssey of discovery for me — fascinating new insight into Dad and Mama's lives and hearts, and the saga of Aunt Grace and her thirty years in China.

Digging into family history was exhilarating; it was captivating; it was painful; it was amusing; it was sad; it was an experience that made me newly thankful that we serve a God of the second chance, who loves us just as we are and wants us to be our highest best for His honor. *Six Yellow Balloons* tells the story from 1897 to 1962, and this volume explores 1962 until 2010. Our two children grew up as MKs (missionary kids), blessed by two worlds, and facing challenges many American children never even consider. They emerged from it stronger and more resilient because of what they saw, learned, felt, and experienced. I love being an MK, and when an MK meets *another* MK, we feel an instant bond — even if we have lived on the other side of the world from them.

The Blue Enamel Cup: An MK's China Legacy is necessarily our children's story as well. It's the story of the various mission fields where we lived and served, and the story of incredible people in each of those countries who blessed and enriched our lives. From Taiwan, we moved to Hong Kong, to mainland China, next to the Philippines, to Australia, then on to Singapore, Malaysia, and India before going back to the Philippines. In most countries, we served primarily with Chinese people. They are part of our hearts and DNA. This is also continuing our parents' story, for the larger sacrifice was theirs — in seeing their children leave to go to the other side of the world, and taking their grandchildren with them. For my parents, it was sacrifice in reverse. Long before, they had lost family time with their parents, and now we were taking *their* only grandchildren far away. In retrospect, however, I don't think any of us would have changed it.

The joy of reunions with friends and coworkers from the early years in China was far more wonderful than we could ever have imagined. Trips to China in 1983, 1984, 1985, then living there in 1986, plus frequent visits in the next decade, were like beautiful gifts and just a touch of what the joy of reunions in heaven may be like. What a privilege and honor to have made these pilgrimages and experienced the inexpressible joy of being together again after nearly forty years. These were a serendipitous link in our Baptist legacy, one that spanned the globe and two centuries. Come along on the journey, and let's go home to China.

THE BLUE ENAMEL CUP

An MK's China Legacy

Bob, Alice and Jody in front of the Hunts' first apartment in Taipei

ONE

THE ADVENTURE BEGINS
1962

The giant engines of the British Airways (BOAC) 707 jet roared in preparation for takeoff. I sat with an excited three-year-old Alice on one side, and on the other, our six-month-old Jody was ensconced in his infant seat. Just beyond the baby was Bob with a gleam of anticipation in his eyes. Controlling my emotions was a challenge; all sorts of thoughts and feelings were running into each other in my head, rather like butterflies out of control. After all these years, here we were — actually beginning the journey to which both Bob and I had felt led for years. Looking out the jet's window, my mind was visualizing the last time I left for the Far East. In 1946, I was eight when our family sailed on the *SS General Gordon,* on our way home to China, the land of my earliest memories. I vividly recall the excitement of that faraway morning. Now on this March morning of 1962, I was *flying* with my family to what would be our home in Taiwan, Republic of China.

The eight-year-old Rosalie had packed in her footlocker six yellow balloons filled with American air. This time around, instead of balloons, I was taking rich memories in my heart and relishing the thoughts of renewing memories of China in our new location. (In 1962, Taiwan was about as close to mainland China as foreigners were allowed to go.) I also had my cherished little blue enamel cup, a relic of my first birthday in Yangzhou, China. This would be the blue cup's third time across the Pacific Ocean, symbolizing for me a tangible piece of my first home that was returning to its roots.

I looked over at Alice who was grinning with glee at her "big adventure." She reached out to grasp my hand and said, "Mommy, we are really, really going on this giant airplane!" I joined in her excitement, happy that she was not frightened but rather delighting in her biggest thrill to date. Then glancing at Jody, I gave thanks that he was sound asleep, hoping his nap would last as long as possible. This would be a long and tiring trip for little ones.

Goodbyes had been extremely difficult, but experience had warned me it would be this way. The toughest part was saying goodbye to Mama and Dad at the Wichita airport. They were watching their only grandchildren go 10,000 miles away for five years. Mama controlled her tears as she gave the little ones a last fierce hug, but I could see the iron control she was exerting over her emotions. Dad coughed repeatedly and blew his nose. Both were brave. On the other hand, I was the one who nearly gave way to the anguish of farewells. After the flight was well underway and the children settled, there was finally time to sit quietly and let tears roll down my cheeks. For this moment, Bob and I had longed and planned and prayed. But, even in the certainty of knowing God was leading us, the actual leaving was a wrench.

In those quiet moments, I thought about the contrast between going as a third grader leaving on a new adventure with that of traveling as a wife and mother with responsibilities. Time to ponder life was short, however, with two small children who demanded attention in the subsequent two days to keep both Bob and me well occupied. In Tokyo, we had a huge surprise, for missionary Lucy Smith, "Aunt Lucy" from my childhood in China, met our plane and showed us around Tokyo for the short time we were there.

The following day, with determination, a touch of trepidation, and a heaping helping of exhilaration, we made the last leg of the trip from Tokyo to Taipei, not knowing just what to expect, but knowing we were expected. As the plane came in for a landing at Taipei International Airport, it was hard to say who was most excited. In the 1960s, Taipei's airport was still small enough that those welcoming family or friends could get close to the runway and watch passengers disembark from behind a tall wire fence. Bob had Alice tightly by the hand, and I held a wide-awake Jody as we stepped down the ramp and headed toward the terminal and customs. Looking eagerly around us, we saw scores of people standing behind a wire fence, eagerly waiting to greet family and friends.

However, as we drew closer, it appeared that a good half of them were actually standing there with signs and waving at the newest additions to the Taiwan Baptist Mission. And wonder of wonders, as we drew close, I even recognized some faces, for there was Martha Franks standing by Olive Lawton, both old China hands and classmates of Mama. When Martha Franks first looked at Jody, she exclaimed, "Harold Hall!" She found the resemblance uncanny. Next to them, longtime family friends Pearl Johnson and Jennie Alderman. Pearl likewise took one look at Jody and said, "This baby looks like his grandfather Harold!" Also near the front of the crowd were Carl and Jeanette Hunker, who had been new missionaries to China during Dad and Mama's last term there. The Culpeppers, yet another part of my childhood memories — for Dr. and Mrs. Culpepper had visited us in Zhenjiang in the 1940s, and later, the younger Culpeppers, Charles J. and Donal — had come as well. All four were here to greet us. We were also welcomed by several Chinese Baptist leaders, making the whole arrival experience especially meaningful.

Bob was a little perturbed with customs, feeling impatient with the long wait and exhaustive inspection of our luggage. Recalling the hassles of Shanghai in the turbulent war years, this seemed fairly simple to me, although the inspectors went over all our luggage, even taking Alice's little stuffed animal and unzipping the pouch in its tummy, I guess to check for contraband. Alice looked anxious until the inspector reached over and, with a smile, placed it back in her arms. Finally, we joined the waiting mission family, which became a blur of names and faces. The MKs in the group surrounded Alice with a welcome all their own. Then the Hunkers whisked us away to their home on the seminary campus where we could spend our first week.

Taipei traffic defied description, with buses, trucks, bikes, motorbikes, a sea of red taxis, and masses of cars moving in both directions, more than half of them with blaring horns. Alice was wide-eyed, and we were much the same. That first time we navigated the narrow road leading to the seminary — bicycles, pedestrians, and coolies carrying heavy loads on poles all crowding the road — we got a touch of culture shock. Nonetheless, the scents of spices, Chinese cooking, and a plethora of unidentifiable fragrances assaulted our senses, and, again, I felt at home. It smelled like China. The noise of honking horns mixed with voices speaking Mandarin was loud and high-pitched but sounded like music to my ears. I caught a familiar word or so, and my heart would skip a beat with excitement. When we arrived at the Hunkers' comfortable home on the side of Seminary Hill, their household help greeted us with the familiar Chinese welcome: *Hwan Ying Hwan Ying*. To be able to answer them in simple Chinese phrases was a comfortable feeling, and they seemed just as gratified as I. Feeling connected became a wonderfully recurrent experience those first weeks; this felt natural. We belonged.

Dr. Hunker was a much-loved professor at the seminary and would later serve as its president. He and Jeanette took a lot of time that first week to help us run errands, get our freight out of customs, and settle in the house designated for our use. Our first order of business was to get in a home and begin language study.

Grace Baptist Church compound — across the boulevard from Tai Da, Taiwan's most prestigious university — included a large structure known as the mission triplex. Lovingly nicknamed the "monstrosities," the triplex provided homes for three mission families. We were to live in the middle unit — with Josephine Ward and Ola Lea on one side, and Hunter and Patsy Hammett on the other. Our eyes grew wide when we first walked in the entrance and stood in the living/dining room. We quickly dubbed it the Hunt football field. Seriously, it was about half the length of a football field, and for some unknown reason, we decided to carpet its terrazzo floor with *tatami* (rice straw) matting. Soon it even *smelled* like a football field. I have vivid memories of our first earthquake in Taipei in that room. That cold winter afternoon, Jody and I were alone in the living room huddled around a little kerosene space heater while I read him a story. The floor, the walls, and all the furniture began to sway. Grabbing Jody, I watched in horror as the kerosene heater began swaying wildly. I ran to a far corner and covered Jody with my body as the tremors kept going. He was squalling by this time — but, thank God, the tremors stopped, and the heater righted itself. We had more moments of earthquakes in our years on *Ilha Formosa* (Beautiful Island), but none quite as terrifying as that first one in a monster of a building that rocked uncontrollably.

The "old China hands" welcomed us warmly, as did the newer appointees like the Hammetts next door. Their son, Joel, was a little older than Alice, and they quickly became buddies. The residents of Grace compound, particularly the church's staff and our neighbors, helped make our adjustment easier. A special piece of Baptist history also lived on the compound — Juliette Mather. Hers was one of the names of national WMU leaders that I had memorized as a young GA — and now, here she was, retired from national WMU, teaching in the university and quickly becoming beloved "Aunt Juliette" to our new MKs. Juliette was part of every birthday and celebration we had our first years on the island.

Along with Juliette was Lillian Lu, a Baptist institution in Taiwan. She

was originally from Shanghai, and the fruit of the ministry of the iconic
missionary Inabelle Coleman, who, as an English teacher at the University
of Shanghai (where Mama had taught her first three years in China), led
countless students to faith — including the two leaders of Taiwan's largest
Baptist church, Grace. Lillian Lu was both musician and student center
director. The other was Dr. Jou (Chou) Lien Hwa, pastor of Grace Church.
He was also personal pastor to Taiwan's president, Generalissimo Chiang
Kai-shek and his wife, Soong Mei-ling. Both Lillian and Dr. Chou were to
have a profound influence on our lives.

Our first order of business was to get into language study. Bob and I
decided that first quarter to study in the same class. For intensive language
study, no more than three in a class is ideal. Bob and I began studying in
the same class. Our language challenges were unique to our backgrounds.
Since I had automatically heard and spoken it as a child, Chinese was never
"foreign" to my ears, and the tones seemed to come naturally. I was also
beginning with a rudimentary vocabulary. On the other hand, Bob faced
the "Southern" challenge, as we dubbed it. One of our first assignments
was to learn the numbers: 1, 2, 3, and so forth. Tones are most important in
saying the right thing. The same sound in the four tones of Mandarin can
mean four entirely different things. Bob declared that it was an additional
handicap to be from the Sand Mountain area of Alabama. The first three
numbers are *Yi, Er, San.* The number three is pronounced like "Sahn." Bob,
in Sand Mountain style, would automatically say "Saan" and drawl it out.
Although tones are perplexing and difficult, Mandarin is truly a beautiful,
musical language. We soon realized, if we wanted to stay happily married,
it might be smart to study in different classes. That we did, right away. It
worked. We have remained happily married sixty-four years and counting.

I began studying at home, and it worked for both of us. He thrived in
the classroom setting — and studying one-on-one was comfortably familiar
to me, because I had studied that way in China as a child. Most of our
teachers were from Peking and spoke beautiful Mandarin, the standard for
the nation. Tsung Syau Jye (Ms. Tsung, as she was professionally known),
was the wife of Colonel Shaw (later a general) in the Nationalist army. She

became a lifelong friend. (After retirement, the Shaws moved to Canada, and, some thirty years later, visited us in Alabama.)

Tsung Syau Jye was a tough taskmaster and would not let me get by with sloppy tones. The four tones of Mandarin are very important, because the same sound in a different tone means something totally different. The sound "ma" in the four tones can mean: *Mama, difficult, horse* or *scold.* It was too easy to accidentally say something quite ridiculous. Thankfully, most of the people with whom we served were very gracious and forgiving of our language mistakes. Not so Tsung Syau Jye. She was a regular drill sergeant, as was true of our best teachers.

Bob and I still remember the loving counsel of one of our "old China hands" — as the younger missionaries identified those who had first been missionaries on mainland China prior to coming to Taiwan when the Communists took control of China. Martha Franks, Mama's college friend, and one of the "aunts" I lovingly remembered from childhood, told us a story that stayed with us and was frequently a comfort to recall. Martha, with her typical beautiful smile, said, "Let me tell you about two missionary colleagues of mine in the early years in Shantung Province. One," she recalled, "had the most beautiful Chinese language of any missionary I have ever known. It just flowed and was admired by all. The other," and she paused and smiled, "struggled from day one. His language was choppy, sometimes monotone, and he continued to struggle, even long after his early language training. But," and Martha paused significantly, "he genuinely loved the people with whom he worked. They knew it. They could feel it. He was the one who made by far the greatest impact on our city, and he was the one who left the lasting mark." Recalling that story helped us to keep going on discouraging days.

Life moved at a different pace in Taiwan, and every day held its own unique challenges. Having household help was a necessity in 1962 Taiwan — otherwise, a missionary would spend the whole day just caring for children, cleaning, going to market every day, building a fire in the heater in order to have hot water, and on and on went the endless challenges. We were most fortunate in being able to secure Gai Shr Fu to cook for us. (*Gai* is the surname and *Shr Fu* refers to head cook.) Gai Shr Fu had worked for foreign families for years and was a splendid cook of both Chinese and American cuisine, as our scales told us all too soon. His wife, Lucy, did the housework, which allowed me time to study and prepare for the work I did on Sundays. Their daughter, Maria, took care of Alice and Jody during language study hours, so fortune smiled on us.

After we had been there a short while, Alice was able to begin a few hours a week in the wonderful preschool and kindergarten right across the compound at Grace Baptist Church. And of course, in typical childlike fashion, she picked up Mandarin quickly and flawlessly. Thankfully she never said to us, as did one little MK (missionary kid) to her language-school parents, "Chinese is so easy. What's wrong with you?" I well remember one early incident of those preschool days. As usual, each time Alice came home from school, I would ask about her day and what she had learned or what little snack they had. One noon she came in, and when asked about her snack, replied, "Mommy, we had raisin muffins today." Then she looked puzzled and with wrinkled brow, added, "But the raisins kept flying away."

As Alice began experiencing life in a new culture, her thought processes often sent me sailing back in my mind to the years in China and how I learned to be part of two cultures. Sometimes it occurs in unexpected ways. I clearly remember the day Alice came in from Grace preschool, crying. *Oh no,* I thought*, she has encountered prejudice.* I put my arms around her and said, "What's wrong, honey? Did someone hurt your feelings?"

"Oh, no, Mommy," and she sounded sad, "I want to know why I can't have straight black hair and eyes that look like my friends." I quickly tried to explain to her that we can't change the color or shape of our eyes and hair, but that we are all just the same on the inside. That worked. (And she has actually spent a lifetime working with others in helping them under-stand that on the inside we are all just alike.)

Another unforgettable moment happened in, of all places, a pedicab. Having grown up in China where rickshaws were a normal mode of trans-portation, I felt quite at home in any of the many pedicabs in Taipei. A pedicab is one step up from the rickshaw, for a "pedicab man" is pedaling a bicycle to pull the cab, rather than having to hold two poles and run to transport his fare. Alice and I were riding home from the market in a pedicab manned by a strong young driver and enjoying the normal sights and smells around us. Out of the blue, Alice suddenly turned serious and asked, "Mommy, do you think this pedicab driver knows Jesus?" I shook my head a bit dubiously, "I doubt it, honey. So few people here know about Jesus." She looked puzzled, "But, Mommy, why don't you tell him, then?" This simple question from our child brought me up short. I silently prayed that God would remind me *every day* of the real reason why we were here.

Gai Shr Fu and Lucy with Alice and Jody

Alice with MK friends

Alice sings a Christmas carol for student fellowship

TWO

CULTURE SHOCK
1962

As we began to settle into a routine, I would often catch a few minutes after the children were tucked in at night to reflect on our new normal. Inevitably, I would compare life in Taiwan, Republic of China, in 1962 with life in China fifteen years earlier. To the ear, both places *sounded* much the same, with Chinese spoken on every hand. I loved the rhythmic cadence of Mandarin, beautiful and musical (and I was secretly glad that we were studying Mandarin — which was much more flowing and graceful, at least to my ears — rather than Taiwanese, with its eight tones and occasional guttural sounds).

The sounds, smells, scents, fragrances, and odors in Taiwan were also much the same as mainland China's. Taiwan had *benjos* (ditches that ran along beside the roads and sidewalks), and the smells emanating from them brought back all sorts of *Dà Lù* (mainland China) memories. Honey buckets were another bit of the familiar. These were the buckets of "night soil" coolies hauled from homes every morning to the rice paddies for fertilizer. Driving through the countryside with the window down right after a rice paddy had been fertilized was an experience that lingered long in the memory (and the nostrils). Whether in Taipei or Zhenjiang, the odor smelled the same.

One particular odor remains imprinted in my mind. Bob and I were with some coworkers and were walking through a newly planted rice paddy, stepping carefully along the narrow paths between paddies. A couple of times, we walked past areas where night soil was stored in giant vats so the farmers could conveniently fertilize newly planted rice seedlings. The odor was overpowering. As we passed one large vat, I held my nose and said to Bob, "If I ever fall in one of these, don't even bother to pull me out." His immediate retort was, "Don't worry. I won't!"

So many sights were identical as well, and late in the evening I would often attempt to decompress from language study and childcare or a busy Sunday and reflect on the lovely feeling of belonging. Taiwan never felt foreign, and that was a gift. Maybe it was just the feeling of being *connected*. There were the same elderly women with bound feet. So many affluent citizens had "refugeed" from China, and all around were women using a cane as they hobbled around on tiny feet. I never saw one of the ladies without a jolt of pity for the pain they were experiencing with every step they took.

Food was another similarity. Topping the list of food delights were the *shau bing* that I found at a little stall not many blocks from Grace compound. I took a deep (and fragrant) breath of satisfaction when discovering the little round black oven in front of a food shop near our compound. Here was another bit of Zhenjiang from my China memories: a man rolling, shaping, and slapping prepared oblongs of bread on the inner sides of the oven, then in just minutes using a long metal spatula to remove them, all crispy and brown, with crunchy sesame seeds emitting their unique fragrance. The bread just *invited* you to hurry up and have a taste. Shades of home — just like in Zhenjiang! Our children quickly developed a predilection for another morning treat: *yòu tyáur*, best described as savory fried doughnuts. They are about ten or more inches long, crispy, warm, and yielding just about as little nutrition as an American doughnut. *Yòu tyáur* became Alice and Jody's go-to treat.

I could also fall asleep at night remembering all the inviting culinary experiences we had nearly every week. It didn't help that Gai Shr Fu, our superb cook, could turn out exquisite entrées — tasting wonderful and looking like they were prepared for a glossy food magazine. He had the "gift." We never before or after tasted such perfect sweet and sour pork (though we are still trying sixty years later), Cantonese chicken with mushrooms, succulent beef and peppers, crispy spring rolls, and toffee bananas, quick fried and covered with syrup that instantly crystallizes them. Just going over a week's menu could bring on weight gain. (And it did that first year — as well as a stomach problem that demanded action.)

On the other hand, the extreme was also true, for there were dishes our stomachs could scarcely handle or contain. Feasts and banquets were a frequent mode of celebration for church groups, and we received many invitations. A real Chinese feast was a sight to behold — and some of the dishes, our occidental stomachs could scarcely handle. Usually at Chinese feasts, we noticed that dishes were brought out a few at a time, with always more to come. And more. We learned the hard way that you need to concentrate on one or two you liked — and that your stomach could handle — and try to politely pick at the others. Some, like sea slugs, field eel, entrails from various animals, pickled jelly fish, and 100-year-old eggs (just like the ones in Zhenjiang forty years earlier), we simply never learned to reconcile to our taste buds.

Bob and I decided pretty quickly in the process of banquet-going that it was a boon when our children were also invited. With some dishes, we could scarcely get past their appearance or smell. It was strategic to place Jody in a chair between the two of us. He was a willing recipient of anything put on his plate. Jody learned to use chopsticks right along with spoon and fork, and often used a single chopstick to spear some interesting-looking tidbit of food. Sea slugs were a dish Bob and I just never learned to swallow, literally. They came in a big steaming pot and looked like cut-up pieces of rubber tires swimming in an oily stew. It is very polite in Chinese culture to personally take care of your guests, so our host would use his or her chopsticks, select a delicacy, and place it on our plates. We would smile and nod and quietly slip it over to Jody's plate. As he swallowed those sea slugs, they looked like nothing so much as a bump-eldy piece of tire rippling down his throat. He thrived, however, and cheerfully did his part. Alice was older and more discerning, so we quickly learned she was not so cooperative.

The language was not as much a culture shock to me as it was for Bob, as is the usual case for those who had never heard spoken Chinese before. His language challenges and mine were different simply because our early backgrounds were so different. He thrived in the classroom setting, and I loved studying one-on-one with a teacher who focused on my particular language difficulties. It was strangely reminiscent of Mama teaching me in my room back in Zhenjiang, one-on-one, and that felt comfortable.

We did have some say in who our teachers were; that was another great thing about the Taipei Language Institute. Most of our instructors were from Peking and spoke perfect Mandarin, the standard for the nation. I was quickly able to request one or two specific teachers who had perfect tones.

Remembering the loneliness in Zhenjiang where there were so few other missionaries or anyone who spoke English, I could fully appreciate some pluses of Taiwan. We had a mission family here with us providing companionship, a listening and sympathetic ear, and occasional much-needed reprimands that kept us from making some silly mistakes. We had all ages and varieties of missionary coworkers. I delighted in knowing a good number from my childhood and often had to remind myself that they were now colleagues and I needed to listen and respond like an adult.

Our next-door neighbors on one side — Josephine Ward and Ola Lea — were friends from early China days and were nearing retirement. In fact, Ola retired our first year on the field, and Josephine moved to a small apartment because the Grace compound triplexes were too large for one person. Right after they moved, Charles Cowherd moved in. His wife and daughters were to follow six months later, so we rather adopted Charles, and he ate with us much of the time (and enjoyed Gai Shr Fu's cooking). Charles was another old friend of mine. He had been a new missionary to China when I lived in Zhenjiang. I remember one memorable weekend in 1948 when he visited Zhenjiang on his motorcycle and took me on the back of the cycle for a ride round the mountains surrounding the city. It was hair-raising. (Would you believe, years later when he lived in Hong Kong, we often visited him, and he drove around the curvy mountain roads around Kowloon in the same breathtaking manner. Our children quickly learned to hold on to the door handles when Uncle Charles was at the wheel.) In a few months, Marian Cowherd and their daughters Virginia (Ginny) and Geenie joined Charles in Taipei, where Marian and Charles did a refresher course in Mandarin.

The Cowherds' story would make a book of its own. In the 1930s, Marian and Charles had been engaged, but, shortly afterwards, broke up. Marian had then married Rufus Gray, a young missionary candidate. The Grays were appointed to China and started language school when World War II forced them to evacuate to the Philippines. Within months, the Grays were captured and interned in a prison camp by the Japanese who assumed control of the islands. Their infant son, William, was just a few months old when they were put in an internment camp. Rufus was tortured and killed, but Marian somehow managed to keep their baby alive under horrendous conditions. Following the Allied victory, a shattered Marian and Charles, just back from service on the war front in Europe, married and were appointed together for China. Both were still shell-shocked, and the following years were turbulent for the couple. We loved the Cowherds and learned much from their years of experience.

Fellowship in a mission station with some twenty or more other missionaries was a blessing, as was their custom of meeting each week for prayer meeting in one of our homes. These were the times when our commodious living room really came in handy. Bob and I were enriched by the wisdom of the "old China hands" and inspired by the experience and knowledge shared by a diverse group of chosen individuals brought together by the same calling. We took turns leading and hosting the meetings. Bob's first birthday in Taiwan was on the station prayer meeting day. Pearl Johnson was hosting the meeting, and we had a station picnic and a surprise cake for Bob. Pearl was one of a kind; I remembered that from knowing her in China when she was my "Aunt Pearl." Pearl was noted for speaking her mind. At Bob's surprise birthday, Pearl offered him a cup of coffee — to which Bob, tongue in cheek, responded, "I don't drink coffee. I'm a Christian." Not missing a beat, Pearl retorted, "I am, too, but *I* didn't let it make a fool of me!"

Station prayer meetings were times of prayer and fellowship, whereas the annual Taiwan Mission Meeting each year was more focused on the business of the mission. Nonetheless, special times of inspiration were the highlights of each summer's sessions. One couple who had been there about four years (and looked like seasoned pros to us) told us about their first mission meeting. The husband had spoken up pretty frequently to express his opinion, and after about his third remark, an "old China hand" with a well-deserved reputation for speaking her mind, rose to her feet, saying, "Sit down, young man. You don't know what you're talking about!" Whereupon he sat down. I clearly recall our first mission meeting, which was held at Yang Ming Shan Baptist Retreat grounds, on Yang Ming mountain just outside of Taipei. I sat in that meeting, remembering similar annual mission meetings as a child in Shanghai. After all, human nature doesn't change a whole lot from decade to decade. Here again, we were hearing a plethora of ideas, suggestions, and opinions. From many of the older missionaries, we kept hearing the phrase, "Back on the mainland, this or that." One of the younger missionaries piped up, remarking, "One of these days, we won't be *hearing* 'back on the mainland, we did this or that.'" I couldn't resist that opening, and spoke up, "However, I am younger than all of you, and I also lived on the mainland — so a long time from now, you may *still* hear the phrase, 'Back on the mainland.'" (Truth be known, we younger ones learned a great deal from those who had experienced so much.)

As the months passed, I began to understand a bit more about what it must have been like for Dad and Mama so many years before when they first went to China. We had so many conveniences now that they never had — but the essential China had not changed, and the needs of people's hearts were just as many and intense. Remembering how important it was to get mail and to maintain the family bond, I wrote home, and to Bob's parents and friends, at least twice a week. Family in America returned the favor and kept the mail and news coming. It was balm to our hearts and helped us step over many a bump in the road of adjustment. Furthermore, we now had airmail and did not have to wait so long for news of family far away.

Bob and I wanted family times of celebration to be important here and create memories for our little ones, so we made a big deal of birthdays, Christmas, and other holidays. Jody started walking about the time of his first birthday, getting into lots of things. It was fun to hear his early mix of English and Mandarin, and he seemed to always know which language to speak to which person. One of his first words was "*bye jyan*," a combination of bye-bye and the Chinese *dzai jyan* (see you again). The children learned the language through their ears, the natural way, and had beautiful, natural tones, whereas their parents often struggled to "say it the right way."

Packages from home were such a treat, and we got plenty. Mama especially knew what to send to please little eyes and ears and hands, but then she had those many years of experience in China and knew what you couldn't buy overseas and what would be most appreciated. I recall the first Easter when she sent jellybeans and coloring and designs for Easter eggs. The children were in raptures. We trained our children early not to rip wrapping paper and ribbons off their presents (this was long before the days of gift bags). If we carefully removed the paper, we could fold it and use it again and again. Nevertheless, we did get a bit tired of the same old paper designs after a couple of years.

Our busiest and happiest day of the week was Sunday, for then we could try to put into practice what we had been studying and feel a little bit "legitimate" as a missionary. Grace Church was a joy, and we both taught a Sunday School class of college students. Bob also had a large group of BYPU (Baptist Young People's Union) students. BYPU was very strong in Taiwan and a huge instrument of evangelism and training. We were fortunate to live right by Grace and have the opportunity of teaching talented students, mostly from the largest and best university on the island — Tai Da. Students tested into schools in Taiwan, and only the top students could attend Tai Da. Furthermore, the best overseas Chinese scholars came to Tai Da as well, and we had occasion to influence students from several countries. Grace's busy student center provided many activities and classes for these university scholars. Bob bonded with many by joining them to play badminton. To a person, they loved the game — and Bob became quite handy with a shuttlecock and racquet, even while he built relationships with the youth.

Our first Christmas was long remembered. We invited Bob's BYPU students to our house for a Christmas party. Our football field of a living room was full of some fifty college students, and Gai Shr Fu polished his reputation as a cook with all the goodies he served. Alice and Jody were the delight of the evening to the students, many of whom who had never been around foreign children. They loved talking with the little ones and trying out their English with non-critical native speakers. The students even charmed four-year-old Alice into singing a Christmas carol for them.

Christmas 1962 in Taipei was very different from Christmas in Zhenjiang. One thing was the same, however — an internal sense of loneliness. I thought of Mama and Dad, and how they would be spending Christmas alone. Our Alabama family would also be missing these little ones who had been with them just the year before. And I recalled China Christmases and felt nostalgic for those long-ago times. Nonetheless, we were starting a new tradition now and wanted to make it special for our two. A memorable part of our first Christmas was having Juliette Mather and Pearl Johnson spend the day with us. The children adored Aunt Juliette and Aunt Pearl, and it made us feel we did have some family there after all. Our churches had special programs, and the student center at Grace was alight with festivities. Christmas offered wonderful opportunities to share the birth of Christ with those who didn't know — and there were many of those.

Our Taipei missionaries had a Christmas celebration and drew names for sharing gifts. Jennie Alderman, our South Carolina friend from China days, had my name and gave me a gift that I am still enjoying some sixty years later. It was Amy Wilson Carmichael's *Edges of His Ways*, which became our all-time favorite daily devotional reading. We wore that first copy literally to pieces and are now using our fourth copy. That India missionary's gripping meditations have given our hearts a lift more times than I can count.

However, a rather unwelcome development from our first Taiwan Christmas was the way my stomach felt all that week of meeting and eating. I tried to figure out what I had eaten and where the bad pain came from. It would take several months and a lot of angst to discover another bit of culture shock and what a move to a new country had done to a digestive system.

Aunt Grace with her great-niece and nephew at Grace Church

Dr. Jou and Bob lead morning worship at Grace Church

THREE

TAIPEI
FIRST YEAR — 1962

The comparisons that evolved in my mind between Taiwan and Zhenjiang seemed inevitable and became something of a daily habit. In Zhenjiang there had been many Nationalist soldiers, but in Taiwan there were not only Nationalist troops but also thousands of American military: Army, Navy, and Air Force. At Calvary — the English-language church on Yang Ming Shan (on the outskirts of Taipei) — the majority of the members were US military personnel. We, like many of the missionaries with children, visited Calvary at night so our children could have a worship experience in English. Bob and I were blessed with many military friends, not a few of whom wanted to be involved in local ministry and who became "aunts and

uncles" to our children. They also showered us with American food items
at holiday times and had toys for Alice and Jody, so we had no sense of
deprivation about anything material. There were a number of US military
snack bars or restaurants, and often American nationals were free to enjoy
them. Baptists in the US military, in turn, appreciated Calvary and its
inspirational worship experiences. As a little girl in China, I had not been
able to attend English services and was so gratified now that our children
could have that experience. We even had a regular "Lottie Moon week"
experience at Calvary that first year, for they had Juliette Mather as the
featured speaker. She was inspiring.

Every now and then, a military wife would invite me to go with her to
an officers' wives' luncheon, or a sergeant's wife would ask me to attend a
tea or gathering with her group. It seemed a bit strange to be surrounded
by American faces and hear only English, but it was a neat experience to
be able to remember there were other things going on besides language
study and learning to be part of a different culture. These women were a
real cross-section of American society — some from small towns and rural
areas in the United States, others from large cities. Many were quite sophis-
ticated and highly educated, while others had come from quite impover-
ished backgrounds. Just like among our young missionaries, some adjusted
quite readily, and others found nothing to like about a strange country so
different from their own. It was refreshing to interact with ladies from such
a variety of backgrounds, and a real learning experience as well. I recall
one Saturday morning listening to a couple of twenty-something-year-olds
chatting over their coffee cups about what it was like to live in the Chinese
culture. One was complaining about how "backward and primitive" things
were in Taiwan, and the other spoke up to disagree, saying, "Well, I think
it's fun. Why, they are almost at civilized as we are!" I had to bite my tongue
— wanting to remind them that the ancient Chinese culture made ours
look like babes in the woods.

Fellowship at Calvary was a big plus, as was fellowship with our fellow
missionaries in Taipei. We also had frequent visits from missionaries living
in other parts of the island, and hospitality was a routine part of our lives

as we frequently entertained missionaries as overnight guests. Often in conjunction with our weekly station prayer meetings, we would have a fellowship meal, and some of the most special occasions were Mongolian barbecue at Martha Franks. For Mongolian barbecue, there were special grills on which a delightful mix of Chinese vegetables and meats were quick-cooked. Martha put labels on all the meats and veggies, including the various and tempting seasonings and sauces. We always grinned when we came to the container marked "cooking stuff," for we all knew this was Martha's euphemistic name for wine.

Yang Ming Shan was not only the location of English-speaking Calvary Church, but also of the Baptist assembly grounds. My first island-wide WMU meeting was at Yang Ming Shan, and it was a bit of China remembered — for the sounds, smiles, praying and comradeship were the same as when attending such gatherings with Mother and Aunt Grace many years earlier. There was nothing much more inspiring than prayer time at large WMU meetings. At frequent intervals, everyone would pray aloud simultaneously. If you had never heard this before, it might seem startling. However, each person soon learned to concentrate on the petition she was personally voicing to God, and the combined sounds of women talking to their Heavenly Father in unison became something of a melody. It was fascinating how the prayers seemed to reach a crescendo and then slowly, gently quiet down to the sound of whispers.

Bob and I were fortunate to be able to invest in the lives of college students at Grace Church each Sunday morning. My Sunday School class varied from ten or so to more than twenty, and included strong Christian young women plus a number who had very little knowledge of God. Still others were hearing about Him for the first time. This presented a huge challenge for the teacher, striving to appeal to all kinds of interests and backgrounds. Bob had much the same experience. His evening group was co-educational and a wonderful spot for training young leadership. Many of Taiwan's future church leaders came from the strong BYPUs in the various churches. On Sunday evenings, while Bob led their largest BYPU group, I took the children to Calvary.

Our usual Sunday practice was to teach at Grace Sunday School and then hurry to downtown Taipei to Hwai Ning Street Church, located near our mission headquarters. This was a vibrant church and a terrific place for us to learn about ministry in this particular culture. Hwai Ning was fortunate to have a strong pastor and a multi-talented woman of faith, Helen Lyou (Liu). She was Bob's first interpreter when he began preaching, prior to the time when he could preach in Mandarin. Lyou Dz Mei (Sister Lyou, as we addressed her), with her excellent English, was always full of enthusiasm. Bob could deliver a whole paragraph of thought, and then she would interpret. I remember many occasions where she was so "into" the message that when Bob would make a strong point, she would exclaim, "*Dweile!* (Right!)" Then she would translate. Helen Lyou was our great encourager. My initial attempt to give a speech in Mandarin was at Hwai Ning that first October, speaking to the WMU women. It lasted all of five minutes but felt more like fifty. The ladies were all gracious and kindly skimmed over my stumbling sentences and mixed metaphors. Along with the feeling of relief that flooded over me when I sat down was the thought, *Maybe next time I won't be so nervous.*

Ever present with us, of course, was language study and the importance of being able to communicate the gospel in the hearer's heart language. Some days were discouraging, and I would think I'd *never* be able to really express my heart. It felt like being a baby again and having to learn to crawl and then walk. I also had to be willing to make a fool of myself — and if I really goofed, just shake it off, start again, and try even harder. I learned to read people's faces to see if they *really* understood what I was talking about, or if they were simply puzzled by some asinine remark I had accidentally made. Our hearers at church might be very polite, but our teachers, especially the really good ones, did not let us get by with sloppy tones or incorrect vocabulary or sentence structure. It's very possible that a leading contributor to the attrition rate among new missionaries was language frustration. I recall one young couple who arrived a few years after we did and who were particularly overwhelmed by the language. The young husband exclaimed in frustration one day, "Why can't all the Chinese just learn English?!" That couple only lasted one term. I also never forgot a remark from a rather uninformed Baptist layman shortly before we left for Taiwan. He didn't want to lose Bob in the work there in Mississippi, and he declared, "Why don't you let someone else go? You're good enough to preach here at home!" We felt like the opposite was true. (Which lends credence to one of the apt quotes of one of WMU's most famous pioneers, Fannie Heck, who declared: "For the hardest fields, God needs the sharpest tools.")

Many odds and ends of new experiences fade from memory, but one clear recollection stayed with me. It concerned prayer. Growing up in a home where the family altar was a natural part of everyday life, prayer was always an important component of each day. Dad and Mama always started their day with prayer time. My brother, Art, and I figured this was the usual practice in every family and only later learned how rare this was. I frequently heard Mama relate how she and Dad became engaged on the same day her name was on the WMU prayer calendar. And Dad matched her story by telling of special protection he had during the fierce closing days of battle on Okinawa in World War II. On his birthday, February 20, his name appeared on the prayer calendar and a vast number of women in America prayed for him. He called it an "especially good day." *This is great,* I thought, *I can't wait until my name is first on that prayer calendar.* That day came, and I approached it with great anticipation. To be honest, it was a pretty lousy day: I couldn't seem to articulate my thoughts in class; the kids were cranky; my stomach hurt; and I was disappointed. Here I had counted on all those prayers. Nothing happened. However, the next day was terrific. The sun shone; the children were little angels (close); all my tones sounded just right in class, and my heart felt like rejoicing. It dawned on me: We were on the other side of the world from America. Taiwan was fourteen hours ahead, and the prayers were just being offered — and answered!

One event our first year on the field was one everyone could have done without, but which was a yearly occurrence in Taiwan — our first typhoon. It was a doozy. Some typhoons are worse than others, and often there is loss of life, and much damage and flooding from the torrential and seemingly unending rains. Flooding did not threaten us as it did so many; our problem was leakage. Within an hour of the storm beginning, the electricity went out and leaking began. On the back side of the house, every window did its best to hold off the wind and rains but without success. Rainwater began seeping in around the edges of the windows, and the trickles soon became more like a stream. What to do? We put buckets and bowls beneath the outer edges of each window, stuffed towels into the window corners, and let the water drip down the towels into the buckets. We spent the night emptying water out of buckets, wringing out towels, then putting them back. Every towel in the house was called into service. The next day, all of us were exhausted, but the damage was minimal. Lesson learned: Never take a typhoon for granted — they pack a punch. My stomach also decided to act up again, and this was becoming worrying. I had never experienced stomach pains like those now recurring regularly.

We learned a number of lessons that first year. One was to allow more travel time than you think you will need. Taipei was a large and sprawling city, and it took a long time to get anywhere. For instance, Calvary was on the other side of the city from Grace compound, and to go to evening service required not just the time of the service itself but also an hour to travel each way. Nonetheless, the fellowship was worth the time. We often took one of Taipei's ubiquitous red taxis. Those drivers must have learned their driving techniques on a racetrack — and the single most important feature on the cab was its horn. Taipei cabbies evidently couldn't drive without constantly sitting on the horn. I remember one day on an extra-crowded narrow street when Bob was driving. He tried to refrain from honking the horn constantly, and this time narrowly missed clipping a man on a bicycle who got too close as we were approaching a red light. The biker got off the bike, came to Bob's window and shook his fist in Bob's face, yelling in his broken English, "Why you no honkie me? You want me die?!"

Sometimes, I would go walking with the children along Shin Sheng Nan Lu, the boulevard in front of Grace compound. There was always something new to see, and Alice, especially, was old enough to look and ask all sorts of questions. When we approached the smaller streets and lanes nearby, there were street hawkers aplenty selling their wares, either goods or food. If there was a hawker selling *yòu tyáur*, the long sticks of puffy fried dough, the children always wanted one. As we walked along, we frequently saw people spitting on the sidewalk; I was not shocked, because back in Zhenjiang, spitting on the ground happened every day. It took a bit of effort to convince the children, "No, we don't spit like that." Then I would hear the inevitable, "Why not?"

Moreover, a stroll along the street was never a restful, quiet affair because there was *always* noise. Something unfamiliar to foreign eyes was the "airing" of gods that paraded down the streets. Many Taiwanese still held on to superstitions and beliefs passed down for hundreds of years. There were a number of lesser gods who had temples or shrines in their honor and who would occasionally be given an outing, or parade. Sometimes people would come watch the processions and make offerings to the deity, all to the tune of loud clanging of cymbals and drums. Many believed that giving honor to these gods would help ward off evil spirits. It was an eerie sight to behold, and a disquieting one. The airing of an idol was a vivid and visual reminder of just why we were here in Taiwan. The children always had many questions. Some of them I could not answer.

Those airings were another memory from childhood, as were the funeral parades. Just as on the mainland, so were there countless Buddhist funeral processions in Taipei, complete with hired mourners and a band that provided the jarring clanging of cymbals and mournful beating of drums. The mourners always wore white to denote their grief. Just like in Zhenjiang, these bands also frequently played Christian hymns as the mourners, wailing loudly, marched along in front of the family members who rode in pedicabs.

Even as we studied and learned more about the culture and became involved in ministry in our two churches, we always remained keenly aware of the impermanence of our lives here. The US Embassy was vigilant in keeping all Americans informed of political realities. The bare truth was that there was always the threat of invasion from the mainland. The two offshore islands of Quemoy and Matsu — close to mainland China, but heavily fortified by Nationalist troops — were bombarded every other day with shelling and mortar fire from forces in Fujian, the nearest mainland province. The US Embassy suggested that, for safety's sake, all Americans should keep $100 in cash available, and a packed suitcase in case of emergency evacuation. Our whole first term, we lived with that cautionary message echoing in our ears. It also made us aware of the need to "speak the message in season and out of season."

Alice and Jody kept the memories of their grandparents and friends alive in their hearts. Nearly every day, and especially when packages came from America, they would talk about "Ho Se Mo and Ho Shien Sun," their name for my parents, or "Granny Ora and Granddaddy Carl," Bob's parents. One day a friend was trying to get others to hurry up and said, "Hup!" Alice spoke up, announcing, "Hup, two, three, four! That's what Ho Shien Sun says!" Another day when we were talking about our families in America, Alice spoke up a bit sadly, "When am I going to see my grandparents again? I miss them so much." This kind of family separation was a part of everyday life and something we learned to deal with, sometimes more gracefully than others.

Grace Church and its staff were like a gift to us, supporting and encouraging these green missionaries, and providing us with significant avenues of ministry. Lillian Lu became a friend for life, and her brilliant musical ability was only exceeded by her people skills and generous heart. Watching Lillian interact with university students provided for us a real-life model for service. She had translated more than a hundred hymns into Chinese, and they were used all over the island and abroad. Our children felt like Aunt Lillian belonged to them. She was part of the amazing Grace team headed by Dr. Jou Lian Hwa. This brilliant man somehow found time to lead in the many ministries of Grace, serve as personal pastor to President Chiang Kai-shek and his wife, preach at the presidential chapel every Sunday after preaching at Grace, and serve as a professor at Taiwan Baptist Seminary. Never before or since has Taiwan had such an extraordinary Christian leader. (We were privileged to work with him again our second term and stood in awe of the man of God he was.)

Also on Grace's staff our first years there was Dr. Teddy Zhang (Jang),

Dr. Jou's co-pastor, who was in charge of the English service and numerous other church responsibilities. Teddy can only be described as a man with a radiant face. He wasn't simply a handsome and charming man; he affected all who came within his aegis. You somehow felt you had been in touch with *goodness* when you were around Teddy. His father was Zhang Qun (Chang Ch'un), secretary-general of the Presidential Office of the Republic, and a close friend and classmate of the Generalissimo (President Chiang). During WWII, Zhang was secretary general of the National Security Council. Mrs. Zhang was a devout Christian and a strong leader in China's powerful Woman's Missionary Union. She raised her children to know and love God, and it showed every day in her son Teddy's life. His children were friends with our little ones, and at parties those early years, there was an interesting mix of English and Mandarin as the children jabbered happily with each other. (The last years of Teddy Jang's long and fruitful life were spent in the United States, where he was vice president of a seminary and pastor of the Mandarin Baptist Church of Pasadena, California.)

Chinese New Year 1963 — the Year of the Rabbit — came in with the usual noise of firecrackers and revelry, bringing back memories of the same noise in childhood New Years' celebrations. I had an additional circumstance this year to keep me awake — that really gnawing stomach pain. It was becoming worrisome. Something was going to have to be done, but when was there time to stop and *do* something about it?

Aunt Grace (Wells) visits Taipei on her way to America and retirement

FOUR

LANGUAGE AND LEARNING
1964

Enough was enough. Having dealt with gripping stomach pain for several months, I finally determined that seeing a doctor and finding out what was wrong was better than worrying and suffering. Donald Dale, a British missionary doctor in Taipei, numbered many missionaries among his patients — and his jovial, positive attitude calmed my imagination down a bit, making me think this might not be life or death. "What does the pain feel like?" Dr. Dale inquired. My closest comparison was, "Like my stomach is a big towel and someone is wringing it out." After beginning with pain medication, Dr. Dale began running tests and advised a bland diet. In a household where Gai Shr Fu cooked wonderful, not-so-bland food, that required giant discipline.

Even when guests came (which was often), I quietly made an effort to eat only bland dishes. That wasn't easy, but bland did help the pain. Guests were also a welcome distraction and kept me from thinking about the delicacies I was missing. Dr. and Mrs. Jou and their three sons, and Teddy Jang and his wife and children, were a special delight. Five-year-old Alice absolutely adored both Dr. Jou and Teddy, and they spoiled her dreadfully. Both pastors had the most wonderful stories to tell about their experiences on the mainland and more recently in Taiwan. They were on a first-name basis with government leaders we had only read about; their tales were fascinating. Bob and I attempted to use Chinese as we chatted around the table — but these couples with their beautiful English, and the two of us with such elementary Chinese, made English the language of choice.

I soon found opportunities to use Chinese in a formal setting, and the practice was invaluable. Most of these revolved around WMU meetings, and the ladies were always encouraging. Meantime, Alice was beginning to play the piano. I had given piano lessons to children in Mississippi, but teaching your own offspring is far different. When the Lord gave the gift of patience, I missed out altogether. It was soon evident that if I didn't want Alice to grow up hating the piano, I needed to stop being her teacher. Then fortune smiled on us. A retired professor from the University of Michigan was a guest lecturer for several months at Tai Da, and his wife, Mrs. Lyles, was a retired piano instructor. She heard Alice play a simple little melody and immediately volunteered to give her lessons while they were in Taipei. Yes! Alice thrived with Mrs. Lyles and learned to love the piano.

Bob was in full-time language study, but on weekends he could do a bit of student work in preparation for his later ministry. One reason

Taiwan missions work had begun so strongly was due to student workers. Several missionaries forced to leave China began their Taiwan ministry with students. Many of Taiwan's strongest Christian leaders came from among those students. Bob went in 1963 to Taichung for his first student retreat. There were at least five single women missionaries involved in student work; Bob was the first man. He learned so much from those ladies, and they, in turn, marveled to see the instant rapport he developed with youth. Each student felt like Bob was focused solely on him or her and was really listening when they talked. His gift with young people was God-given, and he used it spontaneously. Bob conducted his first Lord's Supper in Mandarin with the hundred-plus students at the retreat, and it was a moment he long remembered.

In January of that year, I had a letter from Aunt Grace. She was retiring from the publication work she had begun in the Indonesian mission and was planning to come to Taipei to spend ten days with us. I was so excited I could scarcely sleep. She had never met her great-niece and nephew, and they only knew that their mommy had a beloved "Aunt Grace." All the MKs called missionaries in our country "Aunt" and "Uncle," but I tried to explain to our two that this was a *real* aunt, their Ho Se Mo's (their grandmother's) oldest sister. I had not seen Aunt Grace in twelve years, and memories of our years together in China came flooding back. Her two weeks with us were unforgettable. Aunt Grace formed strong bonds with her great-niece and nephew, telling them stories about their own mommy many years before in China. Aunt Grace herself had old home week those nearly two weeks, for she had reunions with many missionary colleagues she had not seen since China days. When we saw her off at the airport, I wanted to go into hibernation and cry. It would be four more years until we could see her again. Mama and Dad had recently been called to a church in Webbers Falls, Oklahoma, so they had left Wichita and were back in Dad's home state. Aunt Grace was going to visit them, and it warmed my heart to think of them together after so many years.

We continued to have a variety of friends, missionaries, and company from America. We were never bored or needing something to do. One unique visitor that first term was a piece of my China past. Ralph Cauthen — son of Dr. Baker James Cauthen, our Foreign Mission Board director — was finishing his Peace Corps service and stopped in Taiwan on his trip back to America. I had not seen Ralph since both of us were ten, and we reminisced about our childhood in Shanghai and Zhenjiang, trying to catch up on the past nearly twenty years.

Thanks to Lillian Lu's connection with Tai Da (the university close to Grace Church), I was asked to teach a speech class there. Those students were an amazing mixture of overseas Chinese students and the best of Taiwan's young scholars. Teaching them was a blend of challenge and joy, and I loved having contact with students possessing such great ability. One or two were Christians, and it was amazing to see how they could naturally share their Christian experience with the class. I assigned various types of speeches for them to prepare, and one of their favorites was persuasive speech. The top student was from, of all places, North Borneo, and had the best English I have ever heard from a student using it as a second language. Never one time did I need to correct his pronunciation or enunciation. His persuasive speech centered around the power of God in a life. It was profound. I've wondered many times how and where God has used that young man.

Our home in Grace triplex was needed for a newly arriving missionary family, and we agreed to move to the Overseas Crusades (OC) mission compound, located quite near the airport. That house was a single dwelling on a compound with three other houses, and we had a great experience making new friends. The compound was convenient to our various mission duties, and, at the time of the move, Bob began studying at home with a tutor. That worked beautifully; now he could concentrate on the language areas that were most important for his ministry. Our children became big buddies with Rodney and Randy Wait, the children of OC missionaries Les and Ginny. They loved Debbie, too (Rod and Randy's big sister). Norm and Muriel Cook were also living there, and the fourth house had various missionaries come for short periods. Just as Grace Church compound possessed a wall, this compound was surrounded by one as well, with cut glass embedded in the top. Thievery was a problem, and walls provided a layer of protection (supposedly).

Those pesky stomach problems persisted, and Dr. Dale finally determined I had gallstones. The gall bladder had to come out. Our fellow missionary Charles Cowherd quipped, "Well, I always knew you had gall, but I didn't know you let it go to seed!" The surgery was quite straight-forward, but for some reason I lost a lot of blood and needed a transfusion. That ended up causing more pain than the surgery itself, but I eventually got to go home with a bottle of souvenirs — six rather large and colorful gallstones. They looked awfully innocent to have caused so much pain. Dr. Dale noted the cause right away: We had left America and a diet based on using vegetable oil, and had come to a land where animal fat was the oil of choice. Result? Gallstones. Lesson learned. Gai Shr Fu had moved with us to the OC compound, but I learned to be careful what I ate. Lucy decided to retire, but we were fortunate to get the services of Ah Mei, a wonderful young Christian woman who was a capable worker and a warm and loving caregiver for our children. Ah Mei had been an orphan who was adopted by a Christian couple. In her new home, Ah Mei learned about Christ and accepted Him in a life-changing experience. She was a special gift for us; Alice and Jody adored her.

Each summer, we taught classes in Grace Student Center and had terrific one-on-one opportunities with students from various backgrounds, some who came from Christian homes and most who had no concept of a loving God. Alice loved being part of the young children's choir at Grace. It was made up of both MKs and Chinese children whose parents attended the English services. "Aunt" Lillian Lu had a golden touch with children, who responded to her wonderful musicality.

Birthdays for our little ones were a lot more fun than having one ourselves. I reached number twenty-five that year, and the thought was shocking: *A quarter of a century old — but I feel much older.* Nonetheless, just a few years later, I recognized that twenty-five was young indeed. Our children quickly learned another cultural difference when birthdays came. Our American practice is to rip right into the presents, see what we received, and thank the giver. Chinese custom was more difficult for the children to learn and follow. The polite thing to do when receiving a gift is to accept it with both hands, never with just one. Often, one would also give a little bow. Do not open the gift right then. That would be discourteous. However, with the children's birthday parties, we always found it easier just to let them rip in and enjoy.

Not long after moving to the OC compound, we had an experience that we hoped never to repeat. (That ended up a rather forlorn hope.) We woke up one Sunday morning to discover that we had had uninvited visitors while we slept. Sometime during the night, thieves had removed a window in the room farthest from where we slept and helped themselves to many items, including money, cameras, an heirloom watch Bob cherished, as well as other small items easily pilfered. Then the thieves had had the effrontery to simply open the front door and depart, undetected. To make it even scarier, they had opened our bedroom door and taken Bob's watch from the dresser top, just feet from where we slept. We heard nothing. Talk about feeling violated. We discovered they had broken into all four houses on the compound, and we ended up with a lot of nervous adults and children, wondering just what to do next.

No one slept very soundly the next few nights, and we quickly installed an alarm system in each house, putting sensors on all windows, adding to the bars on windows, and having a signal button where each house could alert the others. It took several weeks before we again slept very soundly. About a month after "the robbery," I was lying in bed trying to relax but listening to every little night sound. Bob was sound asleep. First, there was a tiny snap, a short wait, and then another snap. After two more little noises, I grabbed Bob right in the middle of his stomach, hissing, "There's someone out there!" He came up out of that bed, ready to fuss about his rude awakening, when right before his eyes, at the window by our bed he saw a man trying to scale the compound wall. The week before, Bob had put a thick pole under the edge of the bed. Grabbing that pole, he used it to hammer on the window and yell in Chinese at the fleeing intruder. We both decided that guy lost ten years off his life as he scrambled over the pieces of glass lining the top of the thick wall. We immediately hit the alarm button, and missionaries began pouring out of all the houses, clad in a varied array of nightwear. Ours was evidently the first house to be "hit," and we all felt pretty good that the system had worked.

Alice started kindergarten that fall and felt so grownup. She was reading quite well by this time, and on the second day of school, she took one of her favorite books to class with her and read a story to her friends at Bethany School. The principal talked to us the following day, wanting to place her in the first grade. Bob and I quickly decided that wasn't the thing to do. She would be grown up and gone too soon as it was. Alice loved school, and I remember she prayed one night, "Dear Lord, bless me at school and help me learn some stuff." Subsequent years proved how wonderfully that prayer was answered. But, with Alice off at school, Jody was incredibly lonely. He missed his *Jye Jye* (big sister) dreadfully and would often pretend she was there with him and would talk with her as he played.

A real milestone for Bob came that same fall. He preached his first full sermon in Mandarin at Hwai Ning Church, and several men made professions of faith. It was a wonderful affirmation, and, like a gift from God, helped us realize we were where he wanted us to be. This was the first of countless messages Bob was able to preach in coming years, and we always realized that the source of such blessings came from the One who called us. I was pianist at Hwai Ning Jye Church, and it was a terrific way to learn Chinese hymns. Much of what they sang were translations of the great old hymns of the faith, but I quickly realized that hearing them sung in Chinese was a terrific language learning tool.

During the year, a new couple arrived to study Mandarin, and we were asked to host them for their first week. This sort of made us feel like old-timers, since it had just been a bit over a year since we were the newbies. Identifying with what they were seeing and feeling, with everything new and strange, was easy since it was still fresh in our minds. Harry and Vivian Poovey were from North Carolina and had a beautiful little one-year-old named Lisa. We tried to make them as comfortable as possible and worked at remembering what they would need to know about the differences here. For instance, they needed to understand that you couldn't drink tap water or even brush your teeth with it. Water had to be boiled at least twenty minutes to be safe. Consequently, we kept a large plastic pitcher of water in each bathroom to use for brushing teeth. After a couple of days, I noticed that we were filling the pitcher with boiled water several times a day. This was puzzling; these were big pitchers, and normally we brushed our teeth just two or three times a day. I decided to check with Vivian as I inquired, "Is everything OK with the boiled water in the bathroom?" She replied, "Oh yes, it's just that it takes a good bit of it to give Lisa a bath." We quickly explained that tap water was fine for washing — just not for drinking. Bob and I decided that little Lisa was one pure baby, not only cute but also sterilized.

A sad chapter in America's history occurred that fall and is permanently imprinted in our memories. One morning, Norm Cook, head of Overseas Crusades ministries in Taiwan, came out of his front door with an anguished expression on his face. We happened to be outside, and he rushed over to say, "President Kennedy has been assassinated!" Bob and I responded immediately, "Come on, don't joke with us." Norm assured us this was stark reality. Every missionary on that compound was in shock at the horror of such an event, and our sorrow grew as we learned details. It seemed so very far removed from us but hurt with an immediacy that was shocking.

Bob and I were frequently amazed at the special and unusual experiences and people who crossed our paths. Our first New Year's Day at our new compound was one we never forgot. One of the OC families had two special guests for New Year's dinner — Gladys Aylward and her little adopted son, Gordon. We were invited to join them. For many years, we had heard of a celebrated missionary to North China and had read the thrilling story of how she rescued 100 orphans in China, walking them over the mountains to safety in Xian. We not only read the book about her life but also saw the acclaimed movie about her exploits, *Inn of the Sixth Happiness,* starring Ingrid Bergman. We came to know Gladys well and frequently had Sunday lunch with her — but this particular day was memorable, because Alice asked her to relate how she had unbound the feet of the little girls in the villages back when she was the official "foot-unbinder" in her province. Alice and the rest of us sat enthralled as Gladys told how the little girls responded when their feet were finally freed from the painful bindings. Alice and Jody treasure the picture taken of them standing with Gladys and her adopted son. When she was forced to leave China, Gladys moved to Taiwan and established an orphanage in Taipei for deserted children, continuing the same ministry she had done so successfully on the mainland. (Just three years later, Gladys died of pneumonia but left living legacies in the hundreds of children whose lives she had saved.)

Miss Aylward was not the only brush with living history we had during those early years in Taiwan. Thanks to Dr. Jou, we had contact with a man whose fame in Taiwan and on mainland China still lives on many decades later. By dent of his relationship with Chiang Kai-shek, President of the Republic of China, Dr. Jou was presented many opportunities of ministry. Every Sunday after preaching at the early service at Grace, Dr. Jou would hurry across the city to preach at the president's private chapel in the Shr Lin suburbs. One of the prominent people who attended the chapel was Jang Sywe-Lyang (Chang Hsueh-liang), better known as the Young Marshall, the most famous of the powerful warlords of early twentieth-century China. His father, the Old Marshall, had been assassinated in 1928, and the Young Marshall came into power. Born in 1901, Jang was educated by private tutors, then graduated from a military academy, went to Japan for further military study, and became an expert in aircraft. When only twenty-one, he was promoted to major general and was commander of air units. Jang became the leader of the "Northeast Army" upon his father's assassination, and thus the most powerful military force in the entire region.

China was in great turmoil in the late 1920s and early 1930s, with Generalissimo Chiang heading up the Nationalist (Kuomingtang) forces, the Communists seeking to obtain a stronghold in the north, and Japan threatening the entire nation. The Young Marshall became the instigator of the Xian Incident in 1935, when he was persuaded by the Communists that the best thing for China was to arrest (kidnap) President Chiang and thus force him to join forces with them against the Japanese. The Young Marshall, a personal friend of Chiang and his wife, was able to persuade the Generalissimo to come to Xian, whereupon the Communists arrested him and attempted to force him to join forces with them. Chiang had other plans for saving China, and one of those was not trusting the Communists. He attempted to escape and was injured, then developed pneumonia. Word was sent to Madame Chiang that her husband had been kidnapped and arrested in Xian. Furthermore, he was seriously ill with pneumonia. Madame boldly flew to Xian, determined to secure the Gimo's (Generalissimo's) release.

Madame Chiang was also a personal friend of Jang Sywe-Lyang and earnestly pleaded with him to change course and see to her husband's release. She was a strong and persuasive woman and convinced the Young Marshall to help free her husband for the good of the nation. However, Jang understood that if he did so, his own life would be in jeopardy from the Communists. This became known in history as the Xian Incident and ended with Chiang, the Madame, *and* Jang Sywe-Lyang flying out of Xian back to the capital, with Jang himself effectively under house arrest for the rest of his life. Thus was Jang's life spared, and President Chiang went on to defend China as best he could from the Japanese in the years that followed. When the Communists forced the Nationalists out of China and came to Taiwan, Jang Sywe-Lyang came with them and spent the next many years in a lovely villa on the outskirts of Taipei, officially under house arrest. Had he not been protected there, the Communists could soon have done away with him. Under the influence of Dr. Jou, Jang Sywe-Lyang and his wife both came to trust Christ. Jang did not make this decision lightly but determined to study and grow in his faith. That fall, Dr. Jou came to our home and asked, "Rosalie, would you record the Gospel of Luke in English to aid the Young Marshall in his English and Bible study?" My answer was immediate: "Of course. I would be honored." Over the next few weeks, I recorded the entire Book of Luke in English at our new Baptist radio recording studio.

Dr. Jou informed me a few weeks later that the Young Marshall was most appreciative and wanted to pay me for the recording. Horrified, I absolutely refused, explaining what a privilege this was. "Dr. Jou," I told him, "when

I was a young girl in Zhenjiang, my fourth grade reading book contained the story of the Xian Incident, and now, here I am these years later, being able to 'touch' history. The pleasure is *mine*." Dr. Jou loved history, too, and quickly understood these sentiments, reporting to the Young Marshall that I considered making the recording an honor. Some people you can never outgive, however — and about a month later, Dr. Jou came bearing a gift for me from the Young Marshall. It was two beautiful lengths of Chinese silk brocade, one of them hand-embroidered, with a stunning matching stole. I still have that treasure and frequently look at the stole and remember our little brush with history. (A few years after making the recording, I was actually privileged to meet the Young Marshall in person.)

The second big typhoon came during our second year, and unlike the first one, this time our house flooded. The rains came down, the winds blew (some of them 150 miles an hour), and the floods came up. Closing all the doors does not keep water out during a typhoon. Our houses were about three feet above the level of our yards, and here came the water — muddy — swirling — relentless. We put up all the furniture we could by propping them on the hearth and on chairs. What a strange feeling, to see water just seeping up through the floorboards; we mentally held our breath to see how high it would get. Thankfully, it came just so far and stopped. Our family went to bed surrounded by water and put towels at the foot of the bed, so each time we had to get up we could wipe our feet down before crawling back into bed. The finger test worked quite well: We woke up frequently during the night and would stick a finger down to check the flood level. After what seemed like forever, the typhoon moved on and we were left to recover. The odor took longer to leave than did the receding waters. A giant clean-up later, and we had weathered our first flooding.

Early in 1964, the mission asked that we move to Taichung to work with the many university students there. Taichung had two women engaged in student ministry, but no men, and additional reinforcements were needed to reach the tens of thousands of students in the area. We were getting used to moving by this time, so it looked like a new adventure was right around the corner — and down island.

The Hunts in Taichung, 1964

Alice and Jody with Gladys Aylward, New Year's Day, 1964

FIVE

TAICHUNG
1964-1965

By the time our furnishings were packed and sent ahead, Bob and I were exhausted, and the children excited. Having visited Taichung and MK friends there, moving to a new place felt like a special adventure to them. We traveled by train. As a rule, meetings and events in Taiwan tended to start late, but not trains. Taiwan's rail system worked like clockwork, and you could set your watch by their arrivals and departures. Alice and Jody never tired of train trips, and I loved the nostalgic feel a train gave me, taking my mind back to the train trips of yesteryear between Zhenjiang and Shanghai. Here were the same crisp little doilies on the back of each seat and the tea glasses in their holders, waiting for the steward to come by to fill them with tea leaves and boiling water. And yes, the eight-year-old that I had been in China loved those tin boxes with the rice, pork chop, and *jyang you* (soy sauce) egg. I still enjoyed them, and Alice and Jody found tin lunches (as they called them) the highlight of the trip.

Watching the passing countryside was another trip down memory lane. In the bustling city of Taipei, most things looked modern compared to what I had experienced growing up in Zhenjiang. In contrast, watching the passing countryside through the large train windows was eerily like watching the same scenery as a child in China. There were the same miles and miles of rice paddies, farmers in cone-shaped straw hats pushing water buffalo or stooping over planting rice seedlings in the rich soil. However, these farms looked more prosperous, for there were very few houses made of primitive mud brick with straw roofs. Most were substantially built of brick and surrounded by a wall. Several really large farm complexes identified those who were exceptionally prosperous. Everywhere, the landscape was vibrant and green; I found it endlessly fascinating.

We soon realized that Taichung was as special a city as we had been told. It had the reputation of having Taiwan's best climate (that's all relative, of course), and we soon discovered that truth for ourselves. A number of missionaries of various denominations lived in this central island location, headquartering here and working throughout the area. Morrison Academy, a first-rate school founded primarily to teach MKs (missionary kids) also lived up to its excellent reputation. In addition to local MKs, there were children of American military families, and some students from other countries. The teaching staff was provided by the varying denominations who had children enrolled. Dormitories were available for students whose families lived far away. Alice and Jody were beneficiaries of the school's outstanding academics. The most promising aspect of Taichung for us, however, was the limitless scope for ministry among young people, both university and high school.

Taiwan's education system was based on merit, so the pressure on students was tremendous. Entry to the best schools, beginning with middle school, was dependent on test scores. When teaching in these schools, we automatically knew that our classes were made up of the best students. Bob's responsibilities included not only student work but also serving as pastor of several churches. He preached several times each weekend (often four sermons a day) in area chapels and spent weekdays teaching in colleges and engaging in student ministry at the Taichung Baptist Student Center. I taught English at a university as well, and we got our students from various campuses involved in our central student center.

Bob immediately began teaching at a medical college less than a mile from our house (part of a fourplex this time), and he had a big surprise the first day. He had been warned ahead of time that English classes in the crowded universities would not be small, congenial groups conducive to a lot of individual participation. A big part of the Chinese educational system revolved around large classes and memorization. Students could easily memorize a whole paragraph yet not have a clue as to what it meant. When Bob entered his classroom that first day, he found some seventy students seated and looking expectantly toward the door. As he entered, all seventy stood and bowed very formally. Bob immediately turned and looked behind him to see to whom they were bowing. There was no one; they were bowing to their new *Läu Shr* (honored teacher). Teachers were highly respected, and that took some getting used to.

Our new home was just about a block from Morrison Academy, and Alice could literally leave for school in the mornings about five minutes before the bell rang. We had a wonderful gift in her first teacher, a newly arrived missionary associate from Texas, Lola Mae Daniel. She had been a pilot teacher in the Keys to Reading with Phonics program and was a tremendous motivator. We could not have found a better teacher anywhere. Lola Mae loved those children fiercely. Morrison's classes had maybe fifteen to twenty children per classroom, and Alice thrived with "Aunt Lola Mae" (Alice always called her Miss Daniel when at school). Jody was sad that he wasn't old enough to go to school with *Jye* (big sister), but he had plenty of fun at home with our capable and loving helpers, Wu Di Syung (Brother Wu, as we called him) and his wife, who cared for the children when we were at work. They were both Christians, and they addressed us as Pastor Hunt (Húng Mushr) and Mrs. Pastor Hunt (Húng Shrmu). The Wus had two little girls and a baby boy; Jody loved playing with the girls as well as with his friends next door — the Wilson girls.

Mike and Kitty Wilson, along with Lola Mae Daniel, were missionaries of our board, assigned to Morrison. Mike was a teacher and Kitty a nurse; they had six extremely bright daughters, all of whose names started with an "S." Susan and Sarah were the oldest; then Sande, Sally, and Sheri were closest in age to our two. They became bosom friends. (Shelley came along later.) The children conversed in an interesting polyglot of English and Chinese, and sometimes when Jody was jabbering, we couldn't understand him but realized he was speaking Taiwanese, the dialect of the Wus. Sande Wilson had just started school, but Sally and Sheri, the youngest two at the time, were at home and became Jody's special companions. Sally came to me one day with a solemn expression on her face, flatly declaring, "Jody cussed me!" I was shocked. I didn't realize Jody even *knew* a curse word. "What?" I inquired further, "What happened?" She immediately patted her cheek and emphatically repeated, "Yes. He cussed me. He cussed me right *there*." I was a relieved mommy; kissing — I could understand!

Living right next to us in the fourplex were Nan and Alex Herring, wonderful stand-in grandparents for our two children. Uncle Alex told them all sorts of *fascinating* stories about growing up as an MK in China, and Aunt Nan spoiled them dreadfully; they loved every minute of it. Nan was a humble, brilliant, remarkable woman who reminded me of my own mother; they shared the same loving traits.

Just like in Taipei, we were blessed in Taichung with American military who worked in the area and whose children attended Morrison. There were so many that we found a great interest in having an English-speaking service so American children could have a worship experience in their heart language. Calvary Church had provided that in Taipei, but there was none in Taichung. Bob and I were always busy on Sunday mornings and afternoons, but we found a nearby Baptist church that was happy to let us use their facilities for an evening service. Bob became pastor of the fellowship, and Calvary in Taipei, our "mother" church. A number of missionaries in Taichung enjoyed occasionally preaching in English, so there were plenty of people to share preaching time. Taichung had a lot of musical talent, which added inspiration to the services. I retained vivid memories of the mainland China years when I had no opportunity to worship in an English service. Our children could be part of this fellowship. Our MKs, both girls and boys, took up the offering each Sunday evening. We used traditional Chinese offering bags — a twelve-inch velvet bag hanging from a piece of wood with two handles. Jody loved taking up offering; he was so small that he could just walk down each aisle instead of passing the bag along. We enjoyed watching him at work, for it was his habit that if someone did not put in an offering, he would stand there a moment and shake the bag a little bit, as if to say: *OK, put some in.*

Bob and I completed two full years of language study and were now studying part-time — although the more we learned, the more we realized how much we *didn't* know. My great joy was teaching and organizing missions groups. We formed a Sunbeam band that met at our house on Fridays, with Jody and Alice two of the first "beams." Those children were such fun and always eager (and active)! My favorite age group was older youth, but I was quickly discovering that in missions work you end up doing things you never thought about doing and for which you feel singularly ill-equipped. I'd never considered teaching little ones, but through the years that has remained a part of our work.

Bob's ministry with churches and chapels involved preaching, conducting the Lord's Supper, and baptizing new believers. The custom in churches was to have an inquirer's class for new believers, because the great majority came from Buddhist and animistic backgrounds and had no knowledge of a living, personal God. Following the inquirer's class, they were received for baptism, and Bob loved baptizing many new converts. His special joy was witnessing to, discipling, and baptizing college students — and the 1960s was a time when the fields really *were* ripe unto harvest.

Many a Sunday, he preached at least three sermons and conducted the Lord's Supper each time.

I loved working on Sunday mornings at Dż Yóu Lù (Freedom Road) Baptist Church in the heart of the city and learning from Pastor Sye, their extraordinary leader. Here was another man with a special radiance about his face, and it clearly emanated from his heart. I taught primary age Sunday School, and our children came along. It was all in Chinese, of course, but I found the young ones quite tolerant of my frequent Mandarin snafus. Jody would frequently ask me, "Mama, how do you say that in English?" I translated children's Bible songs into Chinese, and the children responded to music. A favorite was "Jesus Loves the Little Children." They *loved* flannelgraph. (I know it went out of favor long ago, but not with me, and I continue to use it six decades later — a kid favorite.)

Dż Yóu Lù Church also became a place for me to minister to high school students. Right next to the church was a large Christian reading room. And within just *blocks* of the church were three massive high schools, with thousands of the best students in attendance. That was a rich field for sowing and reaping. I also began teaching at one of the high schools. English is a great drawing card for students; everyone wanted to study with a native speaker. Of course, when the ideal class size for English conversation is three to five students, and you have seventy in your classroom, it's a definite challenge. With the Chinese educational penchant for memorization, I had to work at helping them understand that it wasn't enough to read a sentence. You needed to understand what you were saying. I loved those eager students, always alert and wanting to learn more. Drawing from these three schools, the students flocked in the late afternoon to the Christian reading room at the church. I began having classes there, but it was clearly too much for one person.

That is where our YWAs came in. Having begun three different age groups — Sunbeams, Girls Auxiliary, and Young Women's Auxiliary — it was hard not to have a bit of a favorite. I loved all three but leaned a little bit toward YWAs, and it was invigorating to organize two groups of YWAs simultaneously. With the student center group, I found eager members among the young university women, and among Morrison students — an exceptional bunch of American girls, the majority of them MKs, excited to be involved. Remembering the loneliness I had experienced in China, I was thrilled that these MKs had such a compatible group of friends.Carolyn Culpepper (born in Shanghai), whose parents *and* grandparents all were part of the Taipei station, was one of the two YWAs from Taipei. Joyce Lynn Hunker (born in Su Jou, China), in whose home we had stayed our first week in Taiwan, was also at Morrison. Nancy Herring, another YWA, was slightly older than the other MKs. Her father, Alex, the son of missionaries, had been born in Tai An, also the birthplace of China's most famous philosopher, Confucius. Alex and Nan were currently living in Taichung, but were developing work in Taitung, on the east coast. Mary Lou Quick (born in Kweilin, China) was the last of the Baptist quartet of MKs. Her father, Oz, had survived a Japanese internment camp during World War II. These four high schoolers were the nucleus of a thriving group of young Americans and were missionaries themselves. The girls had a ready-made missions project right from the beginning. The YWAs came in pairs, two each day, to help with the many students at the reading room who were anxious to learn English. We were equally eager that they learn about God's love as we read and talked together.

In our Morrison YWAs, the girls prepared terrific programs, and we all loved eating together — occasionally going down to the "shacks," little cafés along the riverfront. You wouldn't want to see the kitchens at the shacks, but their sweet and sour pork and beef and peppers were incredible. Amazingly, none of us developed "Taichung Tummy" during these forays. Alice and Jody loved eating at the shacks and often clamored to go.

Organizing Taiwan's first YWA at the student center was really gratifying. The students were eager to share their faith and find paths of ministry. Those were everywhere. Our programs were an interesting mixture of Chinese and English. Material ordered from America took a long time arriving, so we developed topics and Bible studies on our own. Leadership developed within the group, and I could sort of sit back and watch them learn, while I focused my attention on guiding them in tackling new ideas.

A Chinese pastor's wife assisted me as the girls took leadership roles, and the two of us served as advisors. Most gratifying was the mission Sunday School the university YWAs organized. It met in a Christian home on Sunday afternoons and had from forty to fifty children regularly attending, most of whom had never heard the gospel. Seeing those girls take the initiative and accept responsibility was a feeling so good I can't even label it.

Besides language study, teaching at the university, and working with the various missions organizations, there were also missions committees on which both Bob and I served. Committee meetings are the bane of most organizations but something we recognized as necessary for expediting the work. Bob frequently had to take the train to Taipei, usually for a day or so. One such trip remains clear in memory. While Bob was away for some event, the kids and I were headed home from an afternoon class when I somehow managed to run the car into a narrow *benjo* (an open ditch, often used as an open sewer). It was fairly simple to get the car out, but as we drove on home, I *suggested* to the children that they didn't need to tell their father about the incident, since all is well that ends well. Naturally, that suggestion was just asking for trouble. The train arrived, and Bob had no more than gotten in the car until both kids piped up, "Daddy, Daddy, Mama drove the car into the *benjo!*" They sounded like a speech choir.

Each week, I tried to visit one of our area church's WMU meetings. Those dear ladies decided I was their "advisor" simply because I was a missionary. I loved those women, their eager faces and enthusiasm, and I sat at their feet, learning. They always wanted me to speak. It was actually beneficial for my language skills to constantly prepare, speak, and learn to comprehend fast conversations and a variety of dialects. Sometimes we would meet at our home, and the women loved those occasions.

Right after university classes began during our second year in Taichung, the student center held a welcome event, and we were thrilled that twenty students professed faith in Christ. The very next week, Bob began an inquirer's class to ground them in their faith. Those kinds of gatherings were manna to the spirit. Bob especially loved the various retreats each year with daylong one-on-one opportunities to interact and establish deep bonds with students. On one occasion, a young professor came seeking the way of salvation. Dr. Wang earnestly ask Bob, "Shepherd, will you please tell me about the Bible and God? I want to know Him." Wang and his brother both believed. Just one high moment like that will have you keep on keeping on through the dry and lonely stretches.

Alice and Jody were very much part of our work, and the university students loved these little foreigners who conversed with them in a charming mixture of Chinese and English. At one large welcoming gathering at the student center, our dear Wu Di Syung baked 700 cookies, and I remember marveling that there were just seven left at the end of the meeting.

Jody's third birthday party had a sailor's theme, with a sailboat for a cake, a tailor-made Navy uniform, and his Uncle Arthur's sailor's cap from earlier years. Jody informed us, "I'm three now, and when I'm five I'm going on a plane to 'Merica." Of course, our parents missed out on all such milestones in our children's lives. Mama and Dad would sometimes write a letter specifically to the children, and it made them feel important. In one letter, Dad wrote, "We sure would love to see you. Guess we will have to wait for that. When we see the boys and girls in our Sunday School, we think of you." Alice loved school and could scarcely wait to go every morning. We gave thanks each day for that amazing missionary teacher. Lola Mae Daniel was worth her weight in gold, as were Wu Di Syung and Mrs. Wu. We daily counted our blessings.

Another serendipity was availability of goods. Because there were many US military in the area, there was a thriving black market in American products. This meant we could have some American food items if we were willing to pay the inflated prices. Learning how to handle cereal purchases was one of the first food skills we developed. No telling how long some of that American cereal had been around. Stale is the word that comes to mind. Infested is another. We learned a good trick right away: Heat the cereal on a cookie sheet in the oven. It freshens it up — and the heat makes the bugs scurry right off the flakes of cereal. The children were amazed on our first furlough when they could eat cereal straight from the bag! They were a little surprised, though, that in America, you couldn't buy *yòu tyáur* at a food stand anywhere, and there simply weren't any *swān mei* (dried sour plums) to be had. We never quite figured out where their predilection for *swān mei* came from.

I tried to occasionally record fun things the children said or did and write home to their grandparents about little pieces of daily life that they were missing. I remember one Friday night when, miraculously, nothing was on schedule for the following day and we could "sleep in." After we finished our nightly prayer time, the kids crawled into bed, and I exited the room, commenting, "Now, tomorrow is a leisurely day. Don't get up on the crack of dawn." Minutes later, I heard Jody snuffling. Was he crying? Quickly going to the door, I asked softly, "Honey, what's wrong?" He tearfully replied, "Mommy, I don't know where the crack of dawn is — what if I get up on it?" I felt like a mean mother, but we got that question quickly resolved, and sealed it with a hug.

Missions life and conditions in the 1960s were quite different from this new millennium. To call the United States, we had to go to the city's central phone office, reserve an appointment time, and pay a dollar for each minute. Computers were unheard of, to say nothing of email, cell phones, or text messaging. I guess it is all relative. We felt quite modern because we could get an airmail letter from our families in sometimes as little as a week. When Ann and Adoniram Judson sailed to Burma in 1812, it took over three *years* before they had the first letter from home. We planned for months for our first summer vacation off the island. Hong Kong sounded like a mythical wonderland to us, perched right on the doorstep of China. Alice and Jody were both excited. Furthermore, they were going to get to see their Uncle Charles, and we would stay with him. Charles and Marian Cowherd were engaged in Mandarin work in that vast, mostly Cantonese city, although Marian was in the States for the summer. Our two had little concept of what it would be like to go into a store and pick out clothes or toys for themselves. They began counting the days until their first vacation adventure, diligently saving up allowances and birthday money gifts. Truth be told, their parents were a bit excited as well, anticipating our first visit to Hong Kong, the Pearl of the Orient.

Chinese and American YWAs lead a Christmas party at Taichung orphanage

SIX

COMINGS AND GOINGS
1965-1966

Hong Kong lived up to its reputation as exciting and exotic. Our "hotel" was Charles Cowherd's flat (apartment), located conveniently near the main shopping area of Tsim Sha Tswei on the Kowloon side of Hong Kong. The skyline was covered with high-rise housing areas, making it one of the most crowded square miles in the world. Daddy frequently said, "God must have really loved the Chinese, he made so many of them." Hong Kong was a fascinating blend of people from every continent and most countries.

We stood at the Kowloon harbor area watching ferries take people back and forth across the harbor between Kowloon and Hong Kong Island. In just a few minutes, we easily observed a whole cross-section of humanity pass in front of our eyes.

The children loved the ubiquitous red double-decker buses; we could travel anywhere in Hong Kong for just a few cents. Alice and Jody both relished sitting in the top deck and watching the intriguing sights outside the big glass windows. Nothing was much more fun, however, than going into the many plush stores and seeing tempting goods from all over the world. Each of us had a shopping list — so many shops, such limited time! Bob and I enjoyed watching the children choose toys and make decisions. They had learned very quickly in Taiwan that you bargain when shopping and don't pay the first price. That didn't work in Hong Kong. The listed price *was* the price. They were fascinated by the Mei Mei department store — with amazing toys and more dolls in one place than Alice had ever seen. Jody gravitated to the cowboy and Indian toys on display, and Bob and I loved observing their shopping style. Alice knew exactly what she wanted, and, when she saw it, made her purchase. On the other hand, Jody tended to dither. He was prone to wanting it *all* and would wring his hands a bit when it came to deciding. Bob and I likewise enjoyed the stores, with beautifully handcrafted linens from China and countless intriguing antiques.

Baptist work in Hong Kong was flourishing. Many people who had "refugeed" from mainland China were eager to hear about the hope offered in Christ, and our missionaries were busy and encouraged. I reveled in reunions with a number of "old China hands," missionaries I had last seen nearly twenty years earlier in Shanghai. Visiting with Fay Taylor again was serendipitous. Fay was still busy leading young people. She and I enjoyed reminiscing over our sailing together to China in 1946, and she reminded me of how I (at age eight) had called her a green missionary who needed to learn about the Chinese culture.

We returned to Taiwan refreshed and ready to tackle our last year and a half before furlough. The children had a busy summer. Swimming was a favorite sport, but getting Jody started was a challenge. I tried to get him to put his head under water to get a rock, and he kept saying, "I can't." Finally, I reminded him, "If the little engine had said, 'I can't,' he'd never have gotten over the mountain." Jody retorted, "We're not talking about engines — we're talking about swimming!" (We should have known right then he would end up being a lawyer!) Nor were he and his sister shy in expressing their opinions to each other. One night, Jody was complaining because Alice got *more* of something than he did. Bob and I began talking about how much God had given us and how much more we had than did so many others. Alice joined in with, "Yeah, and some people don't have cars, and some don't even have a bike!" Jody muttered, "They could take a taxi then."

When writing to our parents, I often remarked on tendencies and traits we saw in their grandchildren. After one of Jody's feisty little statements, I commented to Mama, "He's a mess — and stubborn! In true family tradition. If he makes up his mind, it takes an act of Congress to change it." One day he got sentimental and began giving us presents — toys he didn't want. He gave Bob three little china rabbits, and Bob said, "Don't give me your *good* rabbits." Jody cheerily responded, "Oh, that's all right. They're Alice's!"

On the other hand, he could be kind and helpful, and regularly took up for the underdog. He loved kindergarten and eagerly went to class each day. About the fourth week of school, a little girl pleaded with him to get a boy off the teeter-totter for her; he had been hogging it. Jody proceeded to drag the little fellow off the teeter-totter, and they went at it. Meanwhile, the girl calmly got on the teeter-totter and enjoyed herself. Jody's result, for both himself and the little boy: bloody noses. When we tried to get the story straight, he matter-of-factly stated, "Oh, we weren't mad. We were just fighting."

The children were thrilled when a missionary friend leaving on furlough asked if they would like to have her adorable little dog, Tiny, for their own. They were in raptures. Tiny was indeed *tiny,* a mixed breed but mostly Pekinese, both beautiful and well-mannered. Nonetheless, the children knew their daddy was not as much "into" dogs as were they. Tiny was a smart little fellow and quickly realized that Daddy was the final word in the house. Bob's policy: no dogs on the beds. However, Tiny loved to get on one of the children's beds and have a good sleep. She had keen ears, though, and recognized steps. I don't even know how many times I watched that little Pekinese raise her head when she heard the front door open. She would trot to the head of the stairs and peer down to see who it was. If Bob walked in, she would politely walk down the steps and greet him. If it was not Bob, Tiny would go back and jump on the bed again. When we left on furlough, a military couple kept Tiny, and, when they themselves were returning to the US, asked if they could adopt Tiny and take her with them to America. And that was how Tiny became a naturalized American Pekinese.

The highlight for our family that year, however, was the Sunday evening when Alice made her profession of faith. A few Sundays later, Bob had the joy of baptizing her. Such special moments were times when we so keenly missed having grandparents and relatives with us to share the experience, but this, too, was part of their sacrifice and ours. Family couldn't be with us, but we did have mission family present, and for that we were grateful. A number of US military families were an active part of our evening services. One special couple became lifelong friends, Bill and Maxine Vandry from Kentucky. Their three daughters — Laura, Ruthie and Janna — were fast friends with our two and were always part of birthday parties and games. Maxine was a wizard with crafts and baking. Her birthday cakes made parties really special. The Vandrys found it amusing that Bob and I often addressed each other by our Chinese "titles." He was my *Lāu Tóu* (Old Head — a very honorary term), and I was his *Tai Tai* (wife). This became a lifelong habit. (For over fifty years, we have kept in touch with the Vandrys and have visited them in a neighboring state in recent years.)

Banquets and dinners were a common form of celebration in Taiwan, whether end of school year or conclusion of a conference. The most memorable banquet in all our years in Taiwan came for me at the conclusion of the school year in Taichung, at a dinner to honor the middle school teachers. I remember it not for the big crowd (more than a hundred teachers) or the speeches, but for the food. We had learned early on that when attending a feast, we should find one or two palatable dishes and politely try to ignore the unknown or noxious. Those were usually identified by either appearance or the fumes emanating from the dish. We were seated ten to each round table. Here came the food, one dish after another — and, as usual, I latched on to one platter, a crispy meat dish that was both tender and lightly seasoned. Delicious. Tender. It crossed my mind that I might be able to prepare this at home, so I asked the young woman seated to my right, *"Jeige hāu chr. She shémma ne?"* (This is so good — what is it?). Custom in Taiwan dictated that if you laughed, you politely put a hand up to cover your laugh. That is exactly what she did. Smiling and giggling, she covered her mouth and shook her head. So, I turned to the teacher on my left and asked the same question. Her response was the same covered-mouth laugh. I went all around the table, and finally, coming to the last young teacher, I implored, "Just tell me what this dish is." She laughed, then uncovered her mouth, and, grinning, said, "Fried puppy dog." Lesson learned. Never again did I ask what I was eating.

The great sorrow of our first term in Taiwan came when Bob's fifty-nine-year-old father suddenly died of kidney failure. In the 1960s, there was no way we could catch a plane and make a quick trip. Just a few weeks earlier, we had received a letter from Bob's mother telling of his pain and their concern because there was no cure for his condition. Learning that he was so ill, and then just weeks later losing him, was a blow. The news came on a Sunday morning. I was in front of our house, waiting for a taxi to pick me up to go teach Sunday School. The taxi was late, and, as I waited, a young telegraph employee, in his green uniform and riding on a bicycle, came in my direction. He checked the address, looked at me and called my name. "Yes, we are the Hungs (Hohngs)," I confirmed, and he handed me a telegram. My heart sank, because telegrams were unusual, and, as a rule, did not bring glad tidings. With trembling fingers, I opened the telegram and read its message. Bob's beloved, gentle father had died. Thank God the taxi had been late, and I was there to be with Bob.

Through our tears, shock and grief, we drove to the telephone/telegraph office to send a reply and reserve a call for the next day in order to be able to talk to Bob's mother. In our sorrow, the 10,000 miles that separated us from family made us feel like we were on another planet. There came flashing into my mind the last weeks we had seen Bob's dad and had marveled at how he sat for hours at a time, just holding Jody, or hugging Alice. It was as if he somehow must have known. By the time we were finally able to speak to Bob's mother, the funeral was already over. Two families from Booneville had learned of Carl Hunt's death and drove to Alabama to be there since we could not. It was a touching gesture. Our great regret was that our two children could not have real memories of this grandfather who loved them so dearly. Our mission family rallied round and supported us in our grief, one after another performing small acts of kindness or just being there for us and listening. In such moments, the loneliness of isolation from family was stark and painful. I began constantly reminding myself of one of Mama's favorite phrases: "Practice the presence of the Lord." We sorely needed that presence.

It was a good thing that our days were so busy. It helped a bit to ease the pain of loss. Working with missions organization groups was amazing therapy. Investing in young lives provided a sense of passing on the message. The YWAs assumed leadership roles, and that sent me to sleep at night with a smile on my face. Both the MK high school group as well as the university YWAs showed real skill in teaching and organizing Sunday School groups for younger children. I spent many hours translating the YWA manual into Chinese, and it proved quite helpful. The university YWAs planned and prepared a farewell luncheon for seniors with a lovely meal and a tribute and challenge to the graduates. I have wondered many times where those young women went and how they have been used by God. One of our special YWA functions was a joint project of the two YWA groups when they put on a Christmas party for a large city orphanage. The girls prepared music, games, stories, goodies and lovely gifts for each child. Alice and Jody came along to help, and the children loved having the "little foreigners" visit and play with them. The faces of the orphans glowed with joy that afternoon, and I doubt the YWAs themselves ever forgot that party.

Just as challenging was organizing Taiwan's first group of GAs and watching their excitement and enthusiasm about helping share the gospel. Several of the university YWAs helped organize the group; it was great leadership training for them. Many of the GAs had brothers who wanted to know if they could come to the meetings as well. Translating the first manual for GAs into Chinese took a number of months. There's no way I could have done it without the help of my language teacher. Mrs. Wang was extremely capable, a devoted Christian woman, and very knowledgeable about Scripture. I grinned a little bit when first seeing the completed manual. It was significantly thinner that the English version; we may have taken a bit of "artistic liberty" in translation.

Equally rewarding was organizing an MK GA group. I vividly recalled being the *only* GA in Zhenjiang, China, so I was doubly pleased that these girls had friends with whom to share experiences. There was one military Morrison student from Texas and five MKs: Barbara Akins, Linda Quick (whose big sister was a YWA), Trudy Robinson, and our next-door neighbors Susan and Sarah Wilson. They were a motivated group of bright girls, and what they lacked in numbers, they more than made up for in enthusiasm and dedication. They loved Forward Steps, and we had grand coronation services. Our GA magazine was regularly at least a month late in arriving, so the girls became super creative. Instead of Christmas in August, we had Christmas in September and sent Taiwan-made items to the Baptist mission center in New Orleans. We designed our own "uniforms," with simple white blouses featuring our emblem and swirly green skirts.

In Taichung, we were right in the middle of all sorts of mission action possibilities. One of the GAs' favorites was assisting at the orphanage, helping with young ones up to six years old. There were even five sets of twins. We regularly took small gifts of clothing and rattlers, and spent time cuddling the little ones and playing with the toddlers. Love had no language barriers, and our GAs were able to speak simple Mandarin phrases. Another highlight was an Easter puppet show we put on in a nearby village, setting up a stage and manipulating clever puppets. All of us sang in Chinese at the appropriate places, and Susan Wilson, who spoke Mandarin, joined me behind stage to do the voices and dialogue. Not just the scores of village children but their parents as well came for the "street show." We shared the gospel story beginning with the birth of Christ and finishing with the account of Easter, while our primary Sunbeams helped by handing out tracts.

It was the custom in the 1960s to have a name for your GA group, and the girls chose to be the Juliette Mather GAs. Our home mission study book for that year was *Taiwan as I Saw It,* and, yes, it was written by Juliette Mather. This was an unusual mission study — a first for all those girls. We boarded a fast train going south, and three hours later we were in Kaohsiung, on Taiwan's south coast. From there we flew on China Airlines to Taiwan's east coast and the city of Taitung, where Baptists had home missions work. Our beloved Nan and Alex Herring worked there. We stayed with them, and they taught our mission study. After visiting our Baptist work, we had a picnic supper and slumber party at the Herrings. Next morning, Alex and Nan served breakfast on their flat roof where we could look out over the shining ocean water and imagine that we could see mainland China in the distance.

Another Taitung highlight was the Herrings' monkey, Vippee, who lived in a cement mixer in their backyard. Uncle Alex, as all the girls called him, also had a pet goat and a wonderful flying squirrel with a long bushy tail. When it jumped, it made a beautiful glide. Socks, their large boxer dog, was a gentle creature. Aunt Nan told the girls that when Alex had been a little MK growing up in China, he had loved animals and told his mother, "Mama, when I grow up, I want to have one of every creature God made." Nan assured the girls that he had come close on that goal.

At the annual mission meeting in Taipei that summer, we had a GA coronation service with the entire mission as the audience. Our little GA group had reached out to MKs all over the island who participated by long distance, and nine MK GAs received recognition. When GA Focus Week arrived the following spring, we celebrated in a big way. At noon on Mother's Day, we had a Mother-Daughter luncheon, and that night a coronation with the theme "The Light of the World." The church was alight with candles. Every girl had worked hard on their Forward Steps, and all had achieved a step — with several crowned as Queens, and each girl receiving a charge from her own mother. I remember going to bed that night with a singular smile on my face, reliving the looks on the faces of those girls who were already making a difference in their world.

There was opportunity for ministry not only among the Chinese but also in the American military community. We found some terrific Baptist families in the various service branches, and they were a special part of our English service ministry. I was invited to join the Officers' Wives Club as an auxiliary member, and it offered unique opportunities to share the gospel with American women who had little or no spiritual background. Talk about a variety of backgrounds — our military had it. I learned so much from those women. One or two other missionaries attended as well, and I believe some of those military wives looked upon us as rather unusual creatures. (We probably were.) One particular experience stands out in memory. The women arranged a trip to Quemoy, the offshore island — which, at its closest point, is less than two miles from Communist China. The little islands of Quemoy and Matsu, nestled closely to mainland China, had remained in the hands of the Nationalists (Republic of China). Quemoy was about 100 miles from Taiwan and was highly fortified. In the years since Chiang Kai-shek and the Nationalist army had shifted from the mainland to Taiwan, these two islands had remained strategic to Free China's interests. Quemoy was bristling with soldiers and with many underground facilities, including their arsenal and a fully equipped hospital. An interesting schedule had developed, with the Communist mainland regularly shelling the island every other day. The Nationalists kept road repair supplies stacked all along the highway system, so as soon as a shell made a hole in the road, it could immediately be repaired.

Due to the "scheduled shelling," the Officers' Wives Club arranged their Quemoy visit on a "non-shelling day." Their president asked that I come along because someone who spoke Chinese was needed as part of the delegation. We flew in on a US Air Force plane, and as we drove along the highway from the airstrip to the military headquarters, I looked with wide eyes at all the road repair material stacked along the highway. The US officers' club president was a colonel's wife, and I became her translator. Vice Admiral Chen of the National Navy hosted the group and took us on a tour of the underground fortifications. (We knew better than to take photographs.) Admiral Chen and his staff next provided a banquet for the American visitors, and we sat at round tables, where everyone could see and interact with each other. Of course, the colonel's wife sat at the table with the admiral. The Navy literally wined and dined us in royal Chinese fashion, with a polyglot of exotic dishes and the famous Quemoy brew that had a reputation for being powerful liquor. Our American colonel's wife was a Mormon and did not drink, so she and I requested *Chi Shwei* (similar to 7-Up) for our drink glasses. Admiral Chen toasted everything and everybody, and got pretty happy at the end of so many toasts. Also in typical fashion, he would have our shot glasses filled again and again, and down it all in one swallow, raising his glass and saying, *"Gan Bei!"* (Empty glass!) The colonel's wife and I were awash in *Chi Shwei* by the end of the hour-long banquet.

For some reason, living overseas made us more aware of our patriotism. Bob and I both noticed a difference in our response to the raising of an American flag, or the singing of the "Star Spangled Banner" or "God Bless America." Our patriotism rose to the fore in a way it never did in the US. We had tended to take our freedoms for granted. Not now. Not when we saw other countries and peoples and the freedoms they did not have.

Increasingly, our thoughts turned to furlough — not only thinking of all the packing, planning and storing that needed to be done, but also realizing the struggle we were having, just thinking about the groups, students and churches with whom we worked, and wondering who would be assuming responsibility. In those five years, we had experienced times of wrenching loneliness, of missing family, and having to grieve for the loss of Bob's father so far away, unable to be of comfort to his mother as she grieved. Now we were just a jumble of mixed emotions; our hearts were firmly attached to Taiwan, and we loved what we did. At the same time, I frequently felt ashamed of the little that I had done in the face of such need and prayed for the wisdom and tenacity I lacked on my own.

It was hard not to feel the children's excitement. Just the idea of getting on a jumbo plane and going to America and seeing their beloved grandparents was enough to make it difficult for them to go to sleep at night. Alice had only a few dim memories of America, and Jody none at all. Somehow, he envisioned America as being full of cowboys and Indians, and both children could scarcely wait to go in a "real American grocery store and buy things myself!" I will admit to anticipating what it would be like to pick out fruit and vegetables and fresh cereal again after five years. Tickets were in hand, and all was ready for departure about the middle of January. Nonetheless, a statement made to Bob in conversation with a seasoned missionary kept preying on his mind. At our annual mission meeting in July, Bob was talking with Carl Hunker about our upcoming furlough, making several references to going home and seeing his mother and family, and all the excitement that was building after five years. Dr. Hunker, such a gentle soul (much like Bob's father, Carl, had been) looked kindly into Bob's eyes and spoke a bit sadly, "Bob, you can't go home again." Bob reacted at once, "Oh, yes, I can! I am going home." (A year later, and a year wiser, Bob saw Carl when we returned to Taiwan and quickly confessed, "Carl, you were right. You really *can't* go home again.") But in January 1966, four excited Hunts boarded a plane bound for Los Angeles and home, thrilled at the thoughts of being with family after five long years.

GAs putting on a Christmas puppet show in a nearby village

With Esther Wu and girls in Virginia during furlough

The Hunts at Foreign Missions Week, Ridgecrest, 1967

SEVEN

REVERSE CULTURE SHOCK
1967

"How many days now?" was the first thing the children said when they woke each morning. January arrived, and our trip was two weeks ahead. Truth be told, all of us were excited. We had not seen family and friends for a full five years, and the last year had seemed at least two years long. Jody wanted to prepare for all the "cowboys and Indians," so in the last letter I wrote to Oklahoma, I relayed his request for Ho Shien Sun (his grandfather) to please take him to the store to buy a gun. "But," Jody added, "I am going to kiss you first!" Bob and I were awash in anticipation of reunions with our families but were simultaneously grieving over the goodbyes to dear coworkers in Taichung. Pastor Sye and other friends showered us with gifts and wishes and frequently brought us close to tears, as we wondered who was going to be helping, leading and filling in gaps. My heart couldn't find an answer for the question of how to gracefully deal with goodbyes.

Our itinerary took us to Tokyo and then Los Angeles, where my brother, Arthur, would meet us. Neither child had ever met Uncle Arthur, their mysterious relative who was just a name. We disembarked at LA airport, and the adventure began. Art gathered his only niece and nephew close and ushered us to his car — America at last. All of us were too excited to notice how tired our bodies were. The highways of Los Angeles were almost overwhelming, with eight lanes all going in one direction, cars whizzing everywhere. Alice and Jody were accustomed to one lane in each direction with buses, cars, trucks, bicycles, pedestrians and oxen all vying for space in the midst of a cacophony of horns and exhaust. Surrounding us now was only the sound of cars quietly swishing by. In a few moments, Jody leaned forward from the back seat and tapped Art on the shoulder, asking, "Uncle Arthur, don't you have a honker on this car?" Art loved it. Jody's next observation was just as surprising. Looking at the masses of high-rise buildings on both sides of the interstate, Jody stared and asked in wonder, "Uncle Arthur, are there cowboys and Indians in *all* those buildings?"

Everything looked different and exciting to Alice and Jody, and they looked around with wide eyes. My heart was mostly eager to get to Tulsa and see Mama and Dad. It had been way too long. Having anticipated this special moment for months, the next morning we dressed the kids up in their finest — Alice in a new dress, and Jody with a sports jacket and tie. We had not been in the air many minutes before the children had shared with everyone in our section of the plane that they were going to see their grandparents for the first time in five years. A number of kind passengers entered the spirit of the moment and joined in their excitement. But wouldn't you know, just as the plane began its descent to land at Tulsa's airport, Jody's excited little stomach did a flip, and he upchucked. Disaster. However, all the surrounding passengers pitched in to help, passing us barf bags and cool cloths, and helping clean him up.

A number of well-wishers hung back and watched sentimentally as the two children were engulfed in the loving arms of their grandparents, and several of the onlookers shed a surreptitious tear or so. That moment was long remembered and made doubly sweet as a gratification so long denied. My heart was home; there was no sweeter moment than seeing my parents hug their only grandchildren to them as if they would never let go. Words tumbled all over each other as all of us talked at the same time. After all, there were five years to catch up on. These grandchildren were not babies now, but active, garrulous, excited, young school children. Driving from Tulsa to Webbers Falls was a treat for the kids, for every sight outside the car windows was something new and different. The houses looked different, the little towns were fascinating, and the open, unclut-tered (comparatively) highways seemed strange. Alice and Jody stared at it all and had a thousand questions for their Ho Se Mo and Ho Shien Sun.

I wasn't surprised that we didn't even make it to Webbers Falls before stopping at a supermarket. When we got to Muskogee, Alice asked the inevitable question, "Could we please stop at a supermarket? I really, really, want to go in one for myself. Please?" Ho Se Mo, ever quick to pick up on others' wishes, spoke up. "We certainly can," she smiled, "and I need some fresh bread and bananas anyway." Ho Shien Sun pulled into the parking lot of Safeway, and two eager children jumped out, Bob and I not far behind. Suddenly, it was every person for himself. I stood near the Safeway entrance and simply breathed in the clean fragrance of an American grocery store. Forgetting about anything but the uniqueness of the moment, each of us wandered off on a pilgrimage of his or her own. I didn't shop — just walked up and down aisles and inhaled the scents. That is, until I heard a commotion at one of the checkout lanes. *Uh-oh,* I thought, *that sounds like Alice.* Moving in the direction of the noise, I saw Alice bargaining with a harried clerk, holding up a pack of three Cracker Jack boxes and saying, "Now, how much do you say I can get just one of these for?" She named a price, and the clerk shook his head and said, "No, you have to buy *all* of them." Alice responded with her final offer, "But I just want to buy *one,* and I'll pay fifteen cents for it." The poor young man looked at her, exasperation written all over his face. Ripping off one of the boxes from the pack, he held it out to her and said, "Here, honey, just take it!" I rushed up to help out, explaining that we had just today arrived in Oklahoma after five years in Taiwan, and this child knew nothing other than to bargain. The young checkout clerk entered into the spirit of the moment; grinning, he handed Alice all three packs and said, "Please, I want you to have these, and welcome to America!" Our child was much pleased with her first purchase in Oklahoma. (See Appendix.)

A whole year of new adventures followed for the children, and Bob and I had an exciting season of reunions with family and with friends in a number of states. There was nothing particularly restful about "furlough," but it was a rewarding year. Watching the children bond with their Ho Se Mo and Ho Shien Sun was pure bliss to see. They were enthralled with Sunday School and worship all in English, and they were particularly pleased to hear their own granddaddy preach. One of the families in the church, Robert and Modean Ross, became special friends of ours, and their five children literally became lifelong friends of our two. (They still visit and correspond half a century later.) Robert's father, Cotton, was a descendant of Chief John Ross of the Cherokee nation. The children thought it highly interesting that Cotton Ross, part Cherokee, had blond hair. Jody especially enjoyed meeting one of the "Indians" of his imagination, even if he only had a bit of Cherokee blood. There were full-blooded Cherokees in the community of Webbers Falls as well, and Jody found them intriguing.

We had worked hard at inculcating manners into the children; sometimes that actually showed. One of the family "rules" was that when you were guests in someone's home and they served you some food you didn't like, you just politely say, "No thank you," and move on. That dictum was put to the test pretty quickly. In one particular home, realizing that we came from Taiwan and would love rice, the lady of the house served some with the main dish. She prepared Minute Rice, and, not knowing what that was, both children took a healthy portion. After one bite, we saw the look on Jody's face. He said nothing but ate no more. When our hostess stepped out of the room, Jody turned to Bob and asked in a loud whisper, "What's *this*?" Never again would our two try Minute Rice, for it was a far cry from the good sticky rice they both loved.

After our week in Oklahoma, we headed for Alabama, where we would be living with Bob's mother. Retrospect revealed how difficult this would be for her. For Ora Hunt, a spotless and highly organized housekeeper, to have four not-so-tidy people suddenly move in with her, especially two active and not-particularly-reserved little people, must have been a shock. She was very gracious though, and she and the children bonded beautifully. Nonetheless, the house seemed strangely empty to Bob, because his dad was not there; he found the reality of his father's absence painful to deal with. Head knowledge and heart response are two very different feelings. It did help Granny Ora to talk to her grandchildren about their granddaddy and how he had loved them. She had quite a flourishing business baking cakes for people — and wonderful creations they were, especially her wedding creations. She always cut the tops off cake layers to make them level and kept them in what our children called "the cake end drawer." It was their favorite after-school treat.

Bob's brother, Joe, and Catherine, his wife, lived just across the street on land that had been part of Hunt Dairy Farm. By this time, their son, Wayne, had two adorable little sisters, Joan and Janis. The cousins now had a chance to know each other and were constant companions. Joe had opened a hardware store shortly before we went to Taiwan. Jody and Alice dearly loved to go to Hunt-Wright Hardware, because Uncle Joe had a wonderful soft drink machine, and he would give each a nickel so they could have an ice-cold soft drink after school.

Since the children were now in Boaz schools, we joined First Baptist Church Boaz, where we were royally welcomed. Our first Sunday "home" is one none of us will ever forget.

The church had a marvelous music ministry led by Glenn Maze, who also headed the music department of Snead, the local community college.

His associate was Rebecca Moore, a young woman with an incredible voice and the ability to sing from the heart as well. We sat in the morning service that first Sunday back, our hearts thrilled to be worshipping with family and friends. Rebecca stood to present the special music, and in her beautiful lyrical soprano voice, sang "Welcome Home Children" — and Bob and I dissolved in tears at such a welcome.

Alice and Jody formed lasting friendships in both Sunday School and Sunbeams. Alice was already anticipating fall arriving so she could be a GA. School was also a smooth adjustment, and Morrison Academy had them more than prepared for classes in America. The McCormick children, Lee Ann and Ken, became their fast friends and treated them to an exciting trip to Six Flags Over Georgia. They talked about their adventure for months.

Bob and I were more than busy with speaking in churches, at conferences, and various conventions, and grateful for family who helped with the children when we were away. In the 1960s, Global Missions Conferences were known as Schools of Missions and lasted for a full week. Being hosted for two meals a day in homes with each new family serving their best dishes was no way to lose weight. However, telling the story of the wonderful people in Taiwan was never like work, but rather a golden opportunity. Going back to Hebron Church in Meridian, Mississippi, gave us the chance to reconnect with special friends and to share the Taiwan story. The Smiths welcomed us with open arms and tables groaning with our favorite dishes, including Ginny Smith's crunchy tea cakes. Lynda, my cheeky little piano student, had blossomed into a beautiful teenager who played the piano like a pro. Likewise, returning to Booneville, Mississippi, and reunions with friends was satisfying to the heart. People in both of these places were the kind who, although you hadn't seen them in a whole handful of years, you could pick up just as if you had seen them the week before. We called them "heart friends." Speaking again in those churches felt like talking with family.

We went to Oklahoma as often as possible for time with Mama and Dad. The Ross children made every trip a special experience for Alice and Jody, and we heard all the time about Dixie, Bobby, Linda, Diane and Peg.

Stuck in the back of my mind is the evening our two and the Ross five came into the living room all at one time, and I innocently inquired of Alice what she was holding cupped in her hands. "Cute little baby frogs," she answered. I automatically reacted, "Oh, goodness. Don't keep those in here," whereupon she obligingly let them go right there on the spot — of course, they jumped and scattered all over the room.

Summer at Ridgecrest for Foreign Missions Week was a terrific reunion with missionary friends from many lands, and Alice and Jody especially enjoyed the afternoon reception for missionaries, with everyone dressing in the costume of their adopted country. Alice was in a Chinese *chi pau* (chee paw) with its mandarin collar, and Jody in the traditional blue cotton Chinese trousers and jacket with frog buttons and a cone-shaped coolie hat. Bob grinned and told me, "If we had a dollar for every picture made of us, we'd be independently wealthy."

Jody began first grade in Boaz schools. The children would have one semester in the States before we returned to Taiwan. Alice and he both loved the social life of school, and Jody had all sorts of "girlfriends" that he claimed, sometimes a new one every week. One Monday when I picked up the children to take them to Sunbeams and GAs, Jody was talking non-stop, full of the happenings in "Mrs. Lackey's room," as he called the class. Mrs. Lackey had been teaching first grade as long as anyone could remember and could handle those children with her hands tied behind her back. Jody reported that they had just elected a class king and queen, "And I'm the king," he reported. "And who is the queen?" was my first question. "Dutchy Malone," he declared, "and I'm going to marry her!" I was properly shocked and immediately asked him, "What about all your *other* girlfriends?" He took me seriously, and burst into tears, snuffling, "But I can't marry *all* of them." He managed to calm down and remained friends with all the girls in the class.

It felt like that about the time we had grown accustomed to all the traveling, speaking, and visiting with family and friends, it was necessary to begin planning our return to the field. That brought up the question of our assignment. Taichung wanted us back to continue with student ministry there, and, of course, we had wonderful ties and more jobs than there was time to do. Yet, about this time, there came a request from Grace Church in Taipei for Bob to be Dr. Jou's co-pastor and for us to work with Lillian Lu and the amazing ministry through the church's student center. There was a long history of problems with church and missionary leadership in the beginning years of that work, and this was a tremendous step forward for missionaries to actually be invited to work alongside outstanding Chinese leadership. Dr. Jou wrote us a letter of invitation, indicating that if we would prayerfully consider the possibility, Grace Church would make a formal request of the Taiwan mission. Bob and I faced a decision between two choices — both of which were appealing — and realized our need for divine leadership. We had a bit more understanding of the dynamics of the Taiwan mission after one term on the field. During those first five years, we had learned that there was a checkered history between Grace and the mission, dating back to the earliest days when there was tension between a couple of the earliest missionaries and Grace Church's leadership. Grace had quickly become self-supporting and able to make their own decisions. A handful of missionaries had residual paternalistic views of their role in leadership that caused a lack of understanding. In light of this checkered history, it was wonderful that Grace was asking for cooperative work with a missionary couple. Our final decision: We would happily work with Grace Church. Alice and Jody were torn; they loved Taichung and their friends there, but they also had friends in Taipei and were happy to hear we would be with "Aunt Lillian" again.

The choice was neither simple nor easy — but we felt at peace with what we should do, desiring the spot where we could do the most good for the most people. With this in mind, we began preparing for a return to what was now "home." At least this time, we had more of an idea about what to expect, and we anticipated the adventures lying ahead. Nonetheless, our final day in Alabama with Bob's mother turned out to be traumatic for Bob. The whole time we had been back in his boyhood home, Bob was ever aware of the emptiness of his father no longer being there. However, that final morning, as he walked out the front door headed to the airport, reality grabbed him in a visceral way: He would never see his father again.

He was gone. The tears began coursing down his face, and he turned and embraced his mother for one last time, and the two wept together. Painful as the moment was, Bob finally had a sense of resolution over his loss.

Just as the children had thrilled to think about going to America, they now were excited about going home to Taiwan and seeing their friends again. Bob and I were eager to get back to the ministry to which we were called and anticipating what God had in store for us in Taipei, the capital city. Past experience had taught us to look for the unexpected and know that new adventures were coming.

Easter at Grace Church — children's choir, Dr. Jou and Bob presiding

Rosalie with choir at Baptist TV Studio, Taipei

Bob photographs the children in a pedicab during typhoon flooding

EIGHT

GRACE
1968-1969

Getting the family comfortably settled on the flight to Los Angeles took a bit of time, but eventually I drew a long breath and leaned back as silent, unbidden tears trickled down my cheeks. Goodbyes made my heart ache. Feeling a touch on my arm, I looked through tears into Alice's anxious eyes. "Mama," she began, then swallowed and began to cry as well. Next, Jody, seated on the other side, joined in our mutual sorrow. After a few moments, I declared, "OK, kids, we'll make it. It's just sort of sad, isn't it, to say goodbye to those we love?"

Being young and resilient, Alice and Jody soon busied themselves with the packet of activities a smiling stewardess gave them, and I gulped a bit and trained my errant thoughts on what challenges God might have ahead of us. Mentally shaking my head, I admitted that goodbyes themselves were one of those challenges that came with the call.

The children were soon speculating on what their Uncle Arthur might have in mind for our day in Los Angeles, the city where he worked. The next day was certainly enough to keep their minds occupied, for Art took us to Marine Land in San Diego, where the children "oohed and ahhed" at the sight of whales and dolphins performing synchronized feats. From there we moved on to explore Knott's Berry Farm, where Alice and Jody stored up all sorts of wonderful sights to share with buddies in Taiwan.

Bob and I spent some time on the long flight over the Pacific talking over what some of our responsibilities at Grace might be. Feeling like old veterans by this time, we knew that language refresher studies would be high on the to-do list. A great part of our excitement came from knowing we would be under the direction of Dr. Jou and Lillian Lu, two brilliant people focused on reaching the lost in their city. We loved this reversal of roles, with Taiwan Christian leadership directing the work of missionaries. They knew the needs better than any occidental possibly could and would know how we might best make a contribution. Grace was involved in multiple outreaches across the area, from jail ministry to a thriving student work among the best university students in the country. Grace's membership was made up not only of many Christians from mainland China but also people from countries around the world, ranging from businessmen to local professionals to embassy personnel. That was one reason the English services were of such importance. After a while, we got used to seeing large limousines flying flags of various countries drive up and disgorge an ambassador or bank president, all coming for the purpose of worship. Grace was truly international and presented us with a fresh challenge every week.

There was no mission housing available, and although plans were underway to build a duplex behind Grace Student Center, it would take precious time, so we found temporary living quarters. Locating an apartment fairly nearby, we were able to settle in by February when our shipment arrived. Using every bit of space in nooks and crannies in the shipping crate, we had tucked in little bits of American goodies. Of course, the little blue enamel cup was tucked in. The morning we unpacked the crate, Bob pulled out a jar of Ho Se Mo's blackberry jelly and handed it to me. I sat down and cried, then gave a long sigh and got back to the task at hand.

Alice and Jody quickly settled into Bethany, the small Christian school in Taipei. Both had to really pay attention because, just like Morrison, this school was academically demanding. The challenge was good for them, and from the beginning, they learned to discipline themselves to study. It paid a lifetime of benefits in their future years of academics. Several other Baptist MKs were also at Bethany, and our two soon had a classroom full of pals. One of Jody's classmates was Jonja Deal, an MK from Malaysia. Her parents, John and Revonda, were in Taipei studying Mandarin. (In one of life's little serendipities, twelve years later, at Samford University, Jody roomed with MK Ken Jacks. Ken and Jonja married and have spent their careers as missionaries in Indonesia.)

In a less uplifting way, however, history repeated itself. We had not been in the apartment a month when we were burglarized during the day when no one was there. That same awful feeling of being violated engulfed us. My jewel box was gone, and Alice's first question was, "Oh, Mama, what will you do? You don't even have a pair of earrings left!" I assured her that costume jewelry was pretty low on the totem pole of valuables, even if my ears went naked. There came ringing into my memory a phrase Dr. Cauthen had used repeatedly at orientation years earlier: "Take your clutter in your hands, not in your heart." The stolen items were just that — clutter. Our apartment was small, and we had no household help, but suddenly we felt vulnerable. The landlord added bars on the downstairs windows, and that helped a bit. Dr. Jou was concerned about our safety and felt a move might be wise; however, considering the new duplex was supposed to be built soon, we were hesitant to move twice.

There was too much going on to spend time worrying over robbers, however, and after a week or two, we began sleeping a little better. Every day was full, especially weekends. Bob preached, directed the English ministry at Grace, assisted Lillian in all sorts of student outreach, conducted a jail service once a week, and carried a heavy load of mission committee work. In addition, he was extremely involved in island-wide student ministry. Bob loved spending time with students as well as preaching, both of which opened doors for personal soul-winning. His one-on-one talent with people was a priceless gift. Bob had many key moments when he could share the gospel and see students and adults come to saving faith. It was the kind of experience where you could end the day with a deep feeling of satisfaction. We often reflected on missionary friends who struggled in lands where they would go for years and see no results. How agonizing. We thought of Adoniram and Ann Judson, and how they studied, struggle, suffered and worked a full six years before seeing the first convert.

Our problem was *too* much to do. Sometimes Bob preached three or four times each Sunday, traveling from spot to spot, conducting baptisms and the Lord's Supper multiple times. On Sundays I played the organ at Grace and taught the junior class (including the Jous' son, Joshua) in Mandarin Bible study. Some Sundays there were as many as eighteen or nineteen, far too many for one class. I also assisted Lillian with the children's choir and worked with Grace's WMU. Marie Jou, Dr. Jou's wife, was the acknowledged guiding light for all WMU women of Taiwan. She was probably the most brilliant, underrated, and self-effacing leader I've ever known. Marie always focused on others, never herself, but she was behind the planning and the work of others, quietly leading by example. She reminded me a lot of a younger version of Mama.

Mrs. Jou knew I had worked with GA and YWA beginnings in Taichung and wanted these groups organized in Taipei and all over the island. Therefore, I worked on materials and sought to find Chinese leadership to work alongside. This was a full-time job, and I simply didn't have the time, just the will; we made a beginning, however, and I worked toward presenting the needs to island-wide WMU leadership. Meanwhile, I taught Speech at the College of Law of Tai Da, the university across the avenue from Grace Church. That took a hunk of time, as did helping at our new radio/TV studio as accompanist. I gave piano lessons to several young Chinese women and felt that this was worthy use of time, for they used their skills to serve in many spots. Simply being organist at Grace was a huge challenge. Knowing all too well my lack of skill on the organ, I had to practice diligently. One Sunday morning, I nervously enjoyed the special music — not because I was playing, but because Alice was at the organ. She and fellow MK David Raley played a duet. David played beautifully by ear, and that Sunday morning he played the piano and Alice the organ. I was one relieved mama when they finished a flawless performance.

House guests were the rule, not the exception, this term — just as in the first. So many missionaries needed to travel to Taipei for medical work, or to the embassy, or for committee meetings that our home was like the Hunt Hostel. The kids learned to pitch in and help, and we needed those extra sets of hands. They loved it when MKs came with their parents, but their favorite company was Aunt Nan Herring. She was their Taiwan grandmother, and she acted the part perfectly, indulging them royally.

Alice was able to get a ride to Calvary Church for GAs and loved it. She and Jody played well together in spite of their age difference, and one of their favorite "play likes" was setting up stores: grocery stores, beauty shops, you name it. They also shared a love of reading and consumed books voraciously. One day, I found Alice going through books in our study. She pulled one out and read the title: *Why God Gave Children Parents*. I overheard her mutter, "I better read that. I've been wondering." Both children had Bible study as part of their curriculum at Bethany School, and Alice frequently presented us with questions about the Bible. One day, she asked, "Mama, where did Cain's wife come from?" I replied, "When you get to heaven, you can ask the Lord that question." She reposted, "I'll just do that." Jody chimed in, "Aw, Alice, that was such a long time ago. I'll bet the Lord's forgotten by now!" I made it a practice to refer the children to their father for such theological inquiries.

I often told Mama and Dad about the children's sayings and doings, knowing how they relished hearing. That spring I wrote, "Jody has an answer for everything. Somebody someday isn't going to take too kindly to some of his remarks!" (I thought about that long-ago tendency when, fifty years later, Jody was serving as assistant attorney general in Washington, DC, and confronted some political types who did not respond happily to adherence to the rule of law. Those early tendencies we saw in our children did develop through the years, and their discipline in study and ability to organize manifested itself in their careers, Jody in government service and Alice as a seminary president.)

We somehow managed to find time for several exciting visits to President Chiang Kai-shek's chapel, thanks to Dr. Jou getting tickets for us. Bob was only able to make it one time because of services at the church, but that spring I was able to enjoy the experience repeatedly. The first visit, I sat with Marie Jou, who kindly pointed out the various pieces of living history in attendance. Seated near us was Mrs. Jang (Chang), the wife of the government's secretary-general, and next to her Jang Sywe-Lyang, the Little General for whom I had made the Bible tapes, and his wife. Then General and Mrs. Ma came in and sat right next to me. Mrs. Ma looked for the world like the Empress Dowager. Mrs. Jou told me after the service that General Ma was a famous and powerful military leader. The general's wife was quite a character and could never find her place in the Chinese hymnal. I obligingly tried to assist her, and when I began singing in Chinese, she just turned and stared at me as if I were some rare kind of creature. I was hard put to keep a straight face. When the sermon started, she went right to sleep. I wrote home about the morning, explaining how the president had arrived: "The MAN himself entered, looking very chipper, and we all stood. He walked down the aisle and turned and smiled in each direction."

Because Mrs. Jou was on a first-name basis with these famous figures of Chinese history, I had an engrossing ten minutes after the service, standing and chatting with them. Mrs. Ma was curious about my speaking Mandarin and asked Mrs. Jou about it. Marie told her I had been born on the mainland. Rather than clarify, I just smiled and acted like I belonged in such rarified company.

The following month I returned to the president's chapel, this time accompanying Alma Hunt. She was on the island to speak at an East Asian gathering of WMU leaders in Taipei, and we had the rare, good pleasure of hosting her in our little apartment. Our children laid immediate claim to their own "Aunt Alma" and became lifelong friends. Alma could spin a wonderful yarn, and Alice and Jody literally sat at her feet and drank it in. We took "Aunt Alma" to our favorite downtown hotel for a facial, manicure and pedicure, all for $1.25. I wrote Mama, "I don't know when I've had such fun watching someone else have fun! I told her the only thing she missed was getting a wig, and she wondered why no one had *mentioned* one to her!" That Sunday, Dr. Jou secured tickets to the president's chapel for us, and Miss Hunt did not miss a moment, taking in the whole experience.

Oh, no — not again. Oh, yes. One Saturday night in June, we sent the kids upstairs to get ready for bed. With reluctant steps, they headed up. Suddenly, Alice called out in a quavering little voice, "Daddy!" "What?" he called out impatiently. "Come here!" she yelled. "Why?" he responded. "Daddy, there's a man in the bathroom window!" Bob took those stairs two at a time. Evidently, the thief had heard the children coming, left the room where he was rifling through drawers, and dashed for the bathroom window to skinny down the water pipe. All four of us nearly had a heart attack, and the children were understandably terrorized. None of us slept that night, and less than a week later, we moved to the overseas compound where a house had just become vacant. The morning following the scare, we told Dr. Jou what had happened. He was upset but so thankful the children had not accosted the thief in the bedroom, because he said it was highly likely the man was carrying a knife. That thought kept us awake more nights. With sighs of relief, we were soon back on the overseas compound, and although our first robbery had been right there, it still seemed much safer than the apartment. The kids were thrilled to be living next to the Wait children again, so good came from the incident. A military family returning to the States gave us their beautiful little white Lhasa Apso terrier, and Meili (her name meant "beautiful") became part of the family. She thought her new home was wonderful, with a yard where she could run and play with the children. Meanwhile, the police traced the young thief by the serial number on our stolen camera. We were required to go to police headquarters and see the man handcuffed to a rail. He looked like a teenager, just a tough kid wanting some excitement. It was *too* much excitement for us.

We took our summer vacation again this year in Hong Kong, staying with Charles Cowherd once more. Bob conducted a revival in a Mandarin church while there. The trip took on special significance for us, because at the invitation one of those nights, Jody made a profession of faith. He had trusted Christ several months earlier and decided on his own that night to make it public. I wrote Mama and Dad, telling of the evening: "Jody plucked me on the sleeve and whispered, 'I want to go down.' 'Why?'" I asked him. He clearly explained — and off he went. At Grace Church the following September, Bob and Dr. Jou together conducted the baptismal service, and I cried happy tears.

Unwelcome incidents seemed to have a way of recurring. Flooding was one of them. The rains came down, and the floods came up. Nineteen inches of rain fell in one day, and with two more days of rain to follow, the water had nowhere to go but into our house. We propped up everything "proppable," and Meili spent the night on a TV tray. The kids found it pretty exciting, and Jody even sailed a little red and white plastic boat down the hallway. We parents were just happy to see the waters finally recede.

The children were eager for Meili to have puppies, and we reluctantly agreed. Several weeks later, she departed for the vets to meet a Pekinese there. Alice and Jody were excited as they awaited the happy event. It coincided with the 1968 presidential election in America and prompted as much household excitement as did the presidential campaign. When Nixon was elected president, there was as much rejoicing in the streets of Taipei as among Republicans in the States. Right after the election, Meili gave birth to three gorgeous little pups, all girls. But, *shock!* One was honey-colored, and two were black! Mind you, Meili was snow white. However, one look at their cute little pug noses assured us that the father was definitely a Pekinese. Those puppies stole the show. Being "election" pups, the two black ones were named for the losers (with a feminine twist) — Wallena (for George Wallace) and Humphrena (for Hubert Humphrey).

The little honey-colored pup was the one we kept; she was named Nixina. She and her mother later became "published," making an appearance in the GA magazine *Discovery*.

The overseas compound had one phone for four houses and used a buzzer system, so whoever happened to answer the phone could buzz the appropriate house. It was a chilly winter, so we had the three puppies indoors near where the buzzer system was set up. One day, I answered the phone, and a very distinguished British voice asked, "May I speak to Mr. Wait?" "One moment," I politely responded, and buzzed the Waits' house, listening to hear if they picked up. Meanwhile, the three puppies were frisking all around the room, and Nixina came over, sniffed at my sandals and nibbled at my big toe. "Don't you bite my toe!" I admonished her, and an offended British voice spoke, "I *beg* your pardon?" I got so tickled I just hung up the phone, message undelivered.

We loved hosting Lillian, the Jous and their sons. I had brought back from the States a reading accelerator to use in teaching English. The teacher could set the calibration of the lap-held machine and cause a marker to move down a page according to how fast the device is set. Knowing Dr. Jou was brilliant, I set it at a speed of 1,300 words per minute. Not explaining, I just asked him to try it out. Mind you, he was reading an English text, and English was his second language. Getting to the end of the page, he politely inquired, "Could you set it a little faster? That's a bit slow." I didn't dare mention what I usually set it on to read for practice. It certainly wasn't near his speed.

Dr. Jou's tales intrigued not only our children, but us as well. It was just a normal part of his week to hobnob with the rich and famous, and he looked with amusement upon a lot of mankind's foibles and took them with the proverbial grain of salt. He often related stories "from the palace," as he called the president's official residence. I wrote home about one of the tales, "The Prince in the Palace," as Dr. Jou dubbed it. Dr. Jou's son, Joshua, had Spitz dogs and gave one to a Miss Lyou, a legislator friend of the Jous and of President Chiang and Madame as well. Miss Lyou also directed Madame Chiang's orphanage. One day when the Madame visited the orphanage, the dog really outdid himself, making up to the Madame and even jumping in her lap. The Madame liked him right back and asked if she could have him — which, naturally, Miss Lyou did not refuse. So Joshua's dog became a royal prince. However, when the terrible rains started, trouble ensued. Every two hours, it was the custom for one of the presidential guards to take the little prince out. Well, the prince refused to go out in the rain. Where did he then decide to mess? First, in the president's own bathroom, second in Madame's study, and third, on the most expensive carpet in the palace! Back the prince went to Miss Lyou! Madame said, "Now, we want the dog back, mind you, but we want him well-trained!" Next, the royal cat got in trouble. The cat had a regrettable habit. It was spoiled and loved to sleep on TOP of a mosquito net, so one night, it decided to sleep on top of President Chiang's mosquito net. Mr. President didn't much care for the idea and shooed the cat off. But when he shooed, the cat jumped and knocked over a priceless Ming vase, breaking it in a thousand pieces. "And now," I concluded the story to Mama, "there is no longer a cat at the palace."

At long last, the duplex was finished, and we moved in; it was right behind the student center and wonderfully close to our work. The children loved the play space at Grace. Harlan and Joann Spurgeon moved into the other apartment. Tim and Twila, their older two children, were so good to our younger ones, and it was a terrific location. Furthermore, we didn't feel as threatened by the possibility of thieves in this section of town.

The following summer was yet another adventure, for the Singapore/Malaysia Mission asked us to come to Malaysia to conduct an MK camp during their annual mission meeting. Alice and Jody had a marvelous time staying in Hong Kong with "Uncle Charles" while we flew first to Thailand and then to Malaysia. The location was on the Straits of Malacca, and we were housed with the MKs in an old rubber plantation owner's mansion. MKs are a breed all their own. Those teenagers were both a joy and a challenge, and they asked some penetrating and difficult questions during Bible studies. We fell in love with them and have wondered through the years what paths their lives have taken. Returning to Hong Kong, we took a side trip with the children to Macau and stood in the territory adjoining

Communist China. As always when thinking of China, and certainly when standing *looking* into it, I wondered if I would ever be able to go home again to that land imprinted so deeply on my heart. Only time would tell. For now, however, it was time to go home to the work before us.

In the yard following a typhoon

Jody admires Alice's piano birthday cake

Neighbor Rodney with Alice and Jody, holding Humphrena, Wallena and Nixina

NINE

KAOHSIUNG

1970-1972

Summer was every bit as busy as the school year, for Grace Student Center conducted continual classes and activities for university students. Many overseas students could not return to their own countries, so they became regulars. We always had students in our classes who wanted to learn English, especially from a native speaker. The students also enjoyed having Bob on their volleyball teams; that setting was a natural for being able to share the gospel in a relaxed atmosphere.

Alice and Jody thrived on time with Aunt Lillian, who lived right next door. One of their favorite outings (and ours) was eating out with Lillian and two other special "aunts," Rita Duke and Lucille Dawdy. Our teacher friend, Lucille, was now teaching at Tai Da University, as was Rita. We all looked forward to forays to Jou Pahngdz's (Fat Joe's). This down-to-earth restaurant was in the heart of a shopping district in the midst of little shops jammed with a bit of everything. Jou Pahngdz specialized in *jyaudzs* (Americans call them pot stickers) — little steamed, boiled, or pan-fried dumplings that were fragrant, succulent, and irresistible. Servers would come to each table with small bamboo steamers brimming with *jyaudzs,* and our children wielded their chopsticks like the pros they were. However, one particular visit to Jou Pahngdz's turned out to be memorable for an unexpected encounter.

Leaving the restaurant, we joined the usual crowds thronging the busy sidewalk — coolies with carts, people, dogs, and plenty of noise. Suddenly, a disheveled man who appeared to be deranged spotted us and headed straight toward Jody, the smallest in our group. Dressed in tattered, filthy rags, thin to the point of emaciation, the fellow was babbling gibberish and holding a plastic juice cup and straw. A mangy dog walking nearby must have sensed danger emanating from the man, for he reared back, bared his teeth, and started growling, the hairs on his back visibly bristling. Confronting Jody, the man repeatedly attempted to thrust his straw into Jody's mouth. All of us were stunned, but Bob quickly grabbed Jody, and we melted into the throngs so the man could not get to him. If I had ever pooh-poohed at the idea of visible evidence of the presence of evil, I never again doubted. It was a spine-chilling feeling that was hard to shake off. Jody never forgot the strange encounter, nor did we.

The editor of *Discovery* (the WMU magazine that is now called *GA World*) was my cousin Iva Jewel Tucker. She loved children and delighted in sharing the story of her young MK relatives. In one issue, Iva Jewel wrote the picture story of "Seven Days with Two MKs," and Alice and Jody began getting fan mail from GAs all over America. It was a novel experience for them.

Sometimes we encountered totally unexpected opportunities to share the gospel. Alice and I, along with fellow missionaries Herb and Emma

Jean Barker, were involved in just such an experience that year. Because we spoke Mandarin, we were asked to be part of the filming of *Queen of the Dark Chamber*, the story of Christiana Tsai. Tsai, along with her missionary friend Mary Lehman, translated the entire Bible into phonetics so it would be accessible to millions. When Bob first heard the movie title, he exclaimed, "Good lands! You're going to act in an X-rated movie?!" Then he learned the real story. Christiana Tsai had been struck with malignant malaria of the eyes, a rare condition that causes blindness and excruciating pain. She was forced to live in a dark room, but her story was a remarkable one of faith and courage. I played the role of missionary Mary Lehman ("China Mary," as she was called). The Barkers portrayed the elder Lehmans, and Alice played the part of Mary (me) as a child. To be sure, it was an unusual experience. Filming was at Dan Shwei, a nearby coastal city, and in central Taiwan at the ancestral home built more than a century earlier by a wealthy Chinese family. Memorizing the script in Mandarin was an exercise in discipline; however, enduring the 100-plus degree weather under bright camera lights was similar to a torture chamber. To my chagrin, the director frequently had to call out, "Cut — ah, cut — ah," and stop the filming for an assistant to mop off the face of this occidental who was perspiring profusely. Meanwhile, the young woman playing Christiana, clad in long sleeves and partly covered by a blanket, sat upright on a bed looking cool and collected. The most rewarding part of the whole experience, however, was the news two years later that a number of people had come to saving faith when the film was shown in several countries.

During our next furlough, the Southern Baptist Convention was held in Philadelphia, and we were thrilled to be able to drive from the convention to nearby Paradise, Pennsylvania, to the Lehman family home. The house itself was historical, for George Washington had been a guest there 200 years earlier. Mary Lehman had died just that past January, but Miss Tsai, now in her eighties, was still living in the house. On the possibility of being able to meet her, we stopped at the Lehman House and knocked at the back door. A uniformed nurse came to the door, and we asked if it would be possible to meet Miss Tsai. She quickly shook her head, saying, "Miss Tsai is unable to receive visitors." Apologizing for intruding, we explained that we came from Taiwan and had recently appeared in the movie about Miss Tsai's life. The nurse paused, looked at us, then asked, "Would you wait a few moments, please?" and went back inside.

Minutes later, she returned, smilingly saying, "Miss Tsai would like to meet you," and we happily followed her into the dark room where Miss Tsai was sitting up in her bed, just like in the movie. We explained our errand, and Christiana was thrilled to hear a firsthand account of the movie. She had not met one person who was in the film and was full of questions. We left that afternoon having felt privileged to have spent half an hour with a missions legacy.

Meanwhile, back in Taipei, more changes were in the offing. The mission asked that we move to Kaohsiung to begin student work there. Our immediate thought was: *No, we love Grace Church, the student work, the multitude of opportunities. We don't want to move.* But we agreed to ponder and pray about it. We sincerely needed direction and sought an answer. Taipei was comfortable. The work was flourishing; openings to witnessing surrounded us. Prayer reminded us, however, that we didn't come to be comfortable. We decided to move and begin work with students in Taiwan's second-largest city. Although Taipei had several missionaries working with the universities, Kaohsiung had none. I fell asleep several nights on the thought: *Here we go again. More change.* But we were not going alone.

Kaohsiung had some unexpected benefits. As Taiwan's southern port city, it was lovely and not as crowded as Taipei. The climate was also a boon, less cold weather and less rain. Furthermore, there was an excellent Department of Defense school for American children. The principal, Bill Reeves, was Alice's new teacher, and, as a bonus, he was a Baptist lay preacher. Tso Ying, the military installation, had a snack bar, bowling alley, and theater to American citizens. Jody was excited about being able to bowl for ten cents and go to a movie for a quarter. He joined Cub Scouts, and Alice became pianist for the junior high choir and joined Girl Scouts. We also organized an Acteens group. At first, Alice was its only member, but then the Spurgeons moved to Kaohsiung, and Twila and several other girls joined in. Our Acteens learned a lot about leadership and loved having "theme" programs, like the time Alice and Twila planned a program on Japan and served *sukiyaki*.

Kaohsiung had tens of thousands of students, and Bob and I looked for the best place to begin. There were two Mandarin and three Taiwanese churches in the city, with many colleges located nearby. Both of us began teaching at Kaohsiung Teacher's College, located very near to Wen Hwa [pronounced *Won Hwah*] Culture Baptist Church. We started with student parties to get acquainted and then organized Bible discussion groups where they could practice English. This was different from Grace, because this time we were starting from scratch.

The Leroy Hogues worked with Mandarin evangelism in Kaohsiung, and their children also attended the DOD school. Thankfully, Alice and Jody had much that was familiar around them. Wouldn't you know — again, a duplex missionary residence was on the drawing board, but we had to wait while it was being built.

Our small mission station decided we needed a service on Sunday evenings so our children and the American community could worship in English. The three missionary men and Bill Reeves from the DOD school each took a turn preaching once a month and happily called themselves "pastors-in-law." We also had Sunday School for the children, and it was a win-win arrangement.

Another bonus was our marvelous language assistant, Mrs. Wen, a devout Christian who spoke wonderful Mandarin. She made it possible for me to prepare messages and translate GA manuals and magazines, plus assisting Bob with work on sermons. Much of our time was spent with Wen Hwa Church and pastor Chen. The Chens spoke not only Mandarin and English but also Taiwanese and Japanese. I taught the women's class; many of the ladies were Japanese and had no other contact with Christianity. Paul preached in Taiwanese, Mandarin, and Japanese every Sunday. Occasionally, Bob led the Mandarin service, but preached every week at the English service. With his black hair and tanned skin, he fit right in. One day, a friend of one of my Bible class women commented to her, "I passed your church last Sunday and the door was open — I could see the preacher, and he had the best English of any Chinese I ever heard!" My class member grinned and explained, "But he *is* an American!"

The Hogues lived in an older mission residence, adjacent to the building site of the new duplex. Again, the Spurgeons were our neighbors. Son Tim and daughters Twila, Ruth and Debbie were great friends with our two. The Hogues had three: Charlie (Alice's age), Tommy (Jody's age), big sister Sue Ann, and Andy, the youngest. Jody distinctly remembers our first parent-teacher conference with Miss Clio Abercrombie, his teacher. Tommy's parents had their conference one day and ours was the next. Tommy warned Jody, "Just be ready. My parents had their conference, and came home and chewed me out!" Jody dreaded our appointment but looked relieved when we came home smiling. Miss Abercrombie had written a short report that followed the listing of his grades. I saved that paper, and Jody now has it framed and hanging on the wall in his law office.

November 5, 1970

Jody Hunt

Jody's work is generally top quality. He has many interests and stimulates class discussions. My only suggestion for Jody is that he try to accept the fact that he can be *wrong* occasionally.

Clio Abercrombie

At the end of the year, he had another superlative report, but she ended with another slight caveat: "Jody sometimes tends to be a trifle smug." In later years, we've enjoyed reminding Jody of those early reports. He once commented, "My goodness, she could read me so well so early!"

Bill Reeves was an outstanding teacher as well. He taught both seventh and eighth grades, allowing students to work on their own at their own speed; it was marvelous training for self-motivation and made a lasting difference in Alice's work all the way through a doctor's degree.

Jody celebrated his third birthday with a sailor party. The hat was a gift from his Uncle Arthur, 1964.

With Wu Disyung's children in Taichung, 1964

Visiting with Vippee, the Herrings' monkey who lived next door, 1964

College YWAs meet with the Hunts at Christmas, 1965

Rosalie examines a YWA magazine with MKs Carolyn Culpepper, Joyce Lynn Hunker, Nancy Herring and Mary Lou Quick, 1965

Two YWA groups lead a children's service in Taichung, 1965

Mrs. Wang and Rosalie with GAs in Taichung, 1965

Some of the GAs receiving awards at a coronation service, 1965

*At a GA coronation
in Taichung, 1965*

*Children at the
Taichung orphanage
Christmas party, 1966*

*The family leaving
for furlough, 1967*

*Enjoying a Chinese
feast with Alma
Hunt, Lillian Lu and
Lucille Dawdy, 1968*

*With Aunt Rhett and Aunt Grace
in South Carolina, 1975*

*Harold Hall performing a wedding
in Tainan, Taiwan, 1971*

*Bob's engineering
students in China, 1981*

*Alice leading a Bible
study in Mombasa,
Kenya, 1981*

With some of our Journeyman friends in Hong Kong, 1981

Alice with Jody at his graduation from Samford, 1982

Exploring the ruins of the old Summer Palace, Beijing, with Jody, 1984

Alice and Harold Hall's fiftieth anniversary, Boaz, Alabama, 1983

The three sisters together in Alabama. It was Alice and Harold's fiftieth anniversary, and Aunt Rhett's first time ever to Alabama, 1983.

Cooking on our one gas burner in Tianjin, China, 1986

Jody gets a cold water shampoo in our Tianjin, China kitchen, 1986

IBC church retreat, 1987

Preschool graduation, IBC,
Manila, Philippines, 1988

IBC international
Bible study, 1988

Luncheon for IBC
preschool faculty, 1988

With our Manila,
Philippines neighbor,
Abel, and his pet,
Susie, 1988

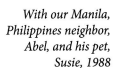

Dr. Eli Sarmiento and Nolyn Cabahug enjoy watching Bob introduce his grandson, Carl, to IBC congregation, 1989

A church picnic in Perth, Western Australia, 1989

Inaugural Christmas Carols by Candlelight, Ballajura, Western Australia, 1990

Children's time at Ballajura Baptist Church, WA, 1990

On one occasion, all of us attended the military chapel at Tso Ying; it was a unique experience for our two Baptist offspring. The chaplain was Presbyterian, and the order of service a bit unfamiliar to our kids. Communion was served that morning, and that's when the unique moment occurred. Parishioners were called by family, or by row, to go to the altar to kneel, and the pastor passed the bread and juice. This was Jody's first Lord's Supper experience outside a Chinese worship service, and he was taking it all in. When the chaplain handed him the little cup, he turned it up and drank it quickly. I'll not soon forget the look on his face. As we watched, his eyes grew big, and we heard him gulp. After returning to our row, he reached up and grabbed my sleeve, whispering, "What *was* that?!" Jody's first taste of wine was a shock.

That evening at home, we talked about the differences in services, and Alice recalled the first time she took communion in an English worship service. Shortly after her baptism, we were visiting at Calvary Church one Sunday evening when they had the Lord's Supper. Alice saw the deacon coming with the plate of bread, so she quickly took the bubble gum out of her mouth in order to be ready. Carefully reaching out to hold the plate, she took a piece of the bread. We all watched with widening eyes as the deacon moved to the next row, trailing behind him Alice's bubble gum that had stuck to the platter.

Occasionally, Bob would be asked to perform a wedding ceremony. The tradition was to follow the wedding with a feast, and it would be a large affair. At one such wedding, we were among some 250 guests. As usual at feasts, we knew to concentrate on two or three tasty but comparatively innocent dishes and smilingly ignore the others, being sure not to ask questions about what a particular dish might be. I distinctly recalled a similar feast to which my Bible class invited us. Bob vowed afterwards that the sea slugs were tasty, but the kids and I agreed that pickled jelly fish tasted like salty rubber bands. When having overnight guests, we often just ate at home; it was less complicated. Always in Taichung and Taipei, we had entertained a lot of company. Now in Kaohsiung, we were glad to host a surprising number of guests who needed a place to stay. One of our favorites was Dr. Jou. I remember one weekend when he came to speak at the fortieth anniversary of the downtown Mandarin church. He stayed with us and had an unending supply of stories that kept the children fascinated. I wrote home, "Dr. Jou is an amazing man. He surely has fingers in more pies than he has fingers on both hands."

The pastor of that Mandarin church, Pastor Lu Bang Di [pronounced *Lou Bahng Dee*], and his wife were a dedicated couple. Among their many ministries was a highly unusual one: a home for polio victims at the back of the church. Lu Shr Mu (Mrs. Shepherd Lu) was its director. A few years earlier, at the height of the polio epidemic, a vaccine became available for most, but one batch was tragically left out of refrigeration and lost its potency. Unknowing medical staff used the vaccine, and many of the vaccinated children got polio. The downtown church took as their ministry to provide care and therapy for these children, helping more than 100 of them get an education and have renewed hope. Doctors volunteered their time and therapists helped with rehabilitation. Our small Acteens group enjoyed making cupcakes and taking them to the home, feeling a small part of making a difference.

The Foreign Mission Board (now IMB) was planning the mission study courses for 1975 to center on medical missions and determined that the study for older children (GAs and RAs) would be the polio ministry in Kaohsiung. I was shocked to receive a letter requesting that I write the book for children. Again, I shook my head, trying to count the number of times I had been confronted with needs on the field in areas where I had no experience whatsoever. Here it was, happening again. I reluctantly agreed to give it a try and attempted to keep all my doubts and misgivings unspoken. What did I know about writing? Precious little.

Board photographer Warren Johnson came to make a series of pictures to be used in the book. A couple of years later, when I held the first copy of *All-Star Pitcher* in my hands, I recognized immediately that the best part of the book was the pictures Warren had made of the courageous children in the polio home. (And I could have no way of knowing that I would end up writing more than one or two other books. Sometimes life can slip up on you.)

While Warren was in Kaohsiung, we took him to photograph another Baptist ministry, Mrs. Wang and her orphanage at Rock Village. Located in the countryside, Rock Village was quite remote from anything but open fields and farms. The intrepid Mrs. Wang ran an orphanage for abandoned children, where they learned how to farm and build things and be part of a self-sustaining village. There were some fifty children, and they grabbed our hearts in a hurry. Warren delighted in capturing their faces and smiles. One of our favorites was Moses. The little fellow had been abandoned near a river by his mother, so Mrs. Wang gave him the appropriate name of Moses. All of Moses's teeth had rotted, but Mrs. Wang got him to a dentist, and, later on, healthy permanent teeth came in. We first knew Moses as a toothless little charmer on whom everyone doted.

That final year before our second furlough was crowned with an unexpected and wonderful surprise. Less than an hour from Kaohsiung was Tainan, where there was a flourishing English congregation pastored by Bob Beard and his family. Numerous US military lived in Tainan — and Trinity Church was a growing one, with both Chinese and American congregations. The Beards were due for furlough, and at just the same time, Ho Shien Sun and Ho Se Mo (my parents) retired from active ministry. The Taiwan mission invited them to come as interims at Trinity. When we first heard the news, it sounded too good to be true. Our children would have their grandparents nearby. Those six months were a special gift from God. Alice and Jody were able to celebrate their birthdays with Ho Se Mo and Ho Shien Sun, go see them each week, have them come visit, and even make a family trip to Hong Kong together.

Dad's Chinese language retention was incredible. Their first Sunday in Tainan, Trinity Church invited him to also preach at the Mandarin service. Dad had not used Chinese formally for twenty-two years, but he preached that morning like his most recent message in Chinese had just been the week before. I sat in the congregation, snuffling and shedding happy tears.

Ever since our first furlough, Bob and I had been discussing the housing situation in America. It wasn't fair to barge in on his mother again. There were churches that provided missionary housing, but none were available in the places near our families. Joe — Bob's brother — helped us find a solution. Being in the hardware business, Joe knew building needs and supplies, and our cousin Melvin, a contractor, lived nearby. We already had a piece of land given to us by Bob's parents that had been part of Hunt Dairy Farm. Joe volunteered to supervise, and Melvin agreed to build. When furlough time came in 1972, we arrived in Alabama to a house already built. It was like living in a dream; wherever we might be in the world, the house would be there for us when we returned.

It wasn't painful to see Dad and Mama leave at the end of 1971, because we knew we would see them again in just months. They would be returning to the house they had built near Webbers Falls, with dear friends living nearby. Meanwhile, Alice and Jody were looking with mounting excitement toward furlough. We had decided to make this the trip of a lifetime, and travel home by way of Southeast Asia, Europe, and the Middle East. For years, the kids had played "travel agency," spending hours going through travel brochures and flight schedules and planning vacations for their "clients." Now, they were working with us on a *real* trip.

Remarkably, we could take the fare the FMB allowed for a direct flight home and apply it to our own itinerary, with the understanding that any additional expense was our own. With long and careful planning, we realized we could buy our tickets in Hong Kong, travel first to Thailand and then travel to numerous countries and end up in the States. Best of all, we could add just $500 to the basic cost and map out our own trip. We decided to each travel with just one carry-on and no checked luggage — and we stuck to it. Not easy, but that journey became a wonderful adventure, leaving us with rich memories.

Shortly before furlough in 1972, Bob went to the Asian Baptist Youth Congress in Bangkok, where he met young pastor Ken Marak from Assam, Northern India. Ken became a lifelong friend. When several people went to the ocean to have a swim, Ken, who had never been on a beach, had no swimsuit, so he simply went in wearing his slacks. (Time would prove that Ken would remain part of our lives.)

Not long before heading to the States, a student in one of Bob's Bible classes asked, "If a man lives a good life and serves others, but does not know about God, will he die and go to hell?" Such penetrating questions brought home to us the terrific responsibility that was ours, wherever we found ourselves — to share the good news in every way we can, while we can. Even as we prepared to leave, I thought long about that young man's penetrating question and wept while praying for wisdom to stay aware of the needs right in front of us all the time.

Rosalie at exam time with her students at Kaohsiung Teacher's College

Alice in her role in "Queen of the Dark Chamber"

At Glorieta for inaugural National Acteens Conference

TEN

***

THE LONG WAY HOME
1972

March 18, and Saturday finally arrived. Four eager Hunts were on the flight to Hong Kong and points around the world. With essentials packed in our little carry-ons, all four of us were ready for new adventures. And we had them — some anticipated, others pure serendipity. Bob and I purposely waited until leaving Taiwan to tell the children about the robber that broke into our house through the locked door to the balcony off Jody's bedroom. While we were at church one Sunday night a few weeks earlier, someone had broken in and rifled through the drawers in our bedroom. Evidently, they were in a rush and got away with very little but left a telltale screwdriver behind on the floor. As we recounted the break-in, the children's eyes grew wide, and Jody spoke up, "I *wondered* why you suddenly installed that heavy metal bar across the balcony door!" Both of the children were alarmed, but since the robbery was history by this time, they soon forgot their fears in their excitement about the trip.

We scheduled two days in Bangkok. The heat was suffocating but worth it to be able to take a small boat ride down the *klongs* (little canals) that ran through Bangkok. Thousands of people lived on houseboats, and some had little shops on boats along the waterways. Visitors could even stop at a pier and get a ride on an elephant. Both Alice and Jody (OK, and their parents, too) were fascinated with the huge pythons at Bangkok's snake farm. We all stood wide-eyed, watching two grown men hold a python and use tongs to feed it the dish (some live creature) of the day. The python swallowed it all, giving all of us shivers.

Our next stop was Delhi. All of us agree, once you have visited India, you can never forget it. The sights, smells, sounds, tastes of that vast land enthralled us. We took a bus to the greatest sight of all — the Taj Mahal. During a stop at 400-year-old Agra Fort, we watched literally hundreds of monkeys climbing over the ancient buildings and ruins. The bus next stopped at a little shop out in the middle of nowhere that sold Indian gemstones. Bob and I were fascinated by the array of ruby star sapphires. We grinned, thinking about the budget on which we were traveling, but we came away with one lovely little ruby star sapphire — for the big price of five dollars. That kind of souvenir fit our budget.

For years, I had heard that the Taj Mahal was one of the most beautiful sights in the world. It lived up to its billing. The thermometer read 100 degrees that day, but I literally had chill bumps at the first sight of that magnificent marble structure. With reflecting pools all down the walkway leading to the entrance, the sight was literally breathtaking. Built as a tribute to his beloved wife by the Emperor Shah Jahan nearly 500 years ago, it was a worthy monument indeed. It staggers the mind to consider the vast number and value of the gems contained in that mausoleum.

The crowds of India were reminiscent of China's crowds, but with a distinctly different flavor. We were stunned at the number of beggars; countless children came up, plucking at our sleeves and saying, "*Me'em Sahib*, a rupee please, please." How can your heart be wrung out so many times in a single day? Many were crippled or blind, and a number of mothers held out their babies to us, begging for help. If tears could have helped, it would have been so easy to spend the day weeping.

Jama Majid, one of India's most iconic mosques, assaulted our eyes and senses. Built by the same Emperor Shah Jahan, it was massive. The head *imam* (priest) had eyes that literally gave me visceral shivers. He insisted we look at the sandals that had been "Mohammed's" and then showed us their most priceless artifact, a red hair from Mohammed's beard. That strained our credulity. As we drew near the back gate, we saw a haunting sight. Lingering in the shadows near the wall was a leper. Alice saw him first, touched my sleeve and whispered, "Mama." We all turned in his direction, and the leper hid his face from us in shame. My heart shrank in helpless sorrow at the hopelessness written on that face. The old, unanswerable question that haunted me time and again returned: *Why?*

The Indian street markets, with scores of little shops littered with wares, would have entertained us for days had we had the time. The bright colors of *saris* flowed all around us, and we found the Indian people beautiful with their large, luminous eyes and graceful fluid movements. Having done a bit of reading up on the countries we were visiting, the children knew about India's caste system and saw evidence of it on every hand. The top sight for Jody, however, was the real live snake charmer, with his hypnotic cobra in a basket and a mongoose to fight with the cobra — all for a few rupees from the crowd. I was just thankful the snake charmer kept his cobra charmed and away from us. Indian food was a favorite with all of us, and the children developed a lifelong appreciation for *na'an*, the round Indian bread baked in a hot, open oven and served piping hot. It reminded us of Chinese *shau bing*, another family favorite.

Next on the itinerary was Israel; we spent most of the next four days in Jerusalem and environs. As with every country, there was simply not enough time to even begin absorbing the wonderful experiences we were enjoying. One reason that we could do such a trip for $500 was the blessing of friends along the way. A missionary family in Jerusalem kindly put up with four wide-eyed guests for four days. Wonder of wonders, we were there for Holy Week — for it was doubly special, remembering what had occurred in that place 2,000 years earlier. On Thursday evening, I went to a commemorative service marking the first Lord's Supper in an upper room. Joining about twenty other pilgrims, we gathered for a service, then walked together down through the Valley of Kidron and up to the Mount of Olives, recalling how Jesus went with His disciples that fateful night when He went to the Garden of Gethsemane to pray, and they to watch (and sleep). We paused in the garden; the night was perfect, clear, quiet, dark — with stars clearly visible all over the sky above Jerusalem. That was a moment for solemn remembrance of the agony of spirit Christ endured as He awaited the approach of the soldiers. The account of Christ's last week, His suffering and His sacrifice, took on a whole new meaning after that night in the garden.

From the Temple Mount and the Wailing Wall, to Golgotha, and then the garden tomb, we drank in one historical sight after another. It was almost too much to absorb, and I constantly wished for more time. The kids loved a camel ride at the Mount of Olives, and we all were thrilled to be able to visit Bethlehem and gaze out over the shepherds' fields. Our missionary friends were also amateur archaeologists and very knowledgeable about Jericho. There had been an unexpected rain the previous week — and driving through the wilderness area toward Jericho, we saw little wildflowers that had sprung up in random display. Our friend explained that at the tells (ancient mounds) at Jericho, visitors were allowed to pick up anything that was at no greater depth than six inches, but no digging was allowed. My mind immediately went back to our front yard in Zhenjiang, China, when I dug up a little piece of jade and dreamed about becoming an archaeologist someday. This was likely to be as close as I'd ever get to that reality. When we got to Jericho, like a child with a toy, I scrambled down the side of a tell (an archaeological dig) to see what I might find in the soil newly loosened by recent rains. A number of yards down, I came across a potsherd (fragment of pottery) of some type, lines clearly etched, the pattern visible. I didn't have a clue as to its original form, but it was nonetheless exciting, being both ancient and biblical. Our missionary friend looked it over and commented that, considering the distance down the tell where I found it, its age was at least 1,500 years old. Looking at my little artifact, I drew a breath of satisfaction, thinking that this was part of something that could have been around when Jesus visited Jericho.

For Alice and Jody, nothing was more impressive and exciting than the Dead Sea. They loved being able to float with no effort. For me, looking toward the Qumran Caves about a mile away was equally exciting, for this is where the Dead Sea Scrolls had been discovered. In fact, there is nowhere in Israel that is not a part of ancient history. Spending months there would not be long enough. We were just grateful for the taste we had and hoped to return someday.

Knowing that more adventures were to come made it easier to leave Israel. We only had two days in Athens, and they were jammed with memories, foremost revolving around the incredible Acropolis, and especially the Parthenon — pure melody in architecture. Place that against a brilliant blue, cloudless sky and perfect weather, and you have a glorious visual memory. On a more mundane level, Greek food was an epicurean delight, even if we didn't always know what we were eating. The whole family stuffed on gyros, *moussaka*, *souvlaki* and *tiropita* (little hot cheese pies) that begged you to eat just one more.

With reluctant feet, and much still unseen, we left Athens and headed for Rome. There, we were met by old friends from Alabama, Fred and Molly Ellen Anderton, missionaries in Naples. Bob and Molly Ellen (Mop) had gone to school together in Albertville and were lifelong buddies. Three of the five Anderton children were young and still at home. Alice and their daughter Jane Ellen established an instant rapport. MKs tend to have a lot in common anyway, and these two certainly did. The Andertons knew exactly the best sights and experiences for a brief but special look at Italy. We did "the quick look" at the Coliseum and forum and were thrilled to see some of Rome's most famous sights during an epochal visit to the Sistine

Chapel. A look at Michelangelo's "Creation," with God's finger about to touch that of Adam, left all of us speechless. There was more to come at St. Peter's Basilica, seeing one famous sculpture after another, crowned by Michelangelo's magnificent Pieta. Our aesthetic senses were on overload long before the wonderful day concluded. Easter Sunday in Italy was another feast for the heart. We attended Easter services in the Andertons' church and were prepared ahead of time for this experience, knowing that the Lord's Supper would be observed using wine. A novel part of this Communion came, however, when the church used a common cup, and all of us drank from the same silver chalice.

Easter afternoon was all my history-loving soul could ask for, as Fred and Molly Ellen took us to Pompeii. We were shocked to arrive only to learn that it was locked up tight. They closed just two days a year, Christmas and Easter. Now what? Fred had an answer. We drove to a rather remote area away from the main entrance, and Fred promptly climbed over a low fence and invited the rest of us to follow. What more could you wish for than a private stroll on ancient streets, no one around, looking at the ghostly remains and remembering the historic eruption that buried the city in ash when Mount Vesuvius erupted in AD 79. We could even hear our footsteps echoing along the streets and didn't spend much time looking over our shoulders to see if some patrol was checking for unscheduled visitors.

Our next-to-last stop was London. Having carefully planned, we made reservations at the China Inland Mission (CIM) compound in Newington-Green, just outside of London. It boggles the mind to recall that for four nights' accommodation and breakfast each morning, we paid a total of thirty-two US dollars. Unbelievable. The kids adored double-decker buses that took us quickly to the heart of London and all the flavor and excitement we found there. Alice and Jody picked up the accent quickly and could sound like a "local." They loved it when a rotund little lady got on the bus, and, shaking the rain from her coat, slipped a bit but quickly grabbed one of the posts to which passengers held as the bus moved. She caught herself, grinned, looked around at all the spectators, declaring, "I don't know what me feet are foh," in perfect cockney English.

Westminster Abbey, Buckingham Palace, a West End play — we took it all in. The public parks were lovely, especially the royal St. James Park. As we walked along, a bird flying overhead had perfect aim, dropping royal poop right in the middle of my hair. The kids found it funnier than I did. It was such a big plop that I had to find a public restroom and mop some of it up. That memory faded however, when we found a street-side stand with amazing fish and chips (they lived up to their sterling reputation). None of us wanted to leave London, especially with so much left unseen, but all four were determined to come back again. By point of comparison, we enjoyed London far more than Paris. It wasn't because Paris wasn't filled with beautiful art and architecture and history on every side; it was rather the unwelcoming atmosphere. Americans seemed to be looked upon with a good bit of disdain, and I must admit, we were a bit tired by this point and getting anxious to get home to America. Nonetheless, the Louvre was incredible. I wish we could have stood a full thirty minutes just gazing at the Mona Lisa.

Now, after three never-to-be-forgotten weeks, we were on the way home, this time first to Alabama and next to Oklahoma. Reunions never get old or lose their thrill. It had been nearly five years since we left, with Alice and Jody ten and seven at the time. Now Jody was nearly eleven and Alice a teenager. I cannot even describe the feeling of driving into Boaz, heading down old Highway 205, drawing near the family land, and seeing right across from the house where Bob had grown up, a brand-new house waiting for us. Joe handed his brother a key and said, "Here's your house." Alice and Jody were a bit overwhelmed to think that here was a place that was *theirs,* not something that was only temporary. It was a feeling beyond words, and we had family to thank for making this possible. For the first time, the kids lived next door to cousins and had a home to which they could invite their friends.

Alice and Jody enrolled in Boaz schools — Alice finishing eighth grade at the junior high, and Jody completing fifth grade. Both recall that understanding Southern accents was a challenge, and both felt completely ignorant when hearing how important football seemed to be. Neither had ever been to a game. They quickly tired of ignorance, so they set about to learn the ins and outs of the game, although it took a season to become true fans. Bob and I observed a trait that stood both our children in good stead. Because of their intuitive ability to observe, Alice and Jody were able to quickly perceive what was culturally important to their peers — football being a fine example. We were immensely grateful that neither child had a real problem with adjusting. Remembering how lonely and *different* I felt when returning to America as a sixth grader, I was doubly thankful for our children's speedy adjustments. However, there was one good experience I shared with them in returning to America and attempting to fit in. They, like I had been, were blessed with a few special friends who piloted them through the adjustments. I remembered my special friend, Barbara Morgan, back in Coweta, Oklahoma, and my friends Jerri, Gail, and Vera Jo. For Alice and Jody, there were kids who had been their friends five years earlier. Jody had Ken, Dwayne, James, Brad, and more. Alice was blessed with several, including Patti, Debbie and Lee Ann, two of them older than she. High school was made smooth (as smooth as turbulent teen years *can* be) by these friends who integrated her into their orbits. I recalled occasional horror stories of terrible adjustments other MKs had experienced, and I was grateful that our two were spared that.

We loved to get to Oklahoma to be with my parents at every opportunity, but that didn't happen often enough. It was 600 miles from Boaz to Gore, so time was always an issue. Having them nearby those months in Taiwan had spoiled us, and we missed that quality family time. They were happily retired in Gore, the little town near where they had a number of friends, but neither was content without being involved in some sort of ministry. We got in some great visits with the Rosses, and our children and theirs picked up right where they had left off five years earlier. Aunt Mellie and Uncle Victor were also near enough to visit as well.

Bob and I were aware that furlough (now called stateside assignment) was not a "rest" as the word "furlough" implies. Instead, it is full of speaking, traveling, conferences, camps, retreats, all the while trying to live in the present and be productive. A trip to Glorieta Baptist Assembly in its beautiful New Mexico setting was a rare treat for the whole family. We had been invited to appear as a missionary family on the program of the first National Acteens Conference (NAC) and share our stories with a thousand teenage girls. National Acteens Director Evelyn Tully became "Aunt Evelyn" to our two and has remained that through the years.

Much of the summer was taken up with speaking at conferences and churches, and along with the speaking, we were able to visit friends in DC and see just enough of the capital to make us eager to get back again. (Jody would end up working in DC for more than twenty years and living nearby.) Not far away was Virginia, and we were thrilled to be able to speak in my special college friend's own church in Lynchburg. Esther Wu was Dr. Wu now (a theological one) — and her husband, Sammy, whom we were finally able to meet face-to-face, a medical Dr. Wu. Such a reunion was food for the soul, and Esther's three beautiful little girls captured a piece of our hearts.

As the furlough progressed, Bob was asked more and more frequently to preach or fill some role in the Boaz church. Earl Chumbly, our pastor, was a gifted minister dealing with a terrible handicap. He had been diagnosed a few years earlier with early-onset Parkinson's disease, and it was slowly worsening. Sometimes two messages each Sunday was more than Earl's body could handle, and he would call on Bob. Like nearly every minister, Bob loved to preach and was grateful for these opportunities. And, typical for Bob, young people gravitated to him; he was soon confidant for several high school boys. Young people instinctively understood that he loved and accepted them, and, consequently, they relied on his opinions and advice. It transpired that events at the Boaz church would have a bearing on our immediate plans.

I had never questioned my call to mission service. In point of fact, neither had Bob. I must admit that my concept of "God's call" was something I could not easily define. (I still can't.) In my thinking at that juncture, God called — and that was it. Many years and a number of experiences needed to occur for me to understand that God's call is not in the past tense, but it is an active, living precept by which His children live. I don't even know the best word for it: *Precept? Concept? Injunction? Tenet?* Maybe it is some of all of those. Time has convinced me that we are "works in progress." I hope and pray never to reach the place where I feel no change is needed. My heart knows better than that. Late in 1972, Bob and I were confronted with decision time. We were just a few months away from decisions about the years ahead. Kaohsiung station wanted us to return. Taipei would like for us to work there, as would Taichung. We loved them all. But for the first time, we did not have peace about the right place, and we earnestly sought what God would have us do. I sometimes wept at night, disturbed to think our decision might not be in keeping with what God wanted.

Boaz Church earnestly desired that we remain, at least for the foreseeable future. Bob was sorely needed. Earl needed help with preaching and church administration, and the youth needed a leader. Bob could fit into both roles and be doing what he loved so much to do — ministering to people and sharing the good news. It was one of the hardest decisions we had ever faced. Bob liked to think in terms of black and white, right or wrong. This choice didn't fit in those categories. We still felt "called." OK. Was a calling just geographical? We grappled with the thought. The Foreign Mission Board was supportive. We discussed the dilemma with our area director and eventually came to the conclusion that we would take a leave of absence and meet this local need for the time being. This is something we could both live with. We were due to return to the field in late March, and it hurt to write the Taiwan mission and explain that we would not be returning right away. The sense of peace we felt with our decision was not easy to either describe or define. It was just there, although it was not what a big part of me wanted to do. Nonetheless, I did know it was the right thing for that time. Now we had a brand-new challenge confronting us, one full of opportunities and the unknown.

One of Rosalie's international students' classes at Snead College

ELEVEN

BOAZ

1973-1974

From the distance of half a century, I can understand more clearly the reason for our need to remain in America in the 1970s. At the time, however, neither Bob nor I could give a clear-cut reason for exactly why that was what we should do. Those eight years in the States held a number of shining moments to be treasured, as well as times containing dark rumbles of approaching thunder. Our new normal was quite different than it would have been in Taiwan. The exact day we would have been flying toward Taipei, we were in Oklahoma with my parents during spring break. Bob and I were still struggling with mixed feelings and moments of questioning our decision. About noon, the phone rang. Our Foreign Mission Board had just received shocking news: Our friend and fellow student worker, missionary Gladys

Hopewell in Tainan, had been discovered murdered that morning. A chill went straight to our hearts; we could read the fright on the children's faces, appalled at the thought of their Aunt Gladys being suddenly and terribly forever gone. In that moment, Bob and I both breathed a prayer of thanksgiving that we were not this very day returning to Taiwan and facing this tragic situation. Mama and Dad had worked in Tainan with Gladys just months earlier. All of us were reminded of the dangers and challenges facing each day and vowed afresh to number our days wisely.

Adjusting to remaining in America was probably easier for the children than for Bob and me. Both made a smooth transition in a new school, Jody in junior high and Alice in high school. For one year, I taught world history at the junior high and ended up having our nephew Wayne for his final semester of world history and Jody for his first. It felt a bit strange to have kin in class, and I bent over backwards to show no favoritism. World history was fascinating to me, and I wanted the students to love it, too. I began the practice of reading a chapter in a good book to the students each day at the extended lunch period, and it's likely some of them later recalled those books more than their history texts. Years later, I had various ones tell me how they loved *The Hiding Place,* Corrie Ten Boom's story. I felt relieved that something stuck in their minds. One thing I learned that year: I'd have to be starving to choose to spend the rest of my career teaching seventh graders. That particular age is a rough one to navigate for most preteens; they needed a patient teacher. I missed that qualification.

Our first full years back in the States brought one of those dark rumbles of thunder that sticks in my memory like Velcro. I acknowledge that my rather unusual childhood gave me a different perspective on race than that held by many people where we now lived. Our backgrounds were so different. Uneasy race relations always gave me a sick feeling in the pit of my stomach, and I couldn't get away from the question of why we had racial problems and strife and what we could do about them. In China, I had grown up as a minority person, labeled as different. Occasionally, I felt the painful edge of condescension and disdain. It was not a good feeling, and I couldn't find anywhere in Scripture that God loved one group of people more than another.

I had read about the Ku Klux Klan and had been touched a bit by that kind of mentality when we lived in Mississippi years earlier. However, until that afternoon in nearby Gadsden, Alabama, we had never confronted it face-to-face. The children and I ran an errand in Gadsden and were headed home when we had to stop for a traffic light. There in the intersection was a group of Ku Klux Klansmen in full gear — white robes and pointed hats, but with their faces clearly visible. My first shocked thought was, *What are they doing here?* I quickly saw what they were doing: collecting money in a bucket as they went from car to car, shaking their containers for a contribution. Here they came, right for us, and this Klansman stuck his bucket in my face, asking for a donation. With purely instinctive response, my face flamed red, and I spoke heatedly, "You know what I should do? I should just run over you with this car!" I gunned the motor and pulled away to the sound of his curses following after us. Alice and Jody sat in stunned silence. After a moment, I heaved a deep sigh and spoke, "I apologize, children. I just saw red. That man made me *sick*." Recalling the moment in Mississippi when Bob and I had been warned that a cross might be burned in our yard, I wondered if that might indeed happen to us now. Alice and Jody both told us later that the incident was seared into their memories, influencing their thinking about race and right and wrong ever after.

Wouldn't you know? A similar incident occurred the next year, this time on Highway 431 between Boaz and Albertville. I was alone in the car and at a red light when I saw Klansmen standing on both sides of the highway. One snaggle-toothed, tobacco-spitting Klansman, clothed in full garb, ambled up to my window and grinned as he stuck the bucket in my face. I clearly hadn't learned much in the past year, because I had the same visceral response. Speaking through clenched teeth, I said, "I'd like to throw up in your bucket!" The light changed, and I took off, hearing his curses echoing against my rapidly pounding heart. I needed to learn something about self-control, but my opinion of prejudice has never changed. I am still as horrified fifty years later to encounter it in any guise and must daily remind myself of being true to the message of God's love lived out in my own life. There is always sweeping that needs doing around the doorstep of my own heart.

About the time I finished that second semester at Boaz Junior High, Snead Community College in Boaz requested that I come direct a program for international students. There were more students arriving than their English program could handle; they were being bombarded with language problems. The spring of 1974, I began teaching internationals at Snead and developing a counseling program. This meant calling on skills developed during ten years of teaching English as a second language and clarified for me that training in counseling was also much needed. I soon enrolled in counseling courses at nearby Jacksonville University. Between teaching, taking courses, and working with youth at the church, our daily routine felt a lot like the schedule we had maintained in Taiwan. Seven terrific years teaching and counseling Snead students were rich in satisfaction. Countless opportunities developed to engage students from some nineteen countries, and to see many of them blossom, learn, and go equipped into their own futures. I earned a master's degree in counseling along the way that helped me to develop a general counseling program for the college. Two years later, another master's degree in English helped broaden my teaching base.

First Baptist Church was remarkable in the way they became involved with international students. A number of households became "host families" for students. Many students participated in a Sunday night fellowship meal and Bible study at the church. Our church hostess prepared a simple meal that gave the students a look into a personal side of America that most of these students had never known. I remember one Sunday forgetting to forewarn the kitchen crew that we never serve ham to Muslim students. Abdul, one of the more vocal students from Saudi Arabia, pulled me aside and diplomatically said, "Mrs. Hunt, we don't eat pork, you know." My face flamed red, and I apologized for the blunder. We ended up that evening eating peanut butter and jelly sandwiches.

Several of the students became part of the church fellowship. Maureen from Jamaica had a lovely voice and joined the choir. Charlie from Nigeria became a regular. When he heard the story of Lottie Moon, Charlie gave his entire week's paycheck from his job at the spinning mill to the Christmas offering. Johnny, also from Nigeria, had the best English of any student I had those seven years. His compositions read like Shakespearean prose. Johnny had an electrifying testimony of how God had called him from a godless and wicked life in the Biafran army and gloriously saved him. He joined our church, saying he felt God's immediate directive to do so. Sophia Kebede from Ethiopia was a sterling student and a young woman of deep faith. She was able to set into motion a means for her fiancé, Melaku, to escape the war in Sudan and make his way to freedom and Snead College. Melaku graduated with a 4.0 grade-point-average that later led to a career as an immigration official in Washington, DC.

About the time I started teaching at Snead, Bob began a ministry with students each week for Bible study. He had numerous experiences confirming the hand of God at work in placing him in Boaz at that particular time. Our pastor's physical condition was precarious, and Bob could assist in instances when Earl Chumbly's health posed extra stress on his ministry. He and Bob made a compatible team, each supportive of the other as they worked in tandem. The work with young people expanded and reached beyond the walls of the church.

Another unexpected blessing came our way. Dad and Mama decided to move to Boaz. Our two were their only grandchildren, and they wanted time with them while they were growing up. What a dividend of grace that became for all of us. We had family property available right next to us, and the folks soon moved into a cozy new house built right next door. For the first time in my married life, I had the joy of having my parents close by, and they had a profound influence on the lives of their only "grands."

That same year, a singular youth ministry developed in Boaz and galvanized the young people of our town. The church was less than a couple of blocks from downtown Boaz, and an empty store building became "the Lighthouse." Many youth in Boaz were reluctant to set foot in a church building, but when they heard of a gathering place for kids their age, with music and laughter, ping-pong and pool tables, friendly and open discussions and all free of charge, the Lighthouse soon became *the* place to go. Several young adult couples, including Billy and Jamie Faucett (who became lifelong friends), helped Bob get supplies and equipment. (The

Faucetts frequently participated in Lighthouse activities, and their first child, Amanda, took her first steps there. Two decades later, Bob had the privilege of performing her wedding ceremony to a gifted young physician.) Bob and Billy scoured the area and found used pool tables at bargain prices, and several friends donated ping-pong tables. Carpet companies donated remnants of carpet, and church youth worked to cover the whole floor surface with multi-colored squares of thick carpet. Large wooden spools were donated and used as tables, with carpet covering for the tabletops and small stools to serve as chairs. The bright carpet, however, became the seat of choice for the scores of teenagers who came.

Hindsight reveals how unusual it was that the main drawing card of the Lighthouse was not its games, music or relaxed fellowship, but keen and engaging Bible studies where students chose the topics, and any question was safe to ask. Weekends were spent at the Lighthouse, and word got around that the students felt safe there, and accepted — just like they were. Not many months passed before some of the youth who had never been willing to go in a church building were now attending Sunday services at First Baptist. By common consent, all would sit together on the left side of the sanctuary, and they filled most of that section. One weekend, we had special meetings at the Lighthouse, and real revival broke out among the youth — resulting in rededications, commitments to life service, and a number of conversions. There was a nearly palpable atmosphere of peace and joy, and it spilled over into the sanctuary of the church when Sunday came. The atmosphere that morning was one I clearly recall fifty years later. Numbers of teenagers made professions of faith at that service, and adults in the congregation were discernibly affected.

That Sunday night, a communion service was scheduled, and many young people participated. Half a century later, the sensations my heart felt during that sacred hour remain vivid. Words can't capture the essence of the communion. The next day, Dad and Mama came over, and we talked about the amazing service. Dad looked visibly moved as he told us, "Last night, I had a moment that I have never before experienced. As I watched row after row of young people go to the front to receive communion, I could see everyone in their glorified bodies." Dad literally came to tears as he tried to put into words that heavenly glimpse. Dad was not given to easy emotion, but each of us had been in that same moment and could understand the power of the remarkable encounter with the presence of God.

Our Boaz youth loved to have fun, but they were never controlled by the need for good times. It was remarkable to note the power of the Word of God to penetrate and change hearts. Bob took them each year on retreats to Gatlinburg in the winter and the Gulf Coast in the summer. Although lots of fun and recreation took place, the main purpose of each trip was growing closer to God and understanding His message to their hearts. At least four young people from that group became ministers, and many more became pillars of their churches in many cities and states.

A half century later, Bob is still running into some of those youth now grown up, many of them grandparents themselves. Over and over, one will say, "Brother Bob, do you remember me?" Bob will often recall the face, even if not the name, and say, "Remind me, please, who you are." The man or woman will explain, saying, "You may not remember me, but forty years ago, you led me to the Lord, and my life has been changed ever since." Another might say, "It was you, Brother Bob, who listened to me when my parents didn't understand, and it changed my life." Sometimes the phone will ring, and an unfamiliar voice will say, "Brother Bob, you don't remember me, but you helped me over the roughest patch in my life, and I just want to thank you." I wish those students could watch Bob's face and realize the blessing such moments bring. Even as then, Bob will say, "Let's just thank God right now," and often have a prayer with them over the phone, or, standing face-to-face, look into their eyes and pray for them in that moment.

I loved working with the Acteens at the church. They especially enjoyed visiting our local nursing home and getting to know the residents by name, going to their rooms every few weeks just to visit or take some sweet treat. The girls particularly loved Mrs. Gladys Lewis, who kept them amused with her funny stories and loved them for bringing homemade cornbread or a dish of peach cobbler. One afternoon, the Acteens visited with residents in their sunroom and sang with them. Alice played the piano to accompany the singing. Old Mr. Mayfield requested a particular hymn that Alice wasn't familiar with, but she bravely struggled through the song. When the music stopped, Alice gave a sigh of relief and announced, "Whew, I'm glad that's over." Mr. Mayfield spoke right up, "So am I, honey, so am I!"

All the youth participated in special projects and often came up with clever ideas. One summer, they had a bike-a-thon for Bangladesh and rode their bikes X number of miles for donations to the cause of raising money to feed refugees in that war-torn nation. Wednesday night Bible study at the youth building (an old house) next to the church provided space for the scores of youth who regularly came for in-depth Bible study. Another serendipity was having Olin Hayes as principal at the high school. A faithful church member and deacon, Mr. Hayes lived what he preached and welcomed Bob to come to the high school each week at activity period. One hour each week was set aside for club meetings, and students could choose what to attend. Bob led spontaneous, open-to-all discussion times. When they grew to 200 or more, they had to move to the auditorium. It was not anything that Bob did. It was clearly the work of God in the hearts of youth. (Decades later, we still hear from many of them who refer to the strength they gained through those unique hours in their high school lives. It was the place where they could talk about anything and feel open and accepted.)

One of our student ventures created memories that none of the some thirty of our eager high school and college students ever forgot: a mission trip to Zuni, New Mexico. In cooperation with the Home Mission Board, our church took on a project to help a struggling new church plant on the Zuni reservation. The Zuni Indian reservation was unique, with the Zuni people living much as their ancestors had for many generations. A good number, especially the older ones, spoke Zuni and worshipped as had their ancestors. The Zuni children used English, and the schools were state schools, but theirs was a culture quite different from the mainstream. The youth all knew Brother Bob (as he was universally called) ran a tight ship, but more was accomplished than anyone expected. Some of the young people did construction work, while others taught Bible school and conducted backyard Bible clubs with the Zuni children. One of our church members took a trailer and headed up the construction crew, with the youth putting up Sheetrock, molding, and other interior work. There was no hot water, so everyone showered in the trailer, with the boys bedding down in sleeping rolls in the building and the girls sleeping in the trailer.

Some of the Zuni children had a bit of Catholic background, but most were from backgrounds centered on traditional Zuni religious tradition. Less than a handful had any knowledge of the gospel or God's love. They were lovable children and attached themselves rapidly to our youth, listening, learning, singing, loving crafts, and gaining truths that would be life-altering.

Our youth spent one memorable evening a little distance out of the community, but still on the Zuni reservation, at the ancient ruins of a long-ago Zuni neighborhood. Gathering around a little campfire in the growing dusk, it became a unique sacred moment for Alabama young adults. The trip home included a visit to the Grand Canyon, and everyone returned to Alabama with a treasure trove of memories. Jody was disgusted to be too young to go since he was still in junior high, but he had a neat consolation trip. He accompanied us as far as Webbers Falls, Oklahoma, and stayed a week with the Ross family. He was actually on a reservation as well, for Webbers Falls was officially part of Cherokee territory. (Forty years later, all except two from that original Zuni trip were able to have a grand reunion at the church and together relive their memories of Zuni in 1974 and how it had impacted their lives.)

Occasionally, we were able to speak on mission needs in churches or conferences, and nothing was more exciting than sharing our passion for ministry with Chinese who did not know the good news. One glorious weekend, we were able to visit my friend from OBU days, Esther Wu and her husband, Sammy. In addition to their full-time vocations, they were deeply involved with their Lynchburg, Virginia, church. We had been able to see Esther and Sammy a couple of times, but this weekend, we spoke in their church. Just before I was to speak, Esther sang, "My Table Is Full But My Field Is Empty." It was so beautiful and challenging that I could barely get beyond the tears to begin speaking. (Esther and I have corresponded for more than six decades, our deep friendship simply another evidence of

God's goodness. See her story in 6 *Yellow Balloons*.)

Bob and I were happily engaged in ministry on many fronts, but knew our time in Boaz was temporary, and, God willing, we would be returning to Asia and our work with the Chinese people. All of those eight years, we were keeping abreast of the work in Taiwan and all of Asia, corresponding regularly with missionaries and Chinese friends. It was somewhat like having your heart in two places; I was already familiar with this feeling, recalling how, as a child, if we were in China, I was also remembering and missing parts of life in America. Now, I was thinking about Taiwan and our friends and life there. I worked at learning to live with a divine discontent. *Maybe we are not intended to just sit around content. Maybe it is this divine discontent that keeps us motivated,* I would sometimes reason with myself. More people and more adventures were going to enter our lives; of that, we were convinced.

Mama and Daddy at their home in Boaz, 1980

Alice with Snead students Sophia Kebede and Miss Li

TWELVE

MORE CHANGES
1974-1980

"Confession is good for the soul" was an expression I grew up on. This China MK had to confess to a "geographical bias" in using the phrase "mission field." Although my mind automatically thought of the field as overseas, I finally began to realize it is any place where God might put us for His purposes. With all the different countries represented by my students at Snead, the "field" was broad indeed. Bob's contacts were widespread as well, with a variety of backgrounds in the collegians who were part of his ministry at Snead; they included far more than just Baptist students.

Along with our work and local involvement, we often had opportunities to tell the mission story in churches and conferences. Coming from Taiwan, with its somewhat different cultural patterns, I thought nothing about wearing slacks and a jacket on Sundays. The first Sunday I dressed in my usual manner raised eyebrows at First Baptist Boaz. After the first service, a friend grinned and remarked, "I've never seen women in pants at our church before." I replied in genuine surprise, "Really? Well, you have now." I did not change my habit. Within a month, a number of young women were doing the same and several expressed their gratitude for my "breaking the ice," although it had been purely unintentional. The same response came the first time I wore slacks when speaking at a neighboring associational meeting; thankfully, other than a few surprised comments, no one really objected. By the end of our years in the States, we noticed it was a common sight in most churches.

I knew that the two graduate programs I completed (in English and counseling) would clearly be useful back on the field. However, they were useful in my work at Snead College also. In September 1974, an interesting new student from Vietnam, Thu Nguyen, matriculated. Colonel Nguyen Dinh Huu, Thu's father, was the official military attaché from the government of South Vietnam to Thailand. (The family surname is Nguyen; however, Colonel Huu was always referred to as "Mr. Huu.") Thu was one of eight children and quickly proved herself to be an outstanding student. The Huus' story was unique. When Saigon fell to the Vietcong in 1975, US troops evacuated, and chaos reigned. The Huus still had one son in Vietnam while the rest were in Bangkok with their parents. A harrowing week followed the fall of Saigon; however, Thu's oldest brother, Peter, miraculously escaped the war-torn country. Following more occasions of divine intervention, the whole family was granted political refugee status and came to the United States. In short order, the Huus became a beloved part of the Boaz community. Our families quickly bonded, and the Huus became our lifelong friends. (See Appendix for an account of the Huus' extraordinary odyssey.)

Those interim years in Alabama in the 1970s had their share of ins and outs, ups and downs, joys and not-so-joys. This family narrative, however, is primarily focused on our overseas experiences. Alice and Jody's complete stories are theirs to tell. I'll just touch on them while bridging the time until our return to Asia. I have learned that it is *hard* to write about the living — whether friends, family, or acquaintances. Examining hearts and stories from another century is much simpler and more precise. Writing about the living is more like figuratively tiptoeing through mine fields.

Our children were favored with the blessing of an excellent school and many friends. Alice was a class officer, involved in several organizations, and took advanced classes. In fact, she had so many credits that she finished a year early and took college courses at Snead.

Between a busy schedule of church youth activities, schoolwork, and busy weekends with their friends, I can't recall a single instance when either child said, "Mom, I'm bored. What is there to do?" Both had after-school jobs, and their social calendar was so busy that we actually posted a sign in the entrance-dining area that stated: "Weekday Visiting Hours Over at 9:30. Weekends — See Manager." (I was the weekend manager, and Bob went to bed whenever he wished, while I stayed up and monitored the visiting hours.) The system worked pretty well — most of the time.

Everybody went in various directions much of the time, but we valued family times together, realizing that this was a blessing that was temporary. Both of our children loved to repeat the miracle of the Easter bunny, knowing it would cause chagrin to their mother. Ever since their Ho Se Mo had started mailing Easter candies (including chocolate bunnies) to Alice and Jody in Taiwan, chocolate bunnies had become an Easter tradition — even when the two were in high school and college. One particular Easter, Alice's bunny was eaten pretty quickly, but Jody propped his up on the dresser top to save it. Slowly, slowly, the ears began to get tiny nibbles. Within a week or so, it was becoming noticeable. One Friday afternoon when Jody came home, he went to his room, then quickly came out to the den where all of us were seated, chocolate bunny in hand. (Bunny was now unable to hear because his ears were completely gone.) Holding Bunny out accusingly, he asked, "All right, who is the culprit? I haven't *touched* my bunny's ears, but they are gone!" He looked stonily into all three faces. When coming to mine, I couldn't keep the guilt or the grin off my face. Piously folding my hands in the position of prayer and raising my eyes heavenward, I intoned, "It's a miracle." That is one confession this mother has never been able to live down.

Alice spent her last two years of college at the University of Montevallo, majoring in math and counseling. She graduated with highest honors in May 1978. In June, she and Kevin Reece, an MK from Nigeria, were married. Don and Gwen Reece — longtime missionaries in Nigeria and friends of ours for many years — had Boaz roots, for Gwen was born in Boaz. Both Alice and Kevin continued with their plans for graduate school.

Jody thrived in high school and got involved in debate, ROTC, and football. He was fortunate to be the Alabama recipient of the Century III Scholarship award from Shell Oil Company and named one of the top ten in the nation. This led to an offer from a large university in south Alabama for a full four-year scholarship. Jody found that tempting, but he had his heart set on Samford University, which came through with an excellent scholarship. He chose to attend Samford.

We were grateful to be in the States during Jody's first year of college and see him settle in and feel at home there. I clearly recall his first semester, when Samford decided to have a missions fair, with each organization on campus setting up a booth and raising funds for the Lottie Moon Christmas Offering. Jody was part of the MK organization, and they figured MKs were a natural for raising money for Lottie. Jody came home the week before the fair and asked what ideas we might have for raising money. He and I collaborated and came up with the idea of oriental cookies, deciding to bake our own missions fortune cookies. We agreed on three different "fortunes" to bake into the chocolate sugar cookies: two round cookies pinched together on the sides, with the fortune tucked inside. I honestly do not recall what evil genius prompted me to suggest putting a little bit of chocolate ex-lax in the batter. If I had thought it through, I'd never have done such a thing. However, my better conscience lost the battle that day, and a bit of laxative went into the mix. I took a sample taste — pretty good! Jody was grinning through the whole preparation time and came up with the "fortunes" to bake inside our Fortune Fudgies from Formosa: "Things will be running smoother soon," "Just sit back and let things ease on by," and "Keep it moving for missions."

Jody came home the following weekend with a report on the missions fair; it was a great success. His two roommates were senior pharmacy students, and one of them insisted on buying two of the cookies ahead of the fair. The rest of the cookies sold out long before the fair ended. The next morning, Jody's roommate told him, "I don't know what is wrong. I feel fine, but I had to get up several times last night." Jody wisely offered no probable cause, but merely commiserated. Then, when he got to his first class, one of his friends kept putting her head on her desk to rest. After class, Jody checked to see if she was OK. "I'm fine," she assured him. "I'm just so sleepy. I got up several times during the night. Oh, Jody, I must tell you," she reached out to grasp his arm, "Those cookies you sold at the fair? They were wonderful. Do you have any left?" Again, Jody kept his counsel, and told her that, regrettably, he was all sold out. When he related the story to us, Bob was quick to note that we might get sued. I did feel a little contrition, but since no one was hurt, I simply gave thanks and decided never to do such a thing again.

Those eight years in Alabama, we were always aware of the special gift of time with family. Having my parents and Bob's mother in one place and watching our lovable nieces and nephews next door as they grew up was a special blessing. Wayne, Joan and Janis now had a brother. Bobby was born in 1970 and named for his uncle. Bob's sister, Dru, had married Misher Almon and lived in a nearby city; their sons, Bill and Link, were adorable little fellows who looked like their mother and had Dru's same sweet smile. Dad and Mama were an active part of our church. Both taught Sunday School classes and became involved in the missions activities of First Baptist Church Boaz. Within a few years, Dad was asked to pastor a small church in the association, and they both loved having a flock to shepherd again. It warmed our hearts that they were so quickly at home in Alabama — but then, they had learned long years before to adjust to new situations. Right next to my parents' house was Mama Hunt's place. Bob's grandmother had lived there many years, and it was like a benediction to have special time with her while we were in the States. She lived until 1977 and the venerable age of ninety-seven. Bob conducted her memorial service, using Psalm 16, which was entirely appropriate for Mama Hunt — for truly we had a goodly heritage.

Alice and Kevin were in graduate school in Birmingham, and Alice on the counseling staff at UAB while taking graduate courses. An unexpected serendipity occurred one semester, for she and I were both in the same graduate counseling class. The professor got a kick out of having mother and daughter studying together.

In 1979, our friends, the Huus, were ready to make a big move. Colonel Huu, this brilliant man who held a master's degree in French literature and had been a leader of men, was willing to do whatever was necessary to support his family. He pumped gas at a local service station and was not too proud to also work on the garbage detail. Mr. Huu somehow found time to attend the University of Alabama graduate program and earn a master's degree in social work, the first Vietnamese to do so. None of us was surprised when he graduated with an outstanding record.

The Huus were at a crossroads now. California was teeming with refugees from Vietnam — thousands with many needs and no social service workers who were Vietnamese. Mr. Huu was sorely needed to head up a program for refugees through social services there. It was ideal for Mrs. Huu as well, because for the first time since their arrival in America, she could be with other Vietnamese families and use her heart language with others besides her own family. California's gain was Boaz's loss. It gave our hearts a pang to have them leave, but all of us knew it was best for the family.

Their children planned to continue their educations there — some still in high school, others in college. The biggest dilemma was for Huan, the third son. He had all sorts of ties at Boaz High School and was a leader in the classroom, in scouting, and on the tennis team. Huan was coming up on his senior year, and leaving at this strategic juncture would be most difficult. Bob and I discussed the situation, then talked with Mr. Huu; we wanted to have Huan live with us his senior year and graduate with his class. (He

graduated with multiple honors, and his subsequent career has echoed that.)
Huan became like a son to us, and he has remained that these forty-plus
years, no matter where he has lived or where we have found ourselves.

During our stateside years, we maintained various contacts with our
mission family in Taiwan, as well as with those in other countries. We daily
prayed to remain open and sensitive at all times to God's leadership. Every
time missionary friends came through for a visit, or came as guest speakers,
we would realize afresh our eagerness to return to the field. There were
numerous opportunities awaiting us in Taiwan, needs in Taipei, Taichung,
and Kaohsiung. But we were also hearing from missionary friends in Hong
Kong, telling of their need for someone to work with Mandarin churches
in that British crown colony, and also the need for student work. They were
hoping we might be open to working with one or both.

Every place had special appeal to us. There was, however, at the back
of my mind a niggling little thought that had never gone away since the
day I left China as a child. I wanted to go back. Hong Kong lay right on
the threshold of mainland China, and living in Hong Kong might expand
our opportunity for getting back to China. In 1980, with Alice and Kevin
teaching and preparing for missionary journeyman service, and Jody at
Samford, we knew we would be leaving without children. It was going to
be different and with a new kind of separation angst.

Bob and I began the painful process of leaving all that was familiar and
loved. Some days we felt philosophical and matter-of-fact about decisions —
but more often, we proceeded with a lump in the throat. We both loved the
youth at the church and at the college. There were challenging opportunities
on many fronts. It took an effort to put aside thoughts of how easy it would
be to stay. Mama and Dad, as usual, were so supportive, even as they felt the
wrench of impending separation. Bob's mother found it more difficult but was
likewise affirming. We were fortunate, realizing that some of our missionary
friends had family who opposed their call and were even bitter about it.

Just months prior to our return to Asia, we had an unexpected
experience. Bob and I were able to take a group of church members to
see the Passion Play in Oberammergau, Germany, performed just once

every decade. It exceeded our expectations. Visiting London, Paris and Switzerland was an added bonus. Over forty years later, I still recall how the sun glistened on the Matterhorn, as we gazed from our bedroom window one morning in Zermatt. That inspiring trip stands as one of our lives' serendipities.

Now it was crunch time. Where should we plant our feet this time? In multiple ways, the decision was a toss-up. Taiwan had many needs, but there were just as many in Hong Kong — and, too, Hong Kong had no organized student ministry, while Taiwan had several. Not without angst, we finally determined to go to Hong Kong. To be honest, one special consideration weighed heavily with both of us, especially me. Hong Kong stood on the very threshold of China — right next door. Furthermore, there might possibly be a tiny crack in the door. The terrible events of the Great Proletarian Cultural Revolution were finally fading into the background. If we were located in Hong Kong, we would be much more likely to have contact with and/or ministry in China once more; this had been a long-standing dream of mine. If possible, we wanted to be part of any opening of the door to ministry there. This was central in both our thinking and our prayers.

The planning and packing process was slightly easier this time. One thing for sure: My little blue enamel cup was going to travel with us again. I grinned to myself as I tucked it in our luggage, speculating on how many times that symbolic little cup had crossed the Pacific Ocean. Alice and Kevin were in Kenya, and Jody was already planning to come to Hong Kong for Christmas. The most painful goodbyes came on our final Sunday at the church and with the family. The two of us and all three of our parents tried not to weep until the goodbyes were over. No one was totally successful. Billy and Jamie Faucett took us to the airport. Leaving them was like saying goodbye to family as well. They had semi-adopted Jody, and we knew they would be there for him during his college years. (A decade later, their only son, B.J., was in Jody's wedding.)

The plane landed at Hong Kong's Kai Tak airport the night of October 14, 1980, one day prior to Bob's birthday. Landing in Hong Kong was an exciting sight as the plane set down on the runway that extended far out into Hong Kong harbor. A million twinkling lights in thousands of buildings along the shoreline beamed a welcome; both of us were as excited as children. At the Hong Kong airport of the 1980s, visitors could come right to the door of where disembarking passengers enter the terminal, and there waiting for us was the entire Baptist mission population of Hong Kong.

Among the missionaries gathered were Jerry and Lynn Barrett. Jerry, a professor at Hong Kong Baptist College, had formerly taught at Samford University in Birmingham. He and Bob's cousin, Harold Hunt — a Samford speech professor — had been colleagues and close friends for years. When Jerry caught sight of Bob, he exclaimed, "As I live and breathe, it's Harold Hunt all over again!" (Bob and his first cousin Harold look more alike than either resembled their own brothers.) Those Hong Kong missionaries became special friends in the years to come. We were invited to a different home each night and heard some amazing missionary stories. I now had the singular joy of being in the same mission again with Fay Taylor, this time as a fellow missionary. She is one of those rare people to whom you could honestly say, "Oh my goodness — you haven't changed in thirty years!" (I confess, in my mind, she was eternally my "Aunt Fay." She lived to be 100!)

Our first Sunday in the colony, we visited North Point Mandarin Church. It was exciting to be worshipping in Mandarin again, and we were thankful that we remembered much of our Chinese, even though we had not used it on a daily basis for eight years. As soon as the service ended, a beaming young man rushed up to Bob and grabbed his hand, saying, "Pastor Hung [pronounced *Hong*], it's wonderful to see you again!" It was Henry Tang, one of Bob's faithful students at Grace Church in Taipei. Henry was back home in Hong Kong and already a deacon at North Point. The pastor and staff were eager for us to be involved with their ministries. They asked Bob to teach a couples' class, and me to begin a class with people newly arrived from the mainland and to also include new believers or inquirers. The possibilities at North Point were exciting and challenging at the same time. Doing Bible classes in Chinese meant a big involvement of time and study for rusty language students. We gulped and accepted, and the studying began right away.

It was abundantly clear that we were back in the Orient. Everything took longer to do, and inconveniences were just a part of everyday life. Our shipment of household belongings had not yet arrived, and the mission apartment assigned to us on the island side was not yet ready for occupancy. We spent a lot of time absorbing the wonderful atmosphere of Hong Kong, a city-colony-country unlike any other on earth. It varied from the most heartbreaking of slums and crowded conditions to the fabulous mansions of the oh-so-wealthy.

It was natural to compare our new home with Taiwan. So many similarities were apparent; after all, by far the largest ethnic group for both was made up of Chinese. However, in Hong Kong, there was also a slice of the whole world. People from scores of nations would pass in review down at the harbor area where ferries and boats took people from Kowloon City on the mainland side to Hong Kong Island just across the harbor. The subway system (MTR) was super-efficient and could whisk us (under the harbor) from island to peninsula in mere minutes. Shopping in Hong Kong was exciting, and prices varied — from the decadently expensive to the night markets and street stalls where a bargain was just waiting. We were impressed by Baptist work in the colony, which included the modern Hong Kong Baptist Hospital, and, right next door, Hong Kong Baptist College. Just a block away was the Kowloon International Baptist Church, an English-language congregation, and in the whole colony, over forty Baptist churches, most of them Cantonese-speaking. There was a growing number of Mandarin-speaking congregations and a few in the Swatow and Hokkien dialects as well. The publishing entity of Hong Kong Baptists prepared materials and provided literature and Bibles for Chinese-speaking people worldwide, and a social service center ministered to thousands of needy people.

Education was a huge part of Baptist work in Hong Kong. Pui Ching and Pui Tou [pronounced *Doh*] Baptist middle schools (high schools in the US) had been founded nearly a century earlier in Canton and were now in Hong Kong and thriving. The mother school of all was the Henrietta

Hall Shuck School on the island side, named for America's first woman missionary to China. The school had several thousand students and a strong alumnae association that was active worldwide.

I began teaching that month and was immediately deeply touched by the students in my new class at North Point. Each of them came from mainland China with unique, and sometimes frightening and sad, stories. Vivid in my memory are the Yang sisters, girls who had just left their teen years, and who had arrived from the mainland only weeks before. On their first Sunday in a free country, they had determined to spend it in an open church — something that had been denied them all their lives. They looked at everything with wondering eyes and had a touching story. During the Cultural Revolution, both parents had been forced by the Red Guards to the countryside to work as "peasants" and be reeducated, as it was called. The girls' grandmother, a devout believer, raised them.

The Cultural Revolution tore the country apart, and fear stalked every roadway and crept into every house. If Christians were caught with a Bible, they were beaten or put in prison — or worse, taken away, never to be seen again. Old Mrs. Yang had bravely hidden her well-worn Bible. Only late at night, with shuttered windows and by the light of a single kerosene lantern, would she unearth it from its hiding place, gather her two little granddaughters about her, and quietly read the Scripture, telling the girls of God's love and care for them and for their parents far away. One of Grandma Yang's Christian friends was discovered with a Bible and taken out in the streets where the neighbors could watch and forced to squat down and use her precious Bible as toilet paper. The evil intent of that act terrified the two little girls as they watched in horror.

Their first Sunday in class, the Yang sisters could scarcely take it in. Here they sat, with other believers, free to hold a Bible in their hands and read it. Both were overcome with the emotion of the moment, as were all of us in that class. As the months passed, I loved watching those girls grow calm and relaxed and finally *really* feeling free. I also noted how they grew from painfully thin young girls who looked small for their ages, to healthy glowing young women, able for the first time in their lives to eat all they wanted. Physically and spiritually, they grew and blossomed and gave me much joy.

This Bible class ran the gamut from those newly arrived in the colony to old-timers who were new inquirers or had little or no spiritual background. Louie and Margaret Wang were two of those. Well-to-do entrepreneurs, Margaret was already a believer, and Louie was just learning. They welcomed us into their home and frequently invited us out to restaurants where we would never have been able to go on our own. It began with relationship, and Bob and I both knew this was the foundation of being able to share the good news.

I recall the meal we had with Bob's couples' class that first Christmas in Hong Kong. We gathered at one of the thousands of restaurants available for a real Chinese feast. Here, the similarities with Taiwan feasts were clearly evident. All sorts of dishes looked dubious, and we politely tried to concentrate on others that we recognized. We both tried sautéed duck's feet, and believe me, we will never do that again. The webbing on the feet is much like rubber. The fellowship with the class, however, was worth the necessity of politely trying to eat what had been put on our plates. We soon learned that Hong Kong had fabulous restaurants, and those specializing in North China cuisine became our favorites.

After a message that Bob preached one Sunday at North Point, a smiling young woman came up to me and held out her hand. "Do you remember me?" she asked as I greeted her. "I'm Esther Er, and I was in your Bible class at Grace Church over fifteen years ago." The slender young college coed was now a lovely, mature woman with a radiant smile. Esther reached in her purse and pulled out a small New Testament. Handing it to me, she said, "You gave me this in 1963, and I have been using it ever since." That was one of those special gifts of a moment God gives, totally unexpected and so uplifting. I had no memory of that long-ago time, but Esther had been blessed — and that gave *me* a blessing.

Bob and I were eager to find the best places to invest our time and efforts, and soon discovered that wasn't going to be easy. But then, whoever expected things to be easy? We should know better by this time. The search for where to plug in began, and both of us hoped the China mainland might be part of the answer.

Bob and Rosalie at Snead College

The family in Alabama, 1980

*Jody with his great-grandmother Martha Moore Hunt
(known to all as "Mama Hunt"), age ninety, in 1972*

Rosalie with one of her English classes at Hong Kong Baptist University

THIRTEEN

HONG KONG AND BEYOND
1980-1981

The "plug-in" place was not obvious. Finding a position for teaching was simple enough; Hong Kong Baptist College needed a psychology teacher immediately. However, the key to student work was not that straight-forward. Everyone in Hong Kong was too busy, especially students. Just getting from one place to another was a lengthy chore; pressure on students was tremendous. Only about 3 percent of high school graduates could get into college. Education was highly prized. One thing I knew at Baptist College: My students were guaranteed to be bright.

Meanwhile, Bob fit right into his usual pattern of instant rapport with young people. Within weeks, he was asked to lead a youth retreat for one of the two thriving English-language churches. During our five years in

Hong Kong, Bob ended up leading multiple retreats. These youth were from many countries, and, at every retreat, a number came to saving faith. Christian youth would bring their friends, and God did the rest.

Just as we had learned in Taiwan (and I, as a young child in China), Christmas is one of the hardest times of year for missionaries, with holiday time so far from family. We had a partial reprieve this year, for Jody came to Hong Kong for a month to participate in a January-term internship with the United Nations High Commission for Refugees. He was providently able to get a working internship assisting in a refugee camp for displaced Vietnamese trying to emigrate to America. It was a fabulous experience for him; he even had eighty-three refugees on his return flight to America. Having Jody in Hong Kong with us for Christmas was an unexpected blessing.

On the other hand, Alice and Kevin were on another continent, spending their Christmas in Mombasa, Kenya. Both were teaching at Mombasa Baptist High School and having a marvelous experience. Being a Nigerian MK, Kevin found Africa familiar territory. To Alice, it was a new slice of culture, and she reaped dividends from the experience, teaching math to high schoolers eager to learn. Bob and I found that planning a trip to Kenya for the following summer eased our angst a bit. We would take our annual vacation weeks to visit them. Kenya sounded so different from Hong Kong, especially when Alice described how they went on safari one weekend and actually saw a pride of lions up close.

We went to work trying to brush up on Mandarin. All around us, we would hear Cantonese, only catching an occasional phrase. However, Mandarin was becoming increasingly popular due to the influence of mainland China right on the doorstep. Meanwhile, several of our missionaries used their contacts to help us find a place for effective student ministry. One contact was with a Christian professor at Hong Kong University (HKU), the elite school in the colony. HKU had a Fellowship of Evangelical Students (FES), and that seemed a possibility. Our friend was clearly frustrated that, despite his time and efforts and the voiced intent on the part of FES, nothing developed. Time and again, the leaders would set a time to meet and plan — but then, over and over, they would change their plans. When Bob was finally able to sit down with FES leaders and talk it through, he learned that they wanted him to minister with them but only if he didn't relate students to churches. This went against every understanding we had of campus ministry: discipling students and getting them involved in a local church. Bob would, of course, relate students to various evangelical churches, but the adult planners objected to *any* church affiliation. They apparently feared that a *Baptist* leader would influence students in the direction of Baptists only. It didn't take us long to realize this was not going to be an option.

Nonetheless, Bob did not wait around cooling his heels but found other ways to minister. He taught at our Baptist Pui Ching High School, where he was blessed with intelligent students plus the freedom to share Christ with them. Then, a professor at Hong Kong Baptist College became ill, and Bob taught his classes. So it was that we found opportunities in places where we had not looked for them. Not only at the high school but also through Church Training (what we called Training Union in the States), Bob had an ideal spot for training Christian youth in discipling. Church Training in Hong Kong met on Saturdays, so we adjusted our schedules accordingly. Bob began leading discipling groups at various churches each weekend.

He was also needed to help out at both English-speaking churches. Hong Kong International on the island side was without a pastor, and while the church searched for one, they asked Bob to be their interim. Between his class at North Point Mandarin and Hong Kong International, Bob's Sundays were always full. IBC also had a mission church at Repulse Bay, where a lot of expats (foreigners) lived, and Bob frequently preached at both locations each Sunday morning.

He and I could seldom travel together because of differing schedules. My Bible class of new arrivals from China was both a challenge and a special joy. Two Sundays were never the same, and I never knew what question I might get or what new story I might learn. One of the members from the mainland had changed his name upon reaching Hong Kong because he feared reprisals from the Communists if they located him. This same earnest man asked me one Sunday during class to explain the Trinity to him. I had to confess that I found that hard, even when explaining in English! I did find a good book written in Chinese that explicated the Scripture dealing with the Trinity.

We quickly discovered another similarity to our work in Taiwan: entertaining guests in our home. We had a constant flow of visitors — our Bible classes, a youth group, a missionary family, or several of our journeymen. When Bob's Sunday School class or my college student classes came to celebrate Christmas, our small flat was filled to overflowing. To a person, they loved looking at our family photo albums, and many an opportunity to witness came from some question they would ask about a photograph.

Hong Kong must have had some of the best journeymen anywhere in the world. They were super, and we fell in love with them. We formed some lifelong friendships with them: Mark Brock, Scott Harris, Celia Seigler, Nancy Tallent, David and Sonya Garrison, Melissa King, and on the list went.

Taylor and Susan Field were two of those closest to our hearts. Taylor and I had an unusual tie. This brilliant young teacher at Hong Kong Baptist College was the son of an MK. Furthermore, his mother had been born in the same house in Yangzhou, China, where my parents first met in 1932. Taylor had a towering intellect and a heart to match. When recounting his experience of salvation and realizing that he came to true faith *after* his baptism, Taylor determined that he wanted to be baptized before leaving Hong Kong. We went out to Clearwater Bay, our Baptist property on the Kowloon Peninsula side in New Territories. (We dubbed it "Baptist Beach.") It was summertime, and several of our Hong Kong journeymen had journeymen friends visiting from other area countries. All of us gathered at the beach, and Bob had the joy of baptizing his friend Taylor; it was a holy moment that none of us present that afternoon forgot. (Taylor and Susan Field became North American Mission Board missionaries, and went on to both found and lead the tremendous Graffiti Ministries in the heart of New York City under NAMB.)

Some of our closest friends in the mission were Benny and Elena Petty. Benny taught at Baptist College, so he and I often saw each other at work. The Pettys hosted us when we first arrived, and their adorable little Elizabeth was born our first February in Hong Kong. She wound herself around our heartstrings without even trying. Elena's cooking put mine to shame, and an invitation to eat at the Pettys was always a treat. We were blessed with missionary friends as neighbors in a couple of locations where we lived, and mission prayer meeting each Tuesday evening was a wonderful time of bonding and praying for one another. Each missionary had an incredible testimony and special gifts. All of them helped us, offering advice, friendship, and sometimes a hand up. Lewis Smith and Don Langford were our two Baptist doctors, and time and again they gave us medical advice and assistance.

Theories of Personality was a challenge to teach at Baptist College, but I was impressed with the caliber of students. Then, when one of our seminary professors had to leave abruptly, I finished his semester's course, teaching Counseling for Ministers. Again, it was no surprise to be doing something for which I felt particularly unprepared. Those were the moments when I depended heavily on the Lord's help, which I should have been doing *all* the time.

North Point's Bible study class taught me lessons every week — about courage, about fortitude, and about trusting God no matter what. Each member had a poignant story and an inspiring testimony. Young Miss Chen, age eighteen and with a glowing face, came from Shanghai, clearly grateful to be free to talk about God. She told the class of the masses of young adults attending open churches in Shanghai, her eyes sparkling as she spoke in broken English. Dr. Lai came from the mainland, as did seventy-seven-year-old Mrs. Yang. They knew little about the Bible but were eager to learn. It smote my heart each Sunday to think of how all these years I just took God and His grace for granted, like they were my due. They weren't. Then three of our class members, who lived in a resettlement area for new arrivals to the colony, were burned out by a devastating fire and lost everything — which wasn't much to begin with. Rather than being in despair, they were thankful to have lived through it. Our class and the church immediately went to work and helped them with clothes, food and furnishings.

Pieces of Taiwan memories came to touch and make our hearts rejoice. Miss Sye, North Point's pianist, was the daughter of Pastor Sye, our dear friend in Taichung. (He was the one who looked so much like my father.) Ever thoughtful, they learned that we were at North Point and sent us a gift by way of their daughter. That first year, another Taiwan friend came to visit. Helen Hsu, one of my friends from a Taiwan Bible class, visited Hong Kong and attended our North Point class. Some years before, Helen had trusted the Lord and grown quickly in her faith. She was the first believer in her family, and soon led her husband to faith and then their three children. Her husband had a deep sorrow; he had not been able to see his parents who lived in Shanghai in thirty years. Furthermore, Helen and Mr. Hsu's oldest son had remained in Shanghai with his grandparents, and they had not seen him since; now he was a grown man. Helen had been able to get a Hong Kong visa, but Mr. Hsu was having difficulty getting one. My class was thrilled when Helen visited and gave her testimony.

Meanwhile, the Hsus' parents and their oldest son in China providentially managed to get permission to come to Hong Kong. Now the family waited together for Mr. Hsu to somehow obtain a visa to come. Every day must have seemed like a month to him. While the rest of the family waited, Helen was able to lead both her in-laws and her oldest son to Christ. The long-awaited visa finally arrived; now after all those years, Mr. Hsu was once again in the same city with his beloved parents and oldest son. When he walked in the door and saw them, in true old-China custom, he knelt on the floor and bowed, signifying his deep love and respect. Helen wept as she described their long-anticipated reunion.

The setting for Bob's various ministries in Hong Kong differed from those in Taiwan, but the end result was the same. He had an uncanny ability to relate to youth — even those he met for the first time, no matter what race or nationality. A young Chinese man at Hong Kong International Church brought his Indian friend Ranjit to a service, his first time in a Christian church. At the conclusion, the young friend introduced him to Bob, and Ranjit excitedly told him, "I have never been in a church in my life, but I felt God moving in my heart. I would like to know Him." Bob was thrilled; he gave the young man a Bible and got his address. Bob was overjoyed when Ranjit returned the very next week, not only listening intently but also professing faith.

The location didn't seem to matter; Bob met scores of young adults and got to know them quickly. One afternoon, he was returning on the Star Ferry from Kowloon to the island, and while waiting for the gates to be opened to board, he began visiting with a young man standing next to him. The man was amazed to hear this foreigner speaking to him in Mandarin. Bob learned that he had left Shanghai two years earlier and now had a job in Hong Kong; he was eager to talk, and Bob was eager to share good news with him. The fellow was clearly interested, and Bob made arrangements to meet him for lunch the following week. Not knowing if he would show or not, Bob took a Bible and arrived at the restaurant. In walked the young man, and here was another opportunity to share one on one. Over and over, we saw God provide such occasions. They weren't just happenstance, but part of a divine plan; we simply needed to be in the right place at the right time.

Much of the time, Bob and I rode double-decker buses to and from various responsibilities, for there was always a shortage of parking places when driving the car. One afternoon, we were returning home when a young student got on the bus. I drew in a breath of surprise and nudged Bob, gesturing with my head in the direction of the young man. Bob did a double take as well. He looked for the world like Huan, our "other" son. I nearly called out, "Huan? Is that *you?*" We knew it couldn't be, for Huan was at Auburn University, but it reminded us yet again of the treasure of friendship and what the Huu family meant to us. Huan wrote beautiful letters and kept us in the loop about his schooling and his family.

In retrospect, the events that followed in 1981 should have been no surprise. They were clearly providential, so why should we be surprised? The frustrations of wanting to see just *where* and *how* to minister kept bugging us, but one day, the phone rang: It was Mr. Chu (name changed) from Kowloon International Baptist Church. John Chu was a Christian businessman in Hong Kong with numerous business ties on the mainland. A China contact in the petroleum industry wanted Mr. Chu to find a native speaker of English to teach twenty select engineering students in a certain south China city. It would be for several months at a time. Immediately, Chu thought of Bob. Both of us felt the chill bumps of recognition, as if to say: So, *this* is why we have been waiting. Here was what our hearts had longed for — a chance to minister in China.

Just as with anything in the Orient dealing with an autocratic government, nothing is simple. This wasn't, but the possibilities were exciting. It took some three months to work out the kinks — but early in April, an excited Bob boarded a plane for Canton and points south. I tried to visualize the situation to my own mind and ponder what this meant for us. Much of it, surely, was simply being ready and being available when God opened doors. I quickly realized this was "being" and not "doing."

I am changing names and not identifying precise locations in order to implicate no one. Even forty years later, we need to err on the side of caution. The events, however, are exactly as they occurred and printed on our hearts. Bob received all sorts of counsel prior to leaving for the mainland: what to do, what not to do, how to be "wise as a serpent and harmless as a dove." Bob was a trial balloon. A couple of missionary women had been able to go for a week or so to teach some students in various cities, but Bob was the first of our missionaries able to go for an extended period. This was rather like sailing into unknown waters, considering the precarious pitfalls that might be swirling around in the seas of an authoritarian regime. I was beyond excited: Bob was going to be able to go to China, and I knew that opportunities on weekends would come for me. More than thirty years ago I had dreamed of just such a time, and I could scarcely believe that dream might actually become a reality. He spent a couple of days in Canton, waiting to meet the man Mr. Chu had arranged to accompany him on the flight to the city where he would teach.

Stanley Fu, a dear friend and a deacon at North Point Church, was a senior military-political analyst at the US Consulate. He was able to give Bob firsthand advice about what to do and what *not* to do when in the mainland. He was not allowed to bring up the subject of God or religion but could respond if he was asked about God. He was never to forget that there were always eyes and ears watching and listening. In fact, he could be sure that someone had been assigned to keep a perpetual eye on him. It was enough to make anyone paranoid, but the opportunity was too special to pass up. Nonetheless, the entire first two months, Bob felt like he was walking a tightrope and did not ever let his guard down.

Bob was astounded with the new sights surrounding him in the storied city of Canton. It looked so different from Hong Kong. Granted, there were the same masses of people, but all those he saw now were Chinese, and he was stared at by everyone. Hong Kong was alive with industry, color, high rises, enterprise. On the other hand, Canton looked like time had stood still for thirty years; it could easily have been the Canton of 1950. Cantonese was heard on every hand, but enough people understood and spoke Mandarin that he felt at home with the language. Bob managed to make a quiet stop at the newly opened church — amazingly, the elderly pastor was there, and the two of them were able to have a picture made together. I was thrilled when Bob recounted the experience, for this was none other than pastor Matthew Tong, the brother of Mama's beloved student at Shanghai University, Moonbeam Tong, some fifty years earlier. The church had just been allowed to reopen, and Bob could clearly detect the sparkle of joy in the eyes of a man of God who had gone through unimaginable perse-cution, his sweet spirit still intact. (Word reached Hong Kong the following November that Pastor Tong had died. We were doubly thankful that Bob had been privileged to meet him and make that incredible link with our family's missions past.)

Bob was careful not to load his luggage with Bibles and Christian liter-ature. Luggage was minutely inspected, and a suitcase full of Bibles would have waved all sorts of red flags. In fact, he said to the inspector, "I have a few Bibles with me. Is that all right?" The inspector was so intrigued that this foreigner was speaking Mandarin that he commented on that rather than inspecting the Bibles. The following morning, Mr. Lee, the man chosen to escort Bob to his city, met him at the airport. When the flight was announced, Mr. Lee said, "Run!" Bob looked puzzled and asked, "Run? Why run? Don't we have reservations?" Mr. Lee repeated, "Just run!" So Bob ran. Sure enough, it was first come first served — and passengers had to scramble to get a seat, climbing over the luggage piled in the aisle to do so. Relieved that they had been able to get a seat, Bob drew a long breath, looked around, and tried to find his seat belt. There was none. Seeing the stewardess walking down the narrow aisle, he asked, "Where is the seat belt?" She beamed as she answered, "Oh, we've ordered them. They should arrive next week." Bob swallowed his surprise and next asked, "What is this hole in the window by my seat?" She responded, "That's the air conditioning; you get air that way." Bob quickly decided it was time for him to pray.

Even writing about his experiences in a letter was dicey, and Bob was also very careful in what he said on the phone when he was able to get a connection to Hong Kong. In turn, I had to be equally cautious, for every phone call and every letter was read and listened to. To come from the conspicuous luxury of Hong Kong into a country that was much as it had been for decades was a shock. The hostel where foreigners were allowed to stay would make a Motel 6 look like the Waldorf Astoria. Bob's bed was a thick box springs — pure lumps. However, the linens were clean and there were plenty of pillows. Nonetheless, the concrete floor was never quite clean. Bob bit the bullet and did his calisthenics on the bed. Later, after observing his students' living quarters, he was grateful to have a commode, sink, and a showerhead. He had a shower drain, but the water ran freely on the floor, so he wore flip flops in the shower. There was no hot water. There *was* a fan — and Bob gave thanks for something to stir the air.

The food was interesting. There was plenty of what there was — mostly seafood, always loaded with garlic, seasoned with plenty of hot pepper, and thoroughly greasy. No sweets were served, although he occasionally had a little fruit. The main vegetable was fried cucumbers, and the first weekend I was able to visit Bob, they were served for every meal. Bob had taken along peanut butter and crackers, and they were as welcome as gold. There was no ice available, something Americans usually take for granted. The heat of the season had already reached that south China city, and Bob dreamed of ice-cold drinks. He also used water-purifying tablets that he had brought from Hong Kong because tap water was not safe, even for brushing teeth.

But the boys … the students. Who cared about spartan living conditions when there is an opportunity to share the best news with people who had never heard? Never in his life had Bob encountered students more eager to learn. The deprivations of the Cultural Revolution had insured that they had missed many opportunities for a solid education; those boys were making up for lost time. There were five or six excellent students, two of whom were outstanding; another handful were capable of learning well; and the remainder would likely never be adequate in English. It would not, however, be from lack of trying. It was also clear that they had been indoctrinated — obvious in the papers they wrote, in their textbooks, and even in their conversation. The party line had been drilled into them. Nonetheless, there was a spirit of inquiry and curiosity evident in the questions they asked. They *wanted* to learn and were fascinated with America, and each, to a person, wanted to go there some day. The students peppered Bob with questions about America, looking at it as something of a promised land.

Jody arrived for his trip to the field provided by the Foreign Mission Board, and he and I excitedly got ready to go to China. This would be Jody's first time in the country about which he had heard so much. This would be many hundreds of miles from my childhood home in Zhenjiang, but just the thought of finally being back in the country I loved so deeply made my heart skip a beat. Stepping off the plane that first afternoon in Canton was deeply emotional. It felt like God had handed me a special gift. After thirty-two years, I was once again in China. Looking around in wonder, I found everything was different but yet the same. Time had stood still. One difference was finding soldiers everywhere I looked. Not only did it feel like everyone was looking at me, they actually were. Foreigners were a rare sight, especially a woman, and when I spoke Mandarin, they would exclaim in wonder.

By the time Jody and I got to Bob's city, I don't know if he was more eager to see us or to see the Hong Kong goodies we brought. He had written about each of the boys, and I was eager to meet them. Bob had suggested things I could bring in for them, so I came supplied with cookies and candy. The most fun came from watching them chew the bubble gum I had brought. They had never had any, and Bob wrote home that never would he have thought that he would include as part of his curriculum a lesson in how to blow bubbles! I had brought each student a T-shirt, and you would have thought they were spun of gold, so excited were they. Bob told me of the different personalities — and I loved meeting Gerald, one of the two with the best English. He never seemed to quit smiling. Huey was forever on the move, so interested in everything and bubbling about his chance to learn English from an American. Conrad joined Gerald in having outstanding learning ability and was full of questions daily. Samuel and Tom wanted to absorb all they could in the time Bob was with them.

All of the students were thrilled to have a real American student their own age to visit. They peppered Jody with questions, and he, in turn, learned much about what was *different* for students in China. Jody and I made the most of every moment we had with Bob and the students, and wished for more time.

There was little chance of privacy in China; only in his room did Bob feel secure from watchful eyes (although he realized there might be a listening device). Everyone took a "siesta" for an hour or so in the afternoon, and Bob developed the habit of walking down to the beach on the South China Sea when no one was around. It was a quiet and peaceful time, and a balm to his spirit. The biggest frustration was not being able to openly share the good news, but he was alert to any opening that might come. One did. Not long before his two-month stint was up, Gerald ended one of his essays with the phrase, "God bless me." Bob's heart skipped a beat. After class he asked, "Gerald, what did you mean, 'God bless me'?" Gerald smiled and said, "That is what I want Him to do." Bob next questioned, "Where did you hear about God?" Gerald proceeded to explain that an older friend in Canton had told him about God, and he learned there was an overseas broadcast, the Far East Broadcasting network, that talked about God. He told Bob, "I want God to bless me." Gerald became the beginning of what would be a harvest in that city, a harvest that would come four months later.

Bob baptizing Taylor Field at "Baptist Beach" in Hong Kong

FOURTEEN

ON TWO CONTINENTS
1981-1983

I could scarcely wait to get back to Hong Kong; I wanted to call Mama and Daddy and tell them of the wonder of being back in China. This would likely be as close to China as they would be able to get, and I wanted them to share the experience. Over the phone, I could hear Mama weeping with excited joy as I described those first impressions of what my eyes saw and my heart experienced. Their sense of call to that land had never changed, so this account was like hearing about home.

Bob returned to Hong Kong after two months in China. He had lost twenty pounds, but was bubbling over with excitement about what he knew God would be doing for those students. They had entwined themselves around his heart, and he was already praying and planning to go back and see God at work. A couple of days after his return, Bob described to Jody and me what had been a singular life experience for him. After he had been there about a month, the loneliness and sense of isolation felt almost unbearable. Being watched all the time and having no one with whom to talk things through was a terrific emotional strain. "I was so lonely," he kept repeating, slowly shaking his head at the memory of that unusual day. It was Sunday morning, and of course, he could not go to church and worship. There was no Christian fellowship, and his sense of isolation was stark. Sitting on one of the two chairs in his spartan room, Bob began reading in Colossians. He struggled to describe what happened next. "There was no one in the room," he told us, "and I didn't hear a voice. In fact, it was eerily silent. But," his eyes glistened with tears, "I *literally* felt the very presence of God with me. It was like I could reach out and touch Him. Right there in that bare, dusty little room," Bob concluded, "I worshipped in a way I never had in all my life. God was *with* me."

A few weeks later, the three of us began our unusual vacation — our first trip to Africa. It meant reunion time with Alice and Kevin. The sun was merciless in Mombasa, Kenya, but we scarcely noticed. All of us were thrilled to be together and see firsthand what journeyman life was like in Kenya. We were dazzled by the beautiful smiles of everyone we met and the welcome we received. Alice and Kevin had both Kenyan and Indian students, and we visited in several of their homes. Church services in Mombasa felt alive and vibrant; although we did not understand Swahili, we were caught up in their contagious worship experience.

Since school holidays were beginning, the five of us traveled to Nairobi to go on safari. I had never dreamed of having such a family time. We were in awe of the wildlife, from elephant families to graceful giraffes, and giant hippos lolling in the water. We ran out of superlatives, especially when coming upon a pride of lions. Then an unexpected treat was added — a reunion with my close friends from Oklahoma Baptist University days. Will J. and Marie Roberts had worked in Kenya for many years. We had not seen each other since their wedding day. We relived memories of OBU and remarked how that seemed a whole lifetime ago.

All too soon, we headed back to Hong Kong and Jody to Alabama for his senior year. I was lined up for a full schedule of classes at the college plus numerous church responsibilities. Bob picked right up on all the preaching and teaching at the various churches, all the time keeping an ear out for word of when he might return to China. That call came in September, and after the usual delays, he headed back to south China, eager to see what God was going to do. Bob knew he couldn't preach there, but he could demonstrate a Christian in action. Bob later wrote Keith Parks, president of the Foreign Mission Board, reporting on the amazing months that followed. He declared, "Those months back in China turned out to be the most remarkable time of my life!"

The students were beyond excited when they heard "Dr. Bob" was back to teach them again. They came to the hostel that first evening, eager to see him again. One student, Gerald, lingered after the others left, walking back into Bob's room with him. He picked up Bob's Bible from the table, smiling as he said, "Yes, we are brothers now!" Bob felt a jolt of excitement, asking, "Gerald, tell me what you mean." Gerald explained that he had continued listening to gospel news on Far East radio, and a couple of months earlier, he had asked Christ into his life. "Now," he paused, "I've been reading the whole New Testament, and I need to be baptized!" Bob was moved to tears as he and Gerald talked and prayed together, and Bob promised they would figure out a way for him to be baptized. Pastor Jang at the little house church was a frail eighty-six years old and could only sprinkle a new believer. Gerald wanted to be immersed, so he and Bob devised a plan.

Bob could scarcely wait to call me and carefully say, "Yes, Gerald *talked* to me today." I knew immediately what he meant, for we were always circumspect about what we said on the phone or put in letters. We talked of finding a time for Gerald to be baptized, and Bob thought we might aim for October when I could travel in.

Whenever I was able to visit Bob, I took a gift for each of the students. This time, Bob took the boys' measurements, and I bought jeans for each one. Their joy over the simple gift was more fun than Christmas for us. None had ever had a pair of "American jeans." They were so thrilled that many put them on right on top of what they were wearing.

The weekend of Bob's birthday, October 15, I could barely contain my excitement. We decided the setting would be the South China Sea, at siesta time when the beach was deserted. Gerald's cousin, James, was visiting from Hainan Island and wanted to be there, too. Gerald had been sharing his story with his cousin, and James was keenly interested. That hot, somnolent afternoon, nothing was stirring, not even the air. Clad in swimming trunks, Bob, Gerald and James waded out into the shallow waters on the beach while I stood on the shore, camera in hand, heart in throat. The sacredness of that moment was profound as Bob raised his hand, calling upon God's blessings on Gerald and his life as a believer. I stood at the edge of the water, silent tears slipping down my face. The camera captured the moment Gerald came up out of the water and declared to Bob, "This is the happiest day of my life." In a paper the next week, he wrote, "Dr. Bob pushed me down into the water and then pulled me up. The feeling I had was astonishing!"

Bob was not able to attend the tiny house church in the home of old Pastor Jang. It would have been dangerous to both the pastor and the other believers. The students could attend, however, and that is exactly what Gerald did. One quiet afternoon, an opportunity came for Bob to visit the dear old man who had shepherded a flock long years before and was eager to help anyone who could come. Bob later described the tiny room where the house church met. There were a few straight-back chairs and two single beds pushed up against one wall. When people sat on both sides, their knees met in the middle, so tiny was the room. The joy that filled the place, however, was not limited by space.

God's Spirit at work quickly became evident, and seeds that had been planted the previous spring began to bud. Bob started each day with antic- ipation, just waiting to see what the Lord would do next. Often in groups of two or three, the boys would come visit Bob in the evening. They were eager to learn more, and a number had penetrating questions. One evening, Michael and Huey came together. Michael said something about God, and Bob responded, "Do you believe there is a God?" Michael spoke quickly,

"Oh, yes! I have a cousin in Hong Kong, and I am going to write and ask him to bring me a Bible." Bob smiled, telling him, "I have a New Testament I can give you *now*." Michael's smile was radiant. "Really? I would love a Bible." Then Bob turned to Huey and inquired, "Huey, what about you?" Huey shrugged and shook his head. "Oh, no. I don't think there is a God." The two boys soon left, Michael clutching his Chinese New Testament. Next morning, as soon as class break came, Huey hurried up to Bob and said, "Teacher, you know that little black book you gave Michael? Well," he grinned, "I read half of it last night, and I have never read anything *like* it. That Jesus in the book," and he plucked at Bob's sleeve to emphasize, "that Jesus is *alive!*" Bob later told me he had chill bumps upon hearing Huey's words. The young man went on to relate story after story he had read of Jesus' miracles, and began asking penetrating questions.

Bob had recently been having a lot of pain with sore, stiff shoulders, but he felt light as a feather after hearing Huey's excitement. One of the boys asked the location of his pain, and when Bob described the ache in his shoulders, Huey spoke right up, "Oh, I'll come over this evening and give your shoulders a massage. I'm really good at that." Sure enough, Huey arrived later that evening and went to work getting the kinks out of Bob's shoulders. All the while, Huey asked Bob questions about "that little black book."

Soon, Huey remarked, "If I can ever go to Hong Kong or to America, I can become God's son, too." Bob assured him, "Huey, you don't have to go to Hong Kong *or* America to trust Jesus. You can do that right here in this city, in this place. I will introduce you to Him." Huey's eyes sparkled. "Really? Oh, yes!" he exclaimed. "That is exactly what I want. Please introduce me." Huey got up, and walking to the little mirror by the sink, straightened his shirt and combed his hair so he would look just right when he was introduced to Jesus. Bob and Huey got down on their knees on the bare concrete floor. Bob prayed first, and then Huey prayed, both in English and in Chinese, simply and eloquently inviting Jesus into his life. As soon as he had finished and they stood up, Bob said, "Huey, now Jesus lives in your heart." Huey's face lighted up again. He put his arms around himself and declared, "Thank you, thank you, Jesus, for coming into my heart." That golden moment for Bob became a treasure he will never lose.

One by one, the young men came; some were closer to being ready than others, yet evidence of God's work in hearts was obvious. One student told Bob his grandfather had had a Bible, and he remembered hearing about Jesus. First one believed, and then another. Samuel came alone at night and talked to Bob, expressing his earnest desire to know the Lord. Bob asked him, "Do you know any Christians?" Samuel smiled and replied, "He never told me he was a believer, but I know Gerald is. I can tell!" Samuel came to faith as well. Many of the students read the New Testament, and because Jesus, the teacher, was called "Rabbi," they began referring to Bob as "Rabbi Hunt." During a break period, one of the older students was eager to tell Bob that he had experienced a special dream in which Jesus visited him. The Sunday prior to Bob's departure, a group of eight students came by to talk and pray. All too soon, Bob stood at his door waving goodbye as the students left, heading to the little house church. He stood watching the young believers as grateful tears slid down his cheeks at such beautiful answers to the prayers of many.

This time, when Bob wrote Keith Parks at the Foreign Mission Board, relating the amazing events of the past months, he explained, "What I had experienced in south China was the closest thing I've ever seen to the New Testament church, so fresh and pure and simple." After returning to Hong Kong, Bob was able on several occasions to receive letters from the boys. Each letter thrilled him. Huey had gone from being at the bottom of the class to handling himself quite well in English. In one letter, he told Bob, "We learn not only English from you but that it is important how to be a kind man during your stay in our city. You already left our class, but your good example has not left us. Especially you introduced me to become an apostle. After that, I have got joy in my heart." Huey concluded his exuberant letter by saying, "Now I tell you a good news that is very happy in my heart. This year's Christmas will advent soon, and I will celebrate my first Christmas." Our best gift of the season was Huey's joyful letter.

Bob was back in Hong Kong in time for a busy Christmas season. He preached three times each Sunday morning — and we hosted a number of Christmas parties at our flat (apartment) for students from our church and discipleship classes, plus my college students. One student, Alice, who had never been in a Western home, asked, "Will this be a tea party or a dance party?" I assured her it was a tea party. We were pleasantly surprised that all thirty students at a time could get in our flat. Christmas was the perfect time and opportunity to share the best news of all. On weekdays, Bob worked with one of our missionaries at a Vietnamese refugee center. He came home one day with a glowing face and told me about the young thirty-four-year-old who had trusted Christ that morning. It tore Bob's heart to note that man had one son with him, but his wife and other three children were all still in Vietnam. We Americans are so quick to take our blessings for granted.

One week, three men Bob had met in China came to Hong Kong on business and at once contacted Bob. He met with them and gave each one a Bible. They came for a meal with us, and we stood in awe again of the openings God provided. None were Christians, but they all were interested in learning. With every opportunity to give a Bible, we thanked God anew for the power of His Word and prayed it would bear fruit.

In April, one of my best college students excitedly called to tell me she was accepted at a university in Texas. I took her to lunch and gave her a Bible. It was a perfect time to talk about her future and what was really important in our lives. Bob and I both were so grateful for all the one-on-one opportunities to share the message, whether with our students or with some chance encounter that was really a divine appointment. I often wished I had kept track of all the times that happened. For Bob, it was a natural avenue to personal encounter, and we were continually amazed at how many times God opened up such an opportunity.

Mr. Chu, the Baptist businessman who had engineered the work with students in China, was most eager for Bob to be part of the business, with numerous opportunities to go into China and serve as a witness just by his presence. Mr. Chu had plans to use Bob's ministry in this way in several cities, and our Hong Kong mission was willing to allow Bob to start with a six-month leave of absence and try this venture. As always when dealing with the government in China, everything was complicated and slower than slow. While Bob waited for details to be worked out, he continued teaching, discipling and preaching. Every week was full. Shortly after Christmas, we moved to a flat at Boundary Street, the building that housed the mission offices. It would be vastly more convenient for my college teaching — and the rooms were larger, making it easier to have students in our home.

Jody, in his final semester at Samford, went to Boaz as often as possible on weekends to check on all three grandparents. He called us one Saturday evening, laughing about his early call that morning. Jody had looked forward to getting a rare Saturday morning to sleep in. But no, at 6:30 that cold February morning, the phone jangled him awake. Fearing an emergency, he answered it quickly. Ho Shien Sun was on the line, saying, "Jody, I need your help." *Oh no, something is wrong with Ho Se Mo* was Jody's first thought. His grandfather spoke quickly, "Jody, I need my lawn mower serviced. Can you take it?" Jody, even knowing how his grandfather wanted everything done yesterday, was still a bit surprised. "Ho Shien Sun," Jody responded, "it's February, and it's 6:30 in the morning." Ho Shien Sun sounded a bit disgruntled, abruptly saying, "OK, I'll just take it myself." Jody answered immediately, "No, Ho Shien Sun, I'm on my way over!" That 6:30 call has become one of the family stories we all like to pass on, a delightful commentary on Daddy's personality.

That winter, Pastor Wu, our friend at North Point Church, had a massive heart attack and had an enforced period away from preaching. This meant still busier Sundays for Bob, with North Point Church on the island side and Kowloon Church a ferry ride away, plus other preaching points. The pastor of each of the thriving English language churches also had heart attacks, though not at the same time. Bob stepped in to fill the gaps as they occurred. Youth retreats were highly popular at both of these churches, and Bob and I loved the special time and opportunities with students from more than a dozen countries.

I had an unexpected experience that Christmas. In the 1970s, when teaching internationals at Snead College, one of my students was Chu Yin Pin, from Hong Kong. One day out of the blue, I had a phone call from her.

She was back in Hong Kong and heard that I was living there. Meeting her at the Star Ferry, I took her to North Point to my Sunday School class and for worship. It was Pastor Wu's first Sunday back in the pulpit, and it was Yin Pin's first time to ever be in a church. It was a thrilling experience, and she seemed keenly interested in all that she heard.

That Christmas was our first ever without any family. It was hard on the children, too, but all of us were looking forward to being together for a few weeks at Jody's May graduation. Bob waited each week to know when he would be returning to China. First one thing and then another slowed the process down. In the end, Bob was in limbo for a full six months, but he was constantly busy while waiting. By summer, we realized this was a no-go. That door was closed — we knew not why, but we *did* know God had plenty of ministry in mind right where we were.

Meanwhile, we were getting disquieting letters from Alice. Something was physically wrong with her, and the doctors in both Mombasa and Nairobi tested her exhaustively but could not pinpoint the cause of her blinding headaches. This went on for nearly three months. One specialist feared a possible brain tumor and felt further testing was needed. It could not be done in Kenya. The Kenyan mission thought it best that Alice seek medical help in the States. It was near the end of their two-year stint, but they reluctantly decided that Kevin would remain until the end of the school year, and Alice return to America. At the same time, Jody wrote that he was concerned about Ho Se Mo (my mother). Doctors could not discover why she was losing weight and was increasingly frail. Bob and I considered the situation and determined I needed to be there for both our ailing family members. We quickly made arrangements to cover the work in Hong Kong while I made a quick trip to Alabama.

I arrived in time to go with Jody to the airport to meet Alice, and there followed months of tests. Mama, as well, was struggling to eat and to maintain any normal activity — but as usual, she never complained, so it was hard to tell how much she was really suffering. Mama was always small, but now she seemed so tiny that she looked fragile to all of her worried kin. Alice's trouble was eventually determined to be a severe endocrine imbalance, and proper medication helped. Bob and I had never pictured events happening as they did, but never were we left feeling that God had given up on us. We didn't understand — but then, we didn't have to. Kevin finished teaching in early May and arrived in time for Jody's graduation from Samford. Bob soon came in from Hong Kong, so a wounded but grateful family rejoiced to be together again. It was like a gift to Jody that Ho Se Mo was well enough to attend the graduation ceremony. She sat there beaming to see her only grandson tapped for the outstanding student award and receive the trophy as valedictorian. My thoughts raced to the realization that the prayers of my mother and father had led to this night. They had prayed for all the days of our children's lives that those lives would honor Christ.

At the end of the month, Bob and I returned to Hong Kong, thankful that Mama felt stronger and Alice had regained her health. She and Kevin would be teaching and in graduate school. Jody was headed to Florida State University to work on a master's degree, and Bob and I were planning to take a short furlough the following year. However, as so often happens, things didn't exactly go according to plan.

Bob baptizing Gerald (name changed) in the South China Sea

Entertaining the Philip Chu family in our Hong Kong flat

FIFTEEN

LIFE HAPPENS
1982-1983

It was satisfying to be back at work with a full schedule of teaching plus ministry at North Point Church, and, in the evenings, at the two international congregations. Bob was active at all three churches, including preaching two or three times each Sunday morning, and frequently at night as well. The children were terrific about writing. We typically received several letters a week from both, keeping us abreast of family news. Jody wrote to tell us of a strange, nearly unbelievable incident that had just occurred. He had been in graduate classes a couple of months and found a weekend when he could get back to Boaz to check on his grandparents. Shortly before dusk that Friday afternoon, Jody was driving on a fairly uncrowded stretch of road when, out of nowhere, a car veered from its lane and headed straight at him.

Eyes wide with horror, he instinctively jerked the steering wheel to the right and ran completely off the road to avoid a head-on collision. The oncoming car missed him by mere inches, so close that he could literally hear the whish of air as it barely missed impacting the side of his car. Trembling with shock and the rush of adrenaline, Jody drew a deep breath and happened to glance at the clock on the dash. It read 4:30. Shaky minutes elapsed before he felt steady enough to continue driving.

Upon reaching Boaz, Jody went immediately to see Ho Se Mo and Ho Shien Sun to tell them of that frightening moment and God's great protection. After the hugs and greetings, Jody launched into his story. When he came to the place where the car missed him, Ho Shien Sun broke in, "What time was it when that car headed straight at you?" Jody recalled looking at the dash and noting it was 4:30. Ho Shien Sun gave an incredulous shake of his head. "Jody," he began, "I was lying down resting this afternoon, and suddenly I came instantly awake on the thought, *I must pray for Jody*. I got right out of bed and knelt down to pray for God to protect you. I was wide awake by then, so I stood up and looked at the clock." His eyes filled with unshed tears as he looked at Jody, and said, "It was 4:30."

Weeks later, the phone rang. We had been back in Hong Kong more than four months, grateful for daily opportunities of ministry. Normally, a call from church leaders or students came later in the day, so we answered the phone, guessing it was probably a call from America. Sure enough, we heard Jody's voice, but we were dismayed at his news. He and Alice were very concerned about Ho Se Mo. She appeared to be failing again. "Mom," Jody sounded anxious, "I think you need to come if you can. Ho Se Mo and Ho Shien Sun need someone to take charge of the situation." Immediately, my mind harked back to the number of times I had remembered Mama so deeply concerned about one or the other of her parents but unable to go help them. However, Mama was blessed with three sisters, so there had been a family member to help out. I had just one brother, far away in California. "Jody," I assured our son, "we'll work something out and find a way." Then I added, "But don't tell Mama and Daddy until we have it firm."

A week later, arrangements in place to cover my work, I headed to the airport, most grateful that our board and the mission were both kindly cooperating in a time of crisis. My heart was racing madly, and I chalked it up to stress. Nonetheless, it was pretty worrisome, because for two months now, I had noticed this accelerated heart rate. We figured it was all the stress and hurry and scurry of life in Hong Kong. Sometimes, my heart sounded so loud in my ears when I tried to sleep that the thump-thump-thump literally kept me awake. Furthermore, for the first time ever, I could eat any and everything and lose weight. That part of the problem was too good to be true. Then after Jody's call, my heart rate went crazy.

First things first. We needed to see what was happening with Mama. I was shocked to find her noticeably frailer than just months earlier. She had never been large, but now she looked tiny. Her doctor had sent her to a couple of specialists, and, thus far, no explanation could be found. Meanwhile, Bob insisted I see a doctor while in the States. Very reluctantly (doctors just being a notch above dentists in favorite things to do), I got an appointment with Dr. Finlay, Dad's cardiologist. Not only was he an excellent and highly respected physician, Andrew Finlay was also a man of deep faith.

It took Dr. Finlay one day to discover that I had thyrotoxicosis. Blood work revealed the level of thyroid in my body was four times what was normal. Something had gone haywire, and the thyroid level in my system was close to lethal. Without delay, I was given radioactive iodine to kill the goiter before it killed me. Thank God I was in the States. Although here because of Mama's illness, I received life-preserving help for myself. The mission board was gracious and supportive and immediately put me on medical leave.

At one of my appointments, Dr. Finlay told me of a moment with my dad that stuck in his mind. "I was giving your dad his annual physical a couple of months ago. I always try to be thorough, and during the exam, I touched the rough callous on his right knee." Dr. Finlay gave a little smile and continued, "I looked at his left knee. It was smooth — no callous. 'Mr. Hall,' I asked, 'why is this callous on your right knee, but nothing on your left?'" Dr. Finlay explained that Dad had looked puzzled and sort of cocked his head, looking at that callous. "Then," Dr. Finlay finished, "his face brightened up and he said, 'Oh, that's the knee I kneel on when I pray.'"

Dr. Finlay told me, "That is the first time in my life I have had a patient who had a callous *caused* by prayer. I will never forget." And I thought, *Thank you, God, for the gift of such a heritage.*

The ensuing months of separation were painful. Slowly I began to get back to normal, although I often wondered what *normal* meant. At the same time, all the family was frustrated not to be able to pinpoint the cause of Mama's alarming fragility. As usual for her, though, no one heard a complaint. This was the first Christmas Bob and I had not been together. At least I had family around — he didn't. Our mission family was wonderful, however; in every letter, Bob wrote of being invited to eat, both at the homes of missionaries and eating out with groups. Nourishment was no problem. Loneliness was.

It was a frustrating puzzle that Mama's problems couldn't be found and treated. She had compression fractures in her back, and the pain from those was nearly unremitting. I could look into her eyes and see her hurting — but her gentle smile never showed it, nor did a single word remark that pain. Now, more than ever, I saw grace at work in a heart. Although not really diagnosed, Mama began to eat a little better, and that encouraged us. She was gently hinting to me every day to "go on back, Rosalie. Don't stay because of me." I assured her I was waiting for the doctor's OK on my condition, and when it came in February, I left with very mixed emotions. I longed to be back with Bob and at the post working, but Mama was so fragile. However, knowing we were taking a short furlough in May gave me the impetus to return to Hong Kong.

We had long ago given up hope of persuading Granny Ora (as all the grandchildren called Bob's mother) to visit us on the field. Very unexpectedly, she told me she would like to see Hong Kong for herself. She would be traveling outside America for the first time ever. To make it even more special, Dru (Bob's sister) and her two sons (Bill and Link) decided to come as well. For two weeks, Bob had the pleasure of his mother, sister, and nephews actually with us in Hong Kong. Dru was thankful that her two teenagers had this experience. "They are learning a *lot* more than they would in two weeks in a classroom!" she proclaimed.

For more than a year, Elena Petty and I had talked of going to China. Bob could not get away from his duties, but Elena planned ahead and found friends to cover for her, as did I for college classes and ministry responsibilities. Elena, a former journeyman in Taiwan, was familiar with Mandarin, so she would be able to understand what was going on as we traveled. My chief aim was to go *home* again, to Zhenjiang, the city where we had last lived, some 150 miles from Shanghai. China was by no means wide open to tourists, but with a lot of planning (and some divine intervention), we were able to make the most of our ten-day odyssey. A friend in Hong Kong discovered the address of my childhood friend, now living in Shanghai with her widowed mother. I wrote to that, hoping my friend would receive it. It had been close to four decades since I had seen her.

Beijing was the start of our China adventure — the ancient capital of the even more ancient kingdom. When the plane landed in Beijing, my heart was thumping so loudly that I wondered if my thyroid crisis had returned; no, it was just the excitement of finally touching down in the heart of history in the country so dear to me. Elena and I must have looked wide-eyed to all the throngs around us. We were stepping into an unknown adventure and didn't want to miss a minute. Beautiful Mandarin flowed from voices all around us. I was excited to hear the musical, tonal language everywhere, from the ticket clerk to the cabbie. The cars whizzing around us looked like they had been in use a long time, and streets were full of cabs, trucks, motorcycles and bicycles. Clothing was drab, and soldiers were everywhere. That was much like I experienced in south China when visiting Bob. What surprised me was the *level* of staring. I had grown accustomed to the stares in south China but had felt that in China's cosmopolitan capital, foreigners would be a common sight. Evidently not. Everywhere we went for the entire trip, we drew stares. After a couple of days, we just came to expect it.

I, in turn, stared at Beijing — amazed at the mixture of ancient walled compounds right next to modern, concrete structures. Our hotel was modern and convenient, plopped down right in the heart of old buildings dating back hundreds of years. When I used Mandarin at the hotel, in the shops, or on the street, there was universal amazement, and someone would ask, "Where did you learn Mandarin?" When I mentioned my early years in China, it seemed to form an instant bond with the inquirer. To a person, they were eager to talk to a foreigner, and the two of us never encountered animosity and disdain. In fact, when answering their question by saying we were from America, the inquirers would start asking all sorts of questions and express a desire to visit our country someday.

Elena and I started off just right by finding a restaurant that specialized in Peking duck. It was every bit as good as advertised. We didn't have a bad meal the whole time we were in China, but we also knew it was important to avoid certain foods; experience through the years had taught both of us that hard lesson. However, finding my beloved *shau bing* (my favorite from childhood — pocket bread with sesame seeds on top) took a long time. It was not until we reached my childhood home that I located some.

Nothing was simple in 1983 China. It was still unused to foreigners, and red tape was honed to a fine art. We made several trips to China travel headquarters to get a permit to even go to Zhenjiang, my childhood home. Since it was not a tourist area, we had to carefully explain our purpose and sign documents. We had decided to travel by train — a long trip, but we could see the countryside along the way. Each day in Beijing brought us new wonders to behold. Tian An Men Square was our first stop, with its giant picture of Mao. (It was on this spot that Mao had stood on the wall in 1966 to kick off the disastrous cultural revolution that left China torn and millions dead. The Tian An Men Massacre was still years away.) Adjacent to the square was the Forbidden City, one of the wonders of the world, with its 9,000 rooms and the three great "halls" of the emperors, each with its own throne. All 180 acres of the city are located right in the heart of Beijing. That first time we were able to take it in, 99 percent of those around us were Chinese, but not so in subsequent visits. Over 600 years old, all this magnificence was surrounded by walls twenty-five feet high.

Before our adventure was over, I had thirty-three pages of notes with each sentence containing another abbreviated story. Our first full afternoon was highlighted by a visit to the Temple of Heaven; it had been Mama's favorite spot when she was a language student in that city in 1932. The perfectly concentric building, with its glowingly beautiful colors, had been constructed over 700 years earlier without a single nail. Just weeks later, I was able to share a picture of us on the spot with Mama, and she felt like it was *her* trip back to a beloved memory.

After a day of walking from one wonder to another, our feet were screaming. The next day wouldn't exactly give them a rest, for we were headed to the Great Wall and the Ming Tombs. Most people visiting these pieces of history went on a tour bus, but we were informed that all buses were filled. Having no option, the two of us determined to go by hired car, which turned out to be about the same price! Elena and I were both taking in unfamiliar sights and were struck by many differences between China and Hong Kong. The whole time we were in Beijing, we never one time saw a pregnant woman. Nor did we see a family anywhere in the city walking around with more than one child. It struck us as unusual, but then we were reminded of China's one-child policy.

In contrast with the great city, the countryside on the way to the Great Wall was quite barren, with occasional spots of peach and apple trees struggling to bud in spite of the chilly winds. We were immensely thankful for the jackets we had thought to bring. There is no other place on earth quite like the Great Wall — so massive and overpowering. As Elena and I walked up the wall to get to a higher tower, the wind went right through to the bone. Wind gusts notwithstanding, the people visiting the wall stared at the strange foreigners in their midst. If I asked someone a question in Chinese, they would burst into laughter and start peppering us with questions. The views from the wall were magnificent, and I could only wonder about the thousands of men who, 2,000 years ago, had spent years of their lives building this towering buttress at the whim of a despotic emperor. I had read about the wall while preparing for this trip, curious about those who built it. Its sheer size was overwhelming, some sixteen-feet wide and over twenty-five-feet high. History recorded that, likely, more than 40,000 men died working on the wall; many of them were buried in it. That was a daunting thought as we climbed the stones laid by workers hundreds of years before. The structure was so massive, it took our breath away.

On the return trip to Beijing, our car took us to the historic Ming Tombs. Thirteen emperors of the Ming Dynasty were buried in splendor and at great expense in an area considered "auspicious" in relation to *feng shwei* (fuhng shway), wind and water in natural balance. In 1983, only one of the excavated tombs was open to the public, and it was mind-boggling to think of the expense and splendor that had gone into the burial of one of the "Sons of Heaven," as the emperors were called. Long marble walkways led to magnificent vaults that contained all sorts of treasures buried with the emperor and his wife and concubines. Even getting to the tombs was amazing as we walked down an avenue guarded by massive stone animals and stone sentries. Elena and I kept running out of words to describe what our eyes were seeing.

The day concluded with a return visit to China's travel service to pick up the all-important visa and tickets for travel to Zhenjiang and home in a couple of days. The shock came upon hearing the ticket price. Foreigners were charged nearly double what the locals paid. I puffed up a bit and turned on my clearest Mandarin to protest the price-gouging. Furthermore, I promised that, when they visited America, they would discover that everyone was the same. *Their* price would be the same as *our* price. This didn't change our exorbitant ticket prices, but I felt a bit better for having let off some righteous steam.

We had a providential encounter with our driver hired for the day. He had a hundred questions and wanted to know if I was a Christian. I assured him I was, and his first response was, "Why?" Perfect opportunity. This led to many more questions about God and His Son throughout the day and at our various stops. I was able to leave some material with him and hoped and prayed it would fall on fertile soil. The visit to the Summer Palace, so adored by the infamous Empress Dowager, was only surpassed by the fun of the Beijing Zoo. The pandas were adorable — dirty, but playful — and we watched with grins on our faces as a giant panda was escorted into an enclosure to have his teeth brushed.

We could easily have spent our entire trip exploring Beijing, but time was limited, and, above all, I wanted to go *home* to Zhenjiang. Just boarding the train Friday evening convinced me the ticket was worth the price. I was actually on a train in China after thirty-five years. My mind immediately harked back to 1948 and that unbelievable train trip, fleeing the threat of war as we escaped Zhenjiang ahead of the Communist troops. That was a nightmare of a memory, but now I could board a train and head back to the city from which our family had fled. (See Appendix for "Tale of the Tapestry.")

Elena and I left our lovely, modern hotel, realizing it would likely be the last time on the trip we would have such fine accommodations and water that we could safely drink. (We had come prepared with Zero-B thermoses that purified water.) The train would be traveling through the night (Zhenjiang is over 600 miles from Beijing), and we were able to get sleeper berths, sharing a compartment with a lady and her daughter.

Shortly after 2:30 Saturday afternoon, we reached Zhenjiang, and I stood again on the platform of that train station for the first time in thirty-five years. My heart was thumping with joy and anticipation; my mind kept repeating, *You are here, you are here once again just like you've dreamed so many years.* Going first to the Jin Shan Hotel (fairly new but nothing like Beijing hotels for comfort), we quickly checked in, washed the dirt and grit off our faces, and headed for the nearest bus stop, about half a mile away in front of Jin Shan Pagoda. I grabbed Elena's arm, pointing to the temple and nine-story pagoda, I described it as I had last seen it thirty-five years earlier. We would certainly explore it, but right now, I wanted to go home to Yin Shan Men (Silver Mountain Gate) where our house had been located. I had no way of knowing if it was still there and had tried to prepare myself for the possibility that it was gone after all these years.

China's crowds clearly exceeded Hong Kong's as we squeezed onto the double-car, old Russian bus. There was no need to try to get a seat. We could just hope to be able to breathe while standing so closely jammed with more people than I had ever seen on one bus. Crowds notwithstanding, everyone stared. Then the talking began, and I recognized much of the Zhenjiang dialect, with its own particular variety of Mandarin. Just hearing it was like traveling back in time. The men and women jammed on that bus began speculating about the two *yang gweidz* (foreign devils) on their bus, commenting on our clothes, our shoes, our skin, and one even said, "Just look at that woman's hair (gesturing toward me). Look how it grows *up* in back instead of down, like normal hair." Another woman retorted, "You oughtn't to talk about people like that in front of them. It isn't *kechi* (polite)." The commentator replied, "Never mind. They can't understand what we're saying!" At this point, I couldn't resist. Turning in her direction, I said in Mandarin, "How are you today?" Her face flamed red. "Oh, no!" she groaned. "She understands!" I told her, "*Mei you gwan syi* (never mind); I like hearing you talk, and I'm just trying to find the way to *Yin Shan Men* (Silver Mountain Gate) because I used to live there."

All those nearby began talking at once. "When did you live here? Why are you here? How old are you? How can you speak Chinese? Are you Chinese yourself?" They peppered me with questions, and as I explained the reason for our coming, they entered into the spirit of the moment. "We'll show you where to get off the bus! We aren't far from there!" Sure enough, in about two or three minutes, the bus lumbered to a stop and helpful hands helped us manage to squeeze off the bus. A number of our new friends began pointing and saying, "Now you just go up the avenue here to the left and turn the corner and there will be Yin Shan Men."

Elena and I got to the sidewalk, took a deep breath, smiled at each other, and turned to walk to the left and around the corner. Wide-eyed, I gazed at all the people and shops and movement surrounding us. It was changed, yet vaguely familiar, this broad avenue leading up to Yin Shan Men. We turned the corner — and there on the side of the hill were the two mission houses, standing much as they had for a century. I stood there, a grown woman in the midst of a busy throng of passersby, tears streaming down my cheeks. I was finally home after thirty-five years. For some reason, my little blue enamel Chinese cup that had been with me since 1938 came to mind, and I thought, *Surely, in this moment, my cup runneth over.*

With Pastor Wu and elderly members of the Yangzhou church

SIXTEEN

GOING HOME
1983-1984

I immediately remembered Thomas Wolfe's bestseller, *You Can't Go Home Again*. In that moment, however, I discovered he was wrong. I was home — and elated. *Yes, you can go home again,* my heart was singing. Grasping Elena's arm, I whispered, "They are still there. The houses are still standing!" She grinned and said, "Come on, let's go look." As usual, passersby were crowding around, and when I smiled and spoke, a chorus of voices started asking questions; they were curious about these foreigners in their city. Pointing to the second house on the hill, I explained, "That was my home when I was a little girl." About a dozen bystanders began following us as we walked up the road to the house. The cobblestone paving at the entrance was still the same. Elena and I walked up the incline as I gazed in wonder at the place where our large yard had been. Now, an awkward-looking apartment building was on the spot where my brother, Arthur, and I had so grudgingly pulled pesky weeds.

However, my eyes immediately focused on the steps leading up to where our front porch had been. The porch was now an enclosed part of the house. A lean-to had been built over half the steps, but the rest were there. I began to climb them, tears trickling down my face again. Heart in throat, I stopped and looked around, my mind's eyes picturing the old leper who had knelt there thirty-six years earlier and begged bread from a little nine-year-old girl. That moment had changed my life, and I was reliving it. A sense of gratitude flooded over me; God had actually allowed me the privilege of returning to the spot and reliving the power of His call on my life.

About this time, a young man came up and politely asked if he could help. His family lived in this house, he explained, along with twenty-nine other families. It boggled my mind to think of that many people housed there, but space in Zhenjiang was at a premium. As we walked around the perimeter of the house, I stopped repeatedly to tell Elena some other story that came to mind. In typical oriental fashion, many of the windows had bamboo poles sticking out of them holding the family's laundry for the day. The entire compound looked weary and rundown, much in disrepair, as if nobody had time to keep it spruce. Revisiting "home," though, was already a red-letter moment in my heart.

The two of us strolled and looked as I reminisced over decades' old experiences. Elena kindly listened to me fondly reliving happenings long gone. Next, we walked back down the cobblestones and viewed the old British consulate building, just back of the Baptist compound. It appeared busy with people walking in and out of the main building, likely a government office now. Wonder of wonders, the old gun emplacement was still standing guard, looking rusty from disuse. The ancient street also remained much as I remembered it. However, the bazaar of street stalls was long gone. We rounded a curve, and I grinned to see the old Yuan Dynasty stone *dagoba* (dome-shaped pagoda) still standing guard over the narrow road beneath. Little had changed in this spot, and it was purely *déjà vu*.

Every new sight was exciting. I know Elena got tired of hearing my superlatives and jumble of memories, but she smilingly endured. The old public square — where the pig parlor had stood, where the operas were performed with clanging of cymbals, where the tooth puller had plied his trade, and where the captured Communist soldier had been executed before the horrified eyes of my brother and me — was long gone. In that spot there now stood a jumble of concrete buildings where hundreds of people were living.

The view down the other road from our house looked much more familiar. I could see the outer shape of our Yin Shan Men church, with its uniquely shaped windows. Walking closer, my eyes fell on the cornerstone, its engraving still legible. This was my day to be a regular watering pot, as I wept over the cornerstone. It looked like someone had tried to X out the date, but I could still read: "First Baptist Church: Organized 1885." I asked a passerby what the building was now used for. "I think it's a factory" was the reply. I choked up again, thinking about the worship services I had attended there, and about my friend's house right next door. I prayed yet again that my letter had reached her and that we could visit when I got to Shanghai.

Elena and I took in one spot after another that Saturday afternoon, from Bei Gu (Bay Goo) mountain and its temple, to Jin Shan and its temple and famous pagoda. Both were little changed — the rickety steps of the pagoda at Jin Shan were harder to climb now — but the same fabulous view of the city and countryside was visible from the top. The temple, with its huge, fierce guardian idols, had aged but was still in use, and the whole place was redolent with the incense burned by those who worshipped there. I was wafted back in time to the years when Arthur and I visited here. The sadness that struck my heart at the sight of such futile worship was the same sorrow I had experienced watching it as a child.

I tried to locate familiar Zhenjiang food. Sure enough, the *jyaudzs* (little dumplings) tasted just the same. I still could not find *shau bing*, that long-remembered bread delight, but I was nevertheless happy to find *lwo bwo Tudzs*, little turnips pickled in *jyang you* (soy sauce). That may not sound good, but to a young MK decades earlier, it had been a savored treat.

The little turnips still tasted as crispy and crunchy as ever.

I questioned a number of people in Zhenjiang about Yangzhou, just across the Yangtze River. "Is there an open church?" I asked first one and then another. The replies varied from, "No, there aren't any," to a shake of the head and a puzzled, "I don't know, but I don't think so." Nonetheless, we planned to be in Yangzhou on Sunday just in case there *was* an open church. The two of us hired a car for the day, and our chatty driver took us across the Yangtze on the vehicular ferry, a one-and-a-half-hour trip. Staff at our hotel recommended that foreigners go to the Friendship Store, a place designed for tourists. That would be our first stop and where we would try to find out about an open church. Lo and behold, along the road, I spied a little outside oven with a man taking *shau bing* out and piling them on a plate. "Stop!" I called out, doubtless startling our obliging driver. He watched in amusement as we bought and devoured the hot, flaky, tasty sesame bread I had searched for ever since landing in Beijing. They smelled the same, they tasted the same — and they still delighted the child that forever remained in me. Maybe this portended an auspicious beginning to our search for roots.

For some unknown reason, I had taken along a couple of pictures belonging to my parents from their years in Yangzhou in the 1930s. Now I was hoping that someone would recognize a face or a place in the pictures. Arriving at the Friendship Store, Elena and I found it nearly empty of patrons but with a surfeit of clerks. Approaching one friendly looking, young salesclerk, I held out the pictures and asked, "Do you recognize this building? Do you know where in the city it might be?" The young lady grew very animated, responding, "Oh, yes, yes! This building is just down this same street, maybe six blocks away!" My next question got to the heart of the matter. "Is it still a church?" I questioned. Our young clerk shook her head and replied, "No, it's a factory now." Then her face lighted up and she told us, "I'll take you there right now!" She had decided that finding these foreigners and talking with them was a lot more fun than boring work. We eagerly agreed and headed for the car. Sure enough, in about six blocks, we could see the building that matched my pictures. As we drew closer, I noticed a new sign in characters posted at the side of the entrance proclaiming this as the city's Protestant church. "Well," our young guide grinned, "look at that. It *is* a church!" We asked the driver to wait, and we headed to the entrance, which was closed.

In less than thirty seconds, there were people milling all around us, staring at the strange *yang gweidzs* (foreign devils) who had suddenly appeared in their midst. Our new guide hammered on the closed door. In short moments, it opened. Standing just inside in the vestibule was a cluster of elderly women with white hair in buns, pearl earrings, several of them with bound feet. They took one look at us and began beaming, *"Hwan Ying Hwan Ying!"* (Welcome!) *"Lai, lai, lai,"* (Come, come, come) they began calling out and gesturing with their hands curled under to beckon us inside. I noticed a basket containing a well-worn Bible on one lady's arm and asked her, "Is this a church? Have you just had a service?" A chorus of little ladies responded, "Yes, yes, yes." I beamed and held out the two photographs as the women eagerly gathered around. "Do you know anyone in these pictures?" I seriously thought someone might have a heart attack, so excited was their response. All began to gesture and point at faces in the pictures and comment on "sister this" or "brother that." I stood there grinning from ear to ear, sharing in their excitement.

"Do you have a pastor here?" They chorused, "Yes, yes, yes," and several of them called out to an elderly gentleman standing down near the podium. *"Mushr! Mushr! Mushr! Lai, lai, lai!!"* they all called out. A dignified gentleman, clad in a sober black outfit and with a hearing aid and cord hanging down, quickly moved in our direction. As he drew nearer, I was struck by the radiance of his face; I had encountered that occasionally, just like our Pastor Sye in Taiwan those years ago. It was the same warm glow that pulled you in to its serenity. The little ladies nearly fell over themselves, all trying to talk at the same time and holding out my two photographs.

The distinguished-looking minister took the proffered pictures, peered at them and quickly looked up to say, "Are these yours?" I smiled and said, "Yes. I used to live here when I was a little girl." Looking intently into my eyes, he asked, "Who are you? What was your father's name?" Smiling, I replied, "Ho" (Daddy's surname). An absolutely radiant smile effused his face, and with trembling voice he switched to beautiful English as he proclaimed, "Your father is Harold Hall. Your mother is Alice Wells Hall, my beloved coworkers." Unbidden tears fell from his eyes, and I, too, began to weep. This was Wu Ji Shao, the brilliant young ministerial student my father had mentored and trained half a century earlier. He had not seen a missionary in thirty-five years.

Pastor Wu began reminiscing as we spoke of long-ago days. "Many's the time I used to eat in your home. You were just a tiny little thing then." He was nearly too overcome to talk, but he continued, "Please give your father a message for me. Tell him I would *love* for him to come back and lead another revival meeting for us." Pastor Wu gestured to a door leading up the stairs, "Come to my office and let us visit." Half the city tried to crowd around and not miss a thing about this unexpected encounter. Pastor Wu closed the door to allow a bit of privacy as we talked over old times, and we spent a glorious hour visiting and talking.

Mrs. Wu joined us, very frail but beaming the whole time. Pastor Wu was most reluctant to speak of the dreadful years of the Cultural Revolution. I was to learn later some of what he endured for those years. Yet, there he sat, beaming and praising God for all the ways He had protected them and brought them through great trials. Pastor Wu wanted no pictures made outside as he escorted us to the waiting car. There were too many eyes and ears, and every place still had informers. We were blessed to learn from him that his sister-in-law in Shanghai was still living, as was his only niece, Wu Wang Ying Kwang. His face looked drawn with sorrow as he told of his brother's death just short months earlier. His brother, Wo Ji Jung, the president of the Baptist seminary in Shanghai, had endured severe perse-cution and humiliation, yet survived the Cultural Revolution. Pastor Wu gladly gave me Mrs. Wu's address in Shanghai, and Elena and I were thrilled to have some Bibles and literature we could give him. So much of theirs was gone, and getting new Bibles was most difficult. When preparing to leave, I told him, "We are going on furlough next month, and I will take fresh greetings from you to my parents." I smiled into his face and somewhat tremulously concluded, "Pastor Wu, remember, not a day has passed since

Mama and Daddy left that they have not thought about you and loved you and prayed for you." The two of us began weeping again. These were tears of joy, however. I realized that, although we had not been able to worship in a church service that day, we had indeed worshipped — as we stood on holy ground in the presence of one of the Lord's true saints. I also knew beyond a doubt that our meeting was providential and one of God's extra blessings. (I assured Pastor Wu I would see him again, and, thank God, I was able to keep that promise, time and again, even a decade later.)

That afternoon, Elena and I located the Yangzhou hospital grounds where I had lived as a tiny child. It was still there, taken over by the government, of course — but the mission residences were still standing, including the house where Mama and Daddy had met for the first time that Chinese New Year of 1932. The house just next to it was my first home in China and where my brother, Arthur, had been born.

As we boarded the train to go to Shanghai the next morning, I looked around the Zhenjiang railroad station one more time and vowed, *I'll be back*. Thankfully, it was a vow that came to fruition. Now, to Shanghai and hopes of reuniting with more pieces of my past. The quaint Park Hotel had stood there at the time of my parents' Shanghai wedding in 1933 and was an old girl now but wore her age with atmosphere. Since it was located not too far from the old business heart of the great city, the Bund area, we planned to visit there the following day. This afternoon and evening, however, were earmarked for finding the Wus and my childhood friend. Armed with the address we had been given, we located the old apartment building where Pastor Wu's widowed sister-in-law lived in one room. Curious neighbors responded that yes, they certainly knew Mrs. Wu and would escort us there.

Climbing three narrow flights of stairs, Elena and I reached a closed door. A knock brought a smiling face in response. The woman standing there looked to be about my age. This was Wu Wang Ying Kwang, Pastor Wu's only niece, and she came this time each afternoon to help her mother. Our timing was perfect. Mrs. Wu was tiny and frail, but with a face that reflected not only the pain of suffering but also the serenity of peace. Again,

Elena and I spent a sacred time with saints. For a solid hour, Mrs. Wu related the story of their last fifty years, especially God's protection through the horrors of the Cultural Revolution. Their house had been taken, their furnishings destroyed, their Bibles and Christian literature ripped apart before their eyes and burned.

Mrs. Wu told of how they had been constantly under surveillance because of their many years of working with "evil Americans." They were publicly beaten and humiliated. We learned from them that Pastor Wu in Yangzhou had been imprisoned for two years. Pastor Wu Ji Jung had survived those horrors, his body broken and weakened, and had died just three months earlier, of cancer. The wounds were still raw as his wife and daughter grieved. I was struck by their calm radiance, their will to survive, both evidence of the depth of their faith and courage. We were able to help them a bit financially, and I silently vowed to return, prepared to do more. It seemed to be cathartic for Mrs. Wu to share her experiences; she probably didn't even realize how her very words were a testimony to her faith and perseverance.

By this time, Elena was completely worn out. We returned to our hotel room, but I couldn't stand the thoughts of actually being in the same city where my dear friend from three decades ago now lived, and not trying to find her. Assuring Elena I would be OK, and agreeing that tomorrow we would both go again, I found a taxi and headed for the address of the old college and seminary on the outskirts of the huge city. I took a deep breath and thought, *I'm actually going to the campus where Mama taught, where she and Daddy were married, where we used to meet for annual mission meeting each summer.*

My long-anticipated reunion with my childhood friend was all I could have dreamed of, and more. She and I were face-to-face for the first time since our childhood. (To my profound sorrow, I am currently unable to tell the story of our reunion. It might endanger the living. It was a stirring experience.) The next morning, Elena and I were able to visit the university grounds (now a state institution), and I wept again when seeing the university gardens where Mama and Daddy had exchanged their wedding vows half a century earlier. Before our departure the next day, we decided to go to the Bund, the famous downtown district of the colonial days in Shanghai. It was a familiar sight to me from childhood days. The Astor Hotel, where Mama and Daddy had stayed, was still there, as were many of the buildings of commerce from colonial days. I was eager to locate the True Light building, which had housed the Baptist Publishing House and offices — so, seeing a likely looking young man standing on the wide sidewalk, I went up to him and spoke in Mandarin, "Could you please give us directions to the old True Light building?" The young fellow stared at me wide-eyed, rather like a deer caught in the headlights. He slowly enunciated, "I. Do. Not. Speak. English." To which I replied, "But I'm speaking to you in Mandarin!" Realization dawned on his face, and, looking relieved, he gave us directions in Mandarin, and we left chuckling.

One last spot: I wanted to see if we could find Rue LaFayette. That street had been in the French Concession in the long-ago years. It was where the two large Baptist residences had stood, the place where our family had sometimes stayed when coming to Shanghai, and also where we lived our last months in China. So much in Shanghai had changed. But then, so much hadn't. Remarkably, we actually found the houses, set back from the road, looking a little the worse for wear but achingly familiar. I turned to Elena and said, "I can't really take it all in, but on this trip, I have blessedly come home! Old places, dear faces. What a treasure trove of memories!"

Just a month later, Bob and I headed home on furlough, and I took fresh pictures, fresh memories, and fresh hugs and wishes from Mama and Daddy's cherished friends from earlier years. Mama sat with her tissue, laughing and crying and asking a hundred questions. Daddy's eyes were suspiciously damp, and he, too, was full of questions, nearly overwhelmed to hear about my visit with Pastor Wu and the messages I brought. As Mama and I sat and pored over the pictures, I told her yet again, "Mama, this trip home to China was your trip. It was truly like you and Daddy were there, too." It was a bare four weeks later that we learned unwelcome news, news that made me eternally grateful for the trip to China. It had come in God's perfect timing.

People gather round the foreigner as she "comes home" to Zhenjiang

Jody with Pastor Wu in Yangzhou, 1984

SEVENTEEN

CHANGES
1983-1984

Just weeks later, Mama was preparing for routine cataract surgery when the bottom fell out of our world. The hospital did blood work prior to her procedure; however, that same evening, they called with unexpected news: Blood tests revealed Mrs. Hall had lymphoma. All of us sat in shock, bereft of words. No wonder Ho Se Mo had been pale, constantly fatigued, and with so little appetite. Daddy was nearly overwhelmed; she had been his rock for fifty years. Mama had her usual response: concern for Harold, not for herself. As Jody wrote in a letter when we told him the news, "Ho Se Mo is the only person I have ever known who immediately — and always

— thinks of others before herself." True to form, she was distressed at how her condition would affect Daddy. After we got over the initial shock, Bob and I gave thanks all over again that we were there with them when this unwelcome news arrived. That selfless nature, such an intrinsic part of who Mama was, revealed itself every day in the weeks and months that followed.

Alice and Kevin, along with Jody, were all in Boaz for the summer, and each moment of family time was doubly precious, as we knew this opportunity was only temporary. I usually managed to save my tears for nighttime, when I lay in bed grieving for the loss that must inevitably come. Jody had a Rotary fellowship that granted him a year of Mandarin study in Taiwan, and he was scheduled to leave in late August. A year of Mandarin study in the country where he had grown up was a thrilling opportunity, but he grieved that he might not see his beloved grandmother again.

Bob and I were on the horns of a dilemma: Our furlough was a short, four-month one. Yet how could we leave my parents, with Mama in such a precarious condition and Daddy already shaken by the imminent loss of his heart's companion? You could read the pain on his face, although around Mama, he maintained as normal a demeanor as possible. Our angst over Ho Se Mo mingled with the pull on our hearts to return to our various ministries in Hong Kong. We knew the mission expected us back in one more month. But Mama was fading every day, and Daddy depended heavily on us for moral support. We prayed, we wept, we deliberated, and came to the only conclusion we could live with. We must take a leave of absence and go without salary for this period — step out in faith and remain in Boaz, caring for Mama as long as need be. Her immediate reaction was so typically Ho Se Mo. She exclaimed, "Oh, no, no, you must not stay because I am unwell!" Bob and I finally managed to convince her that we must follow the Lord's direction, and we could read the relief on Daddy's face. He would not have to face this by himself.

Bob and I were blessed with our support system. Alice and Kevin were nearby and helping. Granny Ora (Bob's mother) was not strong but managing to stay active and help out when she felt able. Joe and Catherine, next door, were mainstays. What had I ever done to deserve such a wonderful sister-in-law as Catherine? She helped in all sorts of unobtrusive ways, always smiling and happy about being *able* to help. (Little did we know then how she would be standing in the gap for us for years to come — a true treasure.) Jody left for Taiwan and his studies with dragging feet. We reminded him of the boon of phone connections and good airmail service. We took advantage of both. Jody also wrote to us and his grandparents three or four times a week. Bob and I wondered how he found time.

Alice was offered a position with a corporation working on contracts with NASA, and she began her new job as a systems analyst at Redstone Arsenal in Huntsville, still near enough to frequently come spend time with her grandparents. Nonetheless, we had sadness of another kind that same year, a year we hoped never to have to repeat. Alice and Kevin came to a parting of the ways, amicably on both sides, but a deep sorrow to all of us who loved them both. Kevin was a dear part of the family and much missed. Again, Mama took what life handed her, and thought of how she could make things better for Alice, even from the confinement of her favorite easy chair. Mama and Daddy's lifelong habit of beginning each day by praying together did not change, even in the face of grave illness and impending death. Their depth of commitment and faith were like beacons of light and hope to all of us who saw the reflected peace that came from their trust in a God who cared more than any of us knew.

Bob and I realized we would need some temporary income. We also knew the Lord had never let us down. Nonetheless, I would often lie in bed at night, trying to fall asleep but wondering, *What are we going to do? We've got to have some income.* As always, God is never late. Bob had a call the following week from a deacon at Union Grove Church, about thirty minutes away. They needed an interim pastor. Could Brother Bob possibly do this? Yes, he could. We simply thanked God and took courage once more. About this same time, several leaders in the Boaz church came to Bob, presenting the need for a chaplain at the local hospital. The hospital could not afford one; however, concerned citizens had formed a committee and were providing the means for hiring a chaplain. Would Brother Bob consider this position? Perfect. Bob had two places to be of service, and we had a temporary income. The work at the hospital was rewarding, as people gained comfort from a caring chaplain. Union Grove Church wrapped itself around our hearts, and we formed lifelong friendships in just a few months. Oh, my, could those women put on a "dinner on the grounds." Their chicken and dumplings were memorable, as were the tables groaning with homemade cakes and pies.

These weren't easy days for our children. Alice was working at adjusting to her new circumstances and a totally different type of employment. Jody was delighted with the opportunity to study Mandarin but distressed at being half a world away when his beloved Ho Se Mo was fading by the day. However, he faithfully wrote of the many opportunities and cultural experiences he was having each week. The Taipei missionaries were wonderful to him, and he had a neat place to stay, thanks to the Leroy Hogues at Baptist Seminary. Jody joined Grace Church and was immediately asked to teach a class of young adults. He also became involved on weekends assisting with various MK functions on the island. Jody's "Aunt" Faye Pearson was an integral part of his year in Taiwan. She indulged him just as she had when he was a little fellow. Dr. Jou at Grace Church was also a special blessing during Jody's year in Taiwan and kindly arranged for him to be able to attend the president's chapel one Sunday, where he was thrilled to meet Jang Sywe-Lyang, the Little General, face-to-face.

Jody's angst was somewhat alleviated when he discovered that the Chinese New Year's holiday in January was long enough for him to fly to the States and be with his grandparents. When he arrived, Mama and Daddy were enthralled to hear tales of the months in Taiwan, especially about the students in his English class. For Christmas, he gave each student a bilingual New Testament and told them why it meant so much to him. The hard part of the holiday came when Jody had to leave Alabama, knowing this might well be the last time he would see his grandmother this side of Glory. She had been a bulwark all his twenty-two years.

The months that followed were a kind of living agony for all of us who loved Mama. She surely must have known her days were numbered, but never one time did she lose a positive spirit; her serenity was balm to our aching hearts. One Saturday morning in April, Dr. Finlay wanted her to come to the hospital for constant observation. She was so weak that she could not walk. I still remember the huge lump in my throat as I watched Bob tenderly pick Mama up and gently place her in the car. The nurses at the hospital were so gentle. There was only a semi-private room available, but, thank God, there was no one in the other bed. Alice came from Huntsville to spend the day, and she, Bob, and Daddy remained until bedtime, when I insisted on staying through the night.

An unusual conversation occurred as Mama slowly began to relax enough to fall asleep. Her voice was weak but audible, and she began motioning with a hand, first in one spot, then moving a bit to the right, then pointing her finger again as she kept repeating, "See the spaces. I see the spaces." I tried to figure out her message; thinking maybe she wanted to be sure I had filled out the admission papers correctly. I explained to her several times, "Mama, it's OK, they are all filled out." Again, and yet again, she murmured, "I see the spaces," then gently and mercifully drifted to sleep. (It would be nearly ten years before I would learn what Mama was trying to tell me.) By dawn on Sunday morning, Mama was too weak to speak, although she was able to take a few sips of water. Bob had called Jody the night before, and that Sunday morning, Jody was able to get a call through to the hospital room and talk to his cherished grandmother one more time. She was too weak to respond, but several times she nodded in response to what Jody was saying. I could only imagine the angst in his heart.

All Sunday, Mama lay there growing weaker, but thankfully in no pain. All of us were with her when she drew her final, gentle breath. Standing there in the midst of overwhelming grief, I could only thank God to have been there with her and with Daddy. He was amazing; he mostly grieved in silence, walking back and forth down the little hallway in their home, stopping to look in one room and then another. He would repeatedly say, "I can just see the dear thing, everywhere I look. She is right there." Time and again, I would see Ho Shien Sun simply shake his head, his eyes welling over with tears that insisted on trickling down his cheeks. He kept saying,

"It's me, it's me, oh, Lord, standing in the need of prayer." Nonetheless, that remarkable resilience came to the fore, and his deep-seated faith was apparent to all of us.

Mama had requested that "The Holy City" be sung at her service. Her pastor, Earl Chumley, ended his eulogy by saying, "When I think of a godly woman, the first one who comes to my mind is Alice Wells Hall." Bob brought the message from Acts, finishing by recalling how Stephen looked up into heaven as he lay dying, and saw Jesus *standing* at the right hand of God. Bob concluded, "I believe this past Sunday night, Jesus was *standing* again." I learned in the months and years to follow that you don't ever "get over" grief. You learn to live with it and grow through it. Not a day has passed in the nearly four decades since her death that I have not wished to sit down with Mama and ask her about this or that, or simply to give her a hug and tell her how much I love her.

Bob and I were amazed at how well Daddy handled the inevitable. His inner core of faith was so evident, even as he went about each day with a lost look in his eyes. It helped him to be able to talk about Mama. As we shared special memories of the long-ago years, Dad's grief seemed to ease a bit. Daddy insisted that we plan to return to the field as soon as we could, and sincerely meant it when he said he would be able to cope. Both then, and increasingly in the years that followed, we gave thanks anew for Joe and Catherine and their kindness and care for Daddy.

Jody was due to finish his Chinese studies at the end of May. When he first learned of his Rotary fellowship, he asked if I'd be able to make a trip into China with him. Both the children had hoped for years to be able to go to Zhenjiang and Yangzhou and see where I had lived as a child. Mama was excited about the possibility of her only grandchildren going to visit her beloved China. When we learned her diagnosis, our plans were put on hold, but she kept wanting the trip to happen. Now, all of us talked it over and decided to honor her wishes. With many a lump lodged in the throat, I made final arrangements to fly to Taipei and meet Jody there.

Often in the subsequent weeks, I thought of my little blue enamel cup and pictured it running over with a wealth of new memories built atop the old. Just landing in Taipei, with our son there to meet me, was exciting. The next three days were filled with renewing rich friendships, visiting our Taipei churches, and sharing Mongolian barbecue with two dozen missionary friends. Then Jody and I flew to Hong Kong, and the little blue cup kept overflowing. Being with my Sunday School class at North Point made Sunday perfect. Friends were excited about our plans to return in early fall, and Jody and I were fed so much that we feared having to pay for extra freight on the flight to Beijing. This was Jody's first visit to China's capital, and it felt like a dream to be able to share the experience with him. He loved being able to use his Mandarin and got rave reviews for his language skills. He was asked repeatedly, "You *are* Chinese, aren't you?" We made the three days in Beijing count, from taking in the Forbidden City to walking on the Great Wall, all interspersed with wonderful Chinese dishes, topped by Peking duck. The time in Zhenjiang and Yangzhou, with old scenes and dear faces, however, dwarfed the wonders of the Ming Tombs and the Temple of Heaven. Jody's language skills made everything that much more meaningful. Our all-nighter train arrived in Zhenjiang on Saturday morning, and we very appropriately started our visit with *jyaudz* (steamed dumplings), a Zhenjiang specialty. Jody agreed that they were the best he'd ever tasted.

Seeing my old house was just as thrilling as the first time I had gone back; in fact, doubly so, since I could show it to our son. We went first to the steps where I relived the Christmas morning on that spot nearly four decades earlier. The man on the steps was a vivid picture in my mind. As we were talking, a young man walked up. Introducing himself as Mr. Jou (Joe), he struck up a conversation. Wonder of wonders, he lived in the house, and invited us in. For the first time in thirty-five years, I was actually standing inside our house again. Of course, like a ninny, my eyes welled up with unbidden tears. This was a precious moment, and I told Jody what each room had been. It was a bit disconcerting to discover that our former kitchen was a family's bedroom. Mr. Jou explained that the government was making the two old houses part of the new provincial museum, and residents were being given two years to find somewhere else to live.

Young Mr. Jou decided to "adopt" us and show us how to get to places of interest. He and another young man helped us rent bicycles to tour the city. I wanted Jody to see the spots dear to my childhood — and we walked the ancient cobblestone streets and viewed the *dagoba*, went to the nearby city park of my childhood memories, and charmed the elderly people relaxing there by chatting with them in Mandarin. Mr. Jou was able to take us to the old European cemetery where Pearl Buck's mother had been buried, and which I remembered from childhood as the burial place of Hudson Taylor. My mind's eye still recalled the day I took "Aunt Fay Taylor" to see Taylor's tombstone. The cemetery as such was gone. All through the former cemetery grounds now were scattered little houses. We explored the alleys between them and found all sorts of old grave markers, many of them British servicemen who had died in Zhenjiang. Some of the stones went back to the 1800s. A little lady came out of a small house and asked if she could help. I explained that we were looking for the grave of the well-known Dr. Hudson Taylor. Her face lighted up like a beacon and she exclaimed, "Ah! *Dai Mokse Yang Gweidz Fuhn!* (Oh, Reverend Taylor, foreign devil man!) I remember his gravestone!" Shaking her head rather sadly, she finished, "It's gone now. They took it away." (Miraculously, I discovered its whereabouts a few years later. See Appendix: Hudson Taylor.)

It was a day Jody and I never forgot, as we biked from spot to spot of my childhood memories, going to the suburbs where Methodist Hill had stood and finding a few of the old missionary residences still around. Sure enough, in the countryside around the old compound, there were still village areas, with mud-brick houses and a few very elderly women moving around slowly on their bound feet. Seeing those feet was like seeing a visage of the past, for binding feet was outlawed around 1911, although in the villages, some didn't stop the binding for several years. Our evening ended with Mr. Jou and friends taking their new foreign friends to one of their favorite restaurants. Jody and I handled the food pretty well, with the exception of the pig's feet, spring eel, and pickled jellyfish. No amount of exposure has made me consider those tasty. Jody and I were so pleased when Mr. Jou and his friends graciously accepted the bilingual

New Testaments we gave them. As we left them that evening, both of us were trusting and praying that they would read their gifts.

Sunday was our Yangzhou day. Upon reaching the church, Jody and I realized the service had already begun. The church was full, but we located a couple of seats on the back row. However, as we entered, the singing stopped as the congregation noticed two foreigners joining the service. First one row, then another, turned to stare curiously at these obvious strangers. We smiled, took our seats, and slowly everyone turned back around and began singing again. Pastor Wu was not in the pulpit; I was concerned when another minister, Pastor Paul, rose and brought the morning message. Nevertheless, it was an awesome hour to be able to sit and worship with dear saints who had remained faithful through trials and sorrows I couldn't even imagine. The closing hymn was "He Leadeth Me," and when they came to the second verse, "Sometimes 'mid scenes of deepest gloom, Sometimes where Eden's bowers bloom, By waters still, o'er troubled sea, Still 'tis His hand that leadeth me," I dissolved in tears. I had sung these words for many years. Now I was hearing them sung by those who had *been* in those troubled seas but had emerged stronger still in faith. It was another holy moment. I glanced in Jody's direction; his eyes had likewise welled with tears.

The instant Pastor Paul prayed the benediction, a veritable array of elderly members flocked to where Jody and I stood, all beaming a welcome and wanting to reminisce about the years when Daddy and Mama had been with them. Tiny little Miss Ho, and her equally elderly friend, Mrs. Dzang, grasped my hands and sent loving messages to their beloved pastor and Mrs. Hall. We asked them about Pastor Wu and learned Mrs. Wu had just had a hip replacement at the former Presbyterian hospital in Zhenjiang. Several of the women from my previous visit came with a multitude of questions and greetings. They all stood waving and weeping as we reluctantly said goodbye. Again, I assured them that, God willing, we would see each other again.

Monday morning, Jody and I took a pedicab to the hospital. My mind raced back thirty-five years to the last time I had been to that compound to visit my friend Penny Moffett. Dr. Moffett, her father, had performed many a lifesaving operation in that place. The buildings were all rundown and derelict, and as we walked the corridor on the surgical floor, we winced to think about the conditions in which Mrs. Wu was trying to heal. Our gentle knock brought Pastor Wu to the door. That same glowing countenance lighted even further upon seeing us, and my heart skipped a beat at the thought of being able to introduce Harold Hall's grandson to him. Pastor Wu immediately focused on how Jody looked like his dear Ho Mushr (Pastor Hall). That made Jody beam. Pastor Wu explained that Mrs. Wu had been in the hospital since January; she lay there, so frail that it looked like a whiff of wind could blow her away. Nonetheless, her smile of welcome made my heart melt. Jody and I were so thankful to be able to help a bit financially, and I quietly slipped Pastor Wu a letter and gift from Daddy. And then, here it happened once more: all of us in tears. Jody and I had also brought along a good supply of chocolates, and those brought big smiles of delight. An hour later, we reluctantly said our goodbyes and assured the Wus that we would return. (Amazingly, in the following twenty years, we had several more emotional reunions.)

Our last stop, Shanghai, brought further joy as Jody had the opportunity to meet more of our dearest Chinese friends. Pastor Wu's niece Wu Ying Kwang, and Mrs. Wu, his sister-in-law, couldn't talk fast enough as they told us all that was on their hearts. I had learned the previous year that Ying Kwang could not get the glasses she needed in China, and I was able to take her a pair. You would have thought I was handing her a gold brick, so thrilled was she. Jody sat wide-eyed as Mrs. Wu relived some of the horrors of the Cultural Revolution, but always focusing on the positive refrain of God's protection and comfort in the midst of pain. Of all the gifts we brought, the one most treasured by Mrs. Wu was the picture Mama and Daddy had sent, the Wus' wedding portrait. She sat and wept, for her pictures had all been destroyed by the Red Guards.

Jody and I then spent hours with my friend from long years earlier and her family, and I long to tell their story. One day it will be safe enough for me to relate that treasured experience. The entire family was astounded at how much Jody looked like his grandfather Hall and that brought me to happy tears. Of course, the emotions of our visit were so overwhelming that sentimental tears stayed constantly near the surface, ready to overflow. We left with priceless moments printed permanently on our hearts. Although new tasks awaited us, we both vowed this would not be our last visit. And it wasn't.

Bob inspects the cornerstone of Zhenjiang Baptist Church, where Pastor Zhang was the leader

At Grace Church, Shanghai, with Dr. Joe Lien Hwa's sister. She is holding her new copy of Dr. Jou's translation of the Good News New Testament in Chinese, 1985.

With Pastor Wu and Nancy, who was Aunt Grace Wells' Bible woman in the 1940s

EIGHTEEN

AND MORE CHANGES
1984-1986

Another visit to China had brought a mixture of joy, nostalgia, and sorrow to my heart: Joy over the reunions, nostalgia over the privilege of making our son part of the memories, but sadness for the burdens and difficulties — both past and present — of our dear China friends. I had a sinking feeling at the thought that had our circumstances been reversed, I would probably not have exhibited the grace and endurance they displayed. It was a lowering thought.

Jody returned to duties at Samford, still struggling to determine the next step. He would love to teach at the university, and that looked like a possibility. Of course, that would mean working on a PhD. Foreign service, possibly with the CIA, was another tempting thought. In the year that followed, he explored both possibilities. Meantime, Alice was busy with her government-related work at Huntsville's Redstone Arsenal. One fascinating assignment was developing software for the Hubble telescope. To this day, she smiles at the thought of that software still at work somewhere out there in space.

Alice and Jody faithfully called and visited Ho Shien Sun and Granny Ora. Catherine and Joe daily helped our parents as well. Catherine was a real godsend to us, helping Daddy with his checkbook, running errands, and frequently having him over for home-cooked meals.

Bob and I moved into a mission flat on Hampshire Road, close enough to walk to our Kowloon Baptist Church (KBC). It was about a mile, so in the spring, summer and fall, we could figure on being soaking wet with perspiration by the time we arrived. Nonetheless, the exercise was terrific. HKBC (Hong Kong Baptist College) was also adjacent to the church, so our work was unusually convenient.

That Christmas, Daddy actually decided to come to Hong Kong for a month. Alice and Jody got the ticket, helped him know what to pack, and got him to the airport. The change of scenery was really good for Daddy, yet I sensed his deep sadness much of the time he was with us. Of course, his grief was still terribly raw, but at least we were together and could talk about wonderful memories. That seemed to ease his heart and mind. My heart grieved, however, to see him often just sort of wander around lost, a wounded look in his eyes. We urged him to let us take him into China, but he turned the idea down. I think he feared returning and finding everything changed. Daddy preached one night at KBC and told of his experiences in China, several of which I had never heard. As usual, sitting there listening, I was a regular watering pot. On the whole, Hong Kong was a good break for Daddy. He reveled in the atmosphere of being surrounded with a Chinese population. He loved finding those who spoke Mandarin, and his continued fluency in the language was remarkable. Daddy's digestion had been messed up ever since the 1930s. For the past forty years, Daddy had proclaimed he simply could no longer eat Chinese food. However, during his month in Hong Kong, Bob and I were both tickled and astounded at the amount of Chinese food he was able to put away. I was careful not to mention "digestive issues," and, thankfully, he had none.

Bob and I were still seeking and hoping for opportunities in China, even as we loved our involvement with three churches and with countless youth in Hong Kong. I taught both English and psychology at HKBC, and I was so grateful for bright students in whom to invest and with whom I had opportunities to share Christ. The contrast of freedom in Hong Kong and the lack of it in China was stark. Bob and I both served on our mission China strategy committee, seeking ways to engage in ministry in a xenophobic Communist nation.

As 1985 arrived, Bob was working nearly full-time with Kowloon International Church with special emphasis on organizing a new chapel at Clearwater Bay, the location of what everyone fondly dubbed "Baptist Beach." Located some forty minutes from downtown Hong Kong, there were several interested families in that outlying area but no church. We began with about twenty people, including children and a young Australian Baptist couple who were eager to help. April, one of my dear university students, had graduated and was engaged to a young professor. They became two of our regulars. We divided the Sunday School into two classes, and I taught the little ones, Bob the adults.

Growth came quite quickly through the year, and our numbers doubled. The little ones were like children everywhere. They adored flannelgraph stories. I had loved flannelgraphs since watching Mama use them long years earlier. Clearwater Bay Chapel was as diverse a group as you could wish for — making it a constant and enjoyable challenge. Dai, a Hindu from India and now an English citizen, was intrigued to hear about an eternal God — and he came with many questions. Also in our little congregation were Filipinos, Chinese, Scottish, English, Americans, and occasionally some people from Singapore and Malaysia. We were a little United Nations.

Our weekly mission prayer meetings were a constant encouragement. I loved being able to work with some fellow China MKs. Flo Fielder McKinney had been born in Honan Province, and Millie Lovegren in Szechwan. Cornelia Leavell, born in Wuzhou, had been my "Aunt Cornelia" many years earlier and was now Hong Kong Mission's extremely competent business manager. A piece of Baptist history came full circle, and all of us were caught up in memories of Bill Wallace of China. Young Dr. Bill had gone to China in 1935 to the Baptist hospital in Wuzhou, Kwangsi Province. Aunt Grace and Daddy and Mama all knew and admired him greatly. He had stayed at the Baptist hospital through the fighting in China during World War II, and exhibited true heroism even as he saved a number of lives. Bill was greatly loved and admired by all with whom he worked.

When the Communists took Wuzhou in 1949, despite growing threats and intimidation from the Communist military, Bill could not bring himself to leave. Conditions deteriorated, and the soldiers became bold in making threats. Dr. Wallace quietly went on about his work as long as possible. The Communists then began openly accusing Wallace of being an "imperialist pig." Unable to find any charges to bring, they secretly planted a gun under his mattress, then "found" it and put him in prison. Within two months, Dr. Wallace had been tortured so severely that he died from his injuries. Missionary Everly Hayes had remained as well but was allowed to leave after Wallace's death. Her testimony was the sole means by which a grieving denomination learned what had really happened in Wuzhou.

Now, thirty-four years later, the Wallace family asked Vice President George H.W. Bush to request the return of Dr. Wallace's remains. The wheels of diplomacy finally turned enough times to bring the request to reality. Cornelia Leavell was able to return to the city of her birth and bring back Bill Wallace's ashes. A moving memorial service was later held in Wallace's hometown of Knoxville, Tennessee. His family could finally have a bit of resolution as the Christian world remembered and honored the heroism of the doctor who loved his people enough to give his life for them. The week following her epic journey home to Wuzhou, Cornelia movingly recounted the experience to our station prayer meeting group, and all of us shared a sense of the historical significance of this moment in Baptist missions.

Then, another piece of my childhood came into focus. We had a guest for our weekly gathering, and I got goosebumps when I heard the name.

C.K. Jang was a piece of my childhood. He was one of the most prominent of Baptist ministers and educators in all of China. Dr. Jang and my parents had been dear friends, and their ties went way back, because Mama was C.K.'s first English teacher at the University of Shanghai. In the thirty-five years since we had last seen one another, I had changed a lot more than Dr. Jang. When he spoke and recounted something of the persecutions and intimidations of the past years, he had his audience spellbound. Then Dr. Jang related how his very first English professor had been Alice Wells, who had so enriched his life. There I sat shedding sentimental tears, wishing Mama could hear those words. That little blue enamel cup of my China memories was once more running over.

Bob and I frequently commented that it was safe to declare that missionary life is never dull. How you *expect* things to happen is seldom how they *actually* happen. We found this particularly true in regard to our time and work in China. One of our prime motivations in the decision to work in Hong Kong was the possibility of going to China and serving there. Both of those happened, but not in the way we *thought* they would. First, Bob had the unusual months in China with young engineering students, followed by plans to minister on the mainland through a business connection. That never developed. Multiple visits into China *did*, however — and unexpected opportunities to reconnect with our family's China ties. We could never have hoped for so much. I got emotional just thinking about being able to take each one of our family members into China to connect with my childhood there — first Jody, then Alice, and right on the heels of that, Bob and I went again.

In April 1985, Alice first came to Hong Kong, and then the two of us headed for China. It was incredible to get the chance to take our only daughter "home" to my China roots and for the two of us to share special moments and memories. I learned a lot more about Jay Hudiburg, one of the aerospace engineers with NASA whom she met through her work in Huntsville. She had mentioned him frequently, but now it appeared to be much more than just a casual acquaintance. It sounded like this might be something serious. Meanwhile, Alice took in Hong Kong for the first time since her visits as a child, amazed at how much had changed, and delighted to find the things that had not. She especially enjoyed reconnecting with several missionary friends in the days before we left for China. I had dreamed a long time of being able to introduce our children to my childhood, up close and personal. Jody and I had relished the contacts just a year earlier. Now, Alice would have the same experience. Lack of time prevented us from going to Beijing and the Great Wall, but our time was spent in the places of great meaning to her grandparents and her mother in those early years.

After flying into Shanghai, we spent a short time looking at tourist places, but concentrated on time with the people who were part of our spiritual heritage. To be able to introduce Alice to my childhood friend and her mother was one of my greatest joys of the entire trip. Nevertheless, because there are still living family members, I am unable in the current political climate to openly share their stories. Alice and I also had beautiful hours of reminiscing with Mrs. Wu Ji Jong and her daughter, Ying Kwang. Again, the lives of her grandparents came into clear focus for Alice as she heard about experiences they had shared with the Wus. She was astounded at how little bitterness she heard from either of those stalwart women.

Next stop on our short odyssey was to go by train to Zhenjiang and Yangzhou. Alice grinned as she noted so many similarities between Hong Kong and Taiwan trains, and then commented on the differences as well. Lack of a feeling of freedom was a nearly palpable contrast. In China, you had to be on guard the entire time, but not so in Taiwan. My favorite moments were being able to actually go with our firstborn to see my childhood church, our house, our neighborhood. She patiently listened to me share story after long-ago story. One of her own favorite moments, likely because it was a piece of her *own* childhood, was finding *yòu tyáur* (fried doughnut sticks) just like she had enjoyed in Taiwan.

Sunday in Yangzhou was another trip down memory lane. Pastor Wu, with his glowing face, was thrilled to meet the granddaughter of his beloved coworkers, and we shared precious moments as he related stories about Mama and Daddy. One distinct difference on this visit: Pastor Wu was willing to be photographed with us in public, something that had not happened in previous visits. Nonetheless, the other pastor of the church was also there, and we had enough wisdom to know to be circumspect about what we said. These could be those "listening ears" of which we had been told.

The biggest problem with our journey was its brevity. However, we cherished each day and each memory, and stored them up to be taken out and relived many a time. Just weeks after Alice returned to Alabama, she called to tell us she was engaged, and we knew a new period of life was beginning for her. She and Jay married late that summer. (Bob performed the wedding ceremony in Huntsville, where they lived. All of us treasured this unexpected extra family time with Daddy, Bob's mother, and Jody.)

Months earlier, our East Asia area director, Dr. George Hays, had asked us to escort two personnel from the mission board to China, particularly to make links with Baptist missions history there. Bob and I could think of no more terrific assignment. We would be taking Minette Drumright, FMB prayer strategist, and Judy Robertson, associate in the East Asia office, to meet our China family. Furthermore, it would be my first opportunity to take Bob to my home in China. Both of us were highly excited about this visit, and it lived up to its billing. In early May, we flew from Hong Kong to Shanghai, beginning an eleven-day trip with the two ladies from Virginia. It was the first time to China for both of them and became a life-changing experience.

Since I had just been in China with Alice, I was able to plan ahead for this visit. As soon as we reached our hotel in Shanghai, I called both my childhood pal and Ying Kwang, making arrangements for all of us to meet at Grace Church the next morning for worship service. There were several legally "open" churches in Shanghai now, each with several pastors. We knew from our friends in Shanghai that at least one of the pastors at each church was the "eyes and ears" of the Communist party. My pastor's wife from childhood days smilingly told me that all churches were non-denominational now. "But," she gave a little grin, saying, "I like to go to Grace, because I know two of the pastors are Baptist." (Grace was my Aunt Grace's church during her years in Shanghai, and I was personally excited about being able to worship there. I knew Aunt Grace would be thrilled about the visit. She was eighty-eight, but her mind was far sharper than her years would indicate.)

It was a beautiful morning, and Grace Church was packed with 1,500 people, plus 500 more seated on stools in the courtyard. They had three services on weekends just to accommodate the crowds. Our hearts sang to see not only the masses of white hair and venerable lined faces, but hundreds of young adults also, eager to worship. The elderly deacon who managed to find us a place to sit in the balcony leaned over and whispered in Mandarin, "You are Baptist, aren't you?" I nodded and assured him we certainly were. He glanced around to see if anyone was listening, grinned, then whispered in return, "I am, too!" When the congregation sang "He Hideth My Soul," I nearly lost it, so moving was it to hear those people, who *knew* firsthand what it meant to "hide in the cleft of the rock," sing the words with such joy. One of the oldest pastors, Reverend Tang, who (along with the famous Watchman Nee) had many years been a leader of the "Little Flock Church," brought a powerful message that belied his venerable years. Of all passages, his text was WMU's watchword: 1 Corinthians 3:9, Laborers Together with God. By this time, my little blue enamel cup couldn't begin to hold the overflow of gratitude for this experience of which we could be a part. Surely, gratitude is the heart's memory.

My little blue cup kept filling up in the hour following the service, as we gathered in the courtyard and visited with both my pastor's wife from long-ago days, and Mrs. Wu and their daughters and families. Minette and Judy were amazed at being able to feel like they were experiencing a moment in Baptist history. And there was more to come. Ying Kwang introduced me to her cousin, saying, "This is my cousin, whose brother is your friend, Dr. Jou Lien Hwa in Taipei." Let me tell you, my chill bumps were big enough for all to see. The lady's face glowed as she said, "You know my brother? Tell me about him. I have not seen him in thirty-five years." My eyes welled up again, and Bob and I had the thrill of relating story after story of the ways God was using her brother to minister to thousands — not only in Taiwan, but literally around the world. Then I had a sudden thought, "You know your brother has recently translated the New Testament into the Good News translation, don't you?" Miss Jou nodded, "Yes, I had heard that." I asked, "Do you have a copy?" She shook her head, "No, I cannot get one here." I couldn't contain my smile a moment longer, as I reached into the large purse hanging on my arm, "I am so happy to say you do now. I have one with me." Joy flooded her face as she bubbled over with gratitude, staring down at the shiny maroon-bound New Testament in her hands. And then, to my further amazement, Miss Jou told me, "When I was young, your aunt, Miss Grace Wells, was my youth leader right here at Grace." My heart actually beat overtime with the emotion of the moment.

Hours-long visits with those longtime friends were timeless moments of jubilation. My heart longed for Daddy to have been here. How Mama would have loved every minute of such fellowship. It crossed my mind that this was just a slight foretaste of what heaven would be like, rejoicing with our dear ones *all* the time, and in the presence of the Savior.

Minette and Judy sat raptly listening to these saints, who personally knew what it meant to suffer, tell with joy how God had spared them and given them courage to simply endure day after day. They had come under special persecution because they had been so closely associated with "evil foreigners" during the years before the Communist takeover. It was a special blessing to be able to give them Bibles and literature and several items they could not obtain in China. There was so little we could really do for them. They, however, had done so much for us, moving our hearts and giving us a firsthand glimpse of what a true saint looks like. These were those who had been in the fire and emerged refined as pure gold.

The wonders of Beijing, the Great Wall and the Ming Tombs, were memorable sights for our visitors, but both agreed that those came nowhere close to the blessing of meeting those precious saints. Bob and I were given a name of a Beijing doctor by our Foreign Mission Board personnel. Dr. Rachel Feng, a pediatrician in the capital city, was active in one of the two open churches there. In her seventies, she knew a little English, but Bob and I did most of the translating. She was thrilled to know that I had been in the movie about Christiana Tsai and asked if I could please send her a copy of the book *Queen of the Dark Chamber*. Dr. Feng's daughter was a professor of political science at one of the large universities and a member of the Communist Party. Upon the death of Dr. Feng's husband two years previously, her daughter had privately acknowledged to her mother that she was a secret believer. She confessed to Rachel, "Mama, pray for me. I am a Nicodemus." (Names are changed to protect the living.)

Leaving Beijing, we flew into Nanjing and planned to take the short train trip from there to my old home in Zhenjiang. I had not been in Nanjing since 1948, and my "history bones" vibrated continually in that ancient city that had once been the capital of China, and where Aunt Grace had studied Mandarin. Visiting the famous Ming Wall, built in the 1300s, was a thrill for all of us. Nonetheless, that was eclipsed by finally being able to take Bob to my China homes, both in Zhenjiang and in Yangzhou. And yes, they had actually moved all of the families out of our two mission houses in Zhenjiang and begun restoration. We were able to go inside my house, and, of course, I had to weep a few tears when showing Bob my bedroom, our living room with its old mantel, and rubbing my hands over the ball on top of the staircase banister. It was just like it had been thirty-five years earlier (though quite a bit dustier).

I loved being able to take our Richmond friends to see the former church building and its cornerstone. Of course, the usual crowds of the curious were gathered around. Several garrulous and friendly elderly men began asking questions as to who we were and why we were there. As I explained, I looked at one smiling old man and asked, "Do you know what this building used to be?" He beamed, "Of course, it was a Ye Su *tang* (Jesus building)." A young man standing nearby asked him, "Ye Su? Who's that?" The old fellow shook his head and said, "You don't know? Then you haven't grown up yet!"

All of us were eager to get to Yangzhou the next morning, for this time I knew there was a worship service and we intended to get there early. Immediately after entering the sanctuary, my eyes lighted on Pastor Wu. His face glowing, he came to greet us, and I had the thrill of introducing

Bob to this saint of a man. Our American guests were amazed at Pastor Wu's beautiful English, to say nothing of his radiant face. The little blue cup was surely running over today, for here came three little ladies who knew Mother fifty years ago and were so excited to meet me. Little Mrs. Chen and her two friends had been teenagers in Mama's Bible study class. When I told them she had gone on to Glory just twelve months ago, tears filled each of their eyes. It was crystal clear that Mama's legacy was much alive.

Shades of the past were not over yet, for next came Nancy Shen, Aunt Grace's fellow Bible woman sixty years earlier. Nancy had been a young adult in 1926, and adored Wei Dz Mei (Sister Wells), who had trained and mentored her. Nancy still lived in Zhenjiang, but the local Baptist grapevine had told her that Sister Wells' niece was going to be visiting, and she left home very early to come meet me in Yangzhou. Providentially, Bob had a picture of Aunt Grace in his wallet. He took it out and smilingly handed it to Nancy Shen. "This is yours to keep," he told her. Thrilled, she beamed, held it to her heart and confided, "You know, I loved to hear Wei Dz Mei preach!"

The service itself was a new worship experience for Minette and Judy, and Bob and I loved hearing the local Chinese dialect. One of the other pastors was preaching the day's message, but Pastor Wu opened the service by quoting Psalm 23, and I could only sit and remember Daddy doing the same in the identical Chinese dialect. Incredibly, during the announcement time, Pastor Wu, who had been so guarded and hesitant just two years earlier, stood and told the congregation that in their midst was the daughter of his beloved missionary coworker of fifty years earlier, his mentor in the gospel, Harold Hall. Then he asked all of us to stand. I was stunned, thinking of how much had changed in just two years, realizing that now he felt safe enough to actually introduce his foreign guests.

I left China overwhelmed by God's bounty in allowing us so many rare and memorable experiences. Only a few years earlier, I could not have imagined being able to renew the family's China ties — not just once, but repeatedly. Furthermore, within a handful of months, another China opportunity was to come our way, one totally unexpected but rich with promise.

Bob and Rosalie on the spot where the beggar knelt

Jody with his graduate students, Nanjing

NINETEEN

TIANJIN
1986

An open door to possible China ministry came in a way we never imagined. A Baptist deacon from America's heartland, active in our Kowloon International Church, had business dealings in several countries and a vision for making a difference spiritually in China, despite closed doors. James Jordan (name changed) learned of our deep interest in China ministry, and his project needed staff with a speaking knowledge of Chinese and an awareness of Chinese customs and mores. "Are you interested?" was James' initial query, and our answer was an immediate, "Yes, we certainly are."

Jordan explained that this was a joint venture with the Chinese government. Their government was to send graduate students to be instructed in technology, management, applied science, language and culture. They would put up half the money, and non-profit philanthropic "Western" sources would give the other half. Jordan would be in charge of providing staffing. By this point, an eight-story headquarters, to include staff apartments and classrooms, was already under construction. There would be a conference center and a staff of some thirty personnel from America. Staff would be on a rotating basis and return briefly to the States once a year, plus periodic trips to Hong Kong. As James explained the plans, Bob and I got increasingly excited. He needed us to provide orientation for the incoming staff and to head up the language and culture training department.

Here was an opportunity to actually live and minister in China. This was a many-years-long dream that seemed almost too good to be true. (As it developed, it was — but hindsight is a marvelous thing.) James Jordan wanted the two of us to go in before the rest of the team. A young man from Tennessee and the two of us would be the vanguard and prepare the way for those who followed. Our Hong Kong mission kindly seconded us to the joint venture. Nonetheless, Bob and I were neither one completely naïve, despite our excitement over this new venture. Having grown up with the knowledge that "oriental" and "occidental" thinking work in entirely different ways, I was aware that what we "understood" about the project policies was likely extremely different from the ways the other half of the joint venture was looking at the project. In Chinese thinking, nothing is ever straightforward (or on time). Chinese thinking tends to go around in circles, whereas we Westerners like to get directly to the point. There are many pitfalls on the road connecting the two; there certainly were in the Tianjin project.

Tianjin is one of China's largest cities, with some 9 million people (and now far more). Located about seventy miles from Beijing, it is an ancient city rich in tradition. Its history in the past 200 years had included the presence of countless foreigners, and there were many remnants of Western colonialism still hanging around. Herbert Hoover was a mining engineer there during his early years after graduating from Stanford. (Months later, I was able to explore the old city and locate Hoover's residence.) Hoover and his wife had managed to survive the Boxer Rebellion, which was aimed at foreigners, many of whom died. The siege of Tianjin came in 1900 and ended

Rosalie with a galah friend at Perth, WA aviary, 1990

Phillip Anderson with Rosalie and Joey, the pet kangaroo, 1990

Eric and Carl with their great-grandfather, Ho Shien Sun,1991

The family in Huntsville, Alabama, 1991

With village children near Bangalore, India, 1991

Nine-month-old Eric practices Kung Fu, 1992

With Pastor G. Samuels and wife, Eve, Carey Bicentennial, Calcutta, 1992

With our Bible study group, Jurong Mandarin Chapel, 1993

*Pastor Ding and Josie
Regacho, with Jedidiah,
Baguio, Philippines, 1993*

*Bob at the gym with Chuck
Norris, Manila, Philippines, 1993*

*Rosalie with Aunt Rhett Wells
at Bethea Baptist Home,
Darlington, South Carolina, 1993*

*Rosalie meets Dennis,
Java, Indonesia, 1993*

*With grandsons Carl and
Eric in Guntersville, 1996*

*FBC Guntersville hosts a retirement
reception for the Hunts. Helen Fling
and Rosalie embrace as Alma Hunt
smilingly looks on, 1996.*

*Alice on an
archaeological dig
at Megiddo, 1996*

*Aidan and Gannon
with their great-
grandfather, Harold
Hall, 1997*

*Eric and Carl holding
their tiny cousins while
Alice looks on, 1997*

*The four grandsons
in sweaters knitted
by their Nana, 1997*

*With Carl and Eric at Adoniram
Judson's boyhood home, Plymouth,
Massachusetts, 1997*

*Aidan and Gannon, eleven
months old, use their "twin-ese"
to discuss a favorite book, 1998*

Gannon and Aidan take a stroll in
Alpharetta, Georgia, 1998

Bob (Papa) with his
four grandsons, 1998

1998: With Hawaii WMU
leadership, including Sue
Saito Nikashima, executive
director emeritus, who was
a young teen at Wahiawa
Church when Harold and
Alice Hall were there in 1938

With Mr. Huu and
daughter Thu, in Stanford,
California, with Adoniram
Judson's great-grandson,
Dr. Stanley Hanna, 2000

Carl and Eric at Paul Revere's grave, Boston, Massachusetts, 1997 …

… And ten years later, in 2007

With Carl and Eric on the steps where the beggar had knelt, 2004

Carl sits astride a Ming Dynasty stone carving at palace ruins near Zhenjiang, China, 2004

Restoration in progress on the two former mission residences, Zhenjiang, China, 2004

Bob with Meg and Ern Avery on a visit to Western Australia several years after serving there, 2009

Standing with the family where the beggar knelt sixty-three years earlier, Zhenjiang, China, 2010

At Syi Lyang Jye church in Yangzhou, with Pastor Wu's granddaughter and great-great-grandson, 2010

up being the bloodiest battle of the Boxer Rebellion. Tianjin came away from the rebellion with a tainted history of distrust and resentment of foreigners. This affected relations with foreigners for many years to come.

Bob and I had a few weeks in the States prior to moving to Tianjin, during which I made a trip to Richmond to help with some documents discovered in the Foreign Mission Board warehouse. These were papers, deeds, and documents from the early 1900s, all relating to missionaries and missions in China. The board asked a Chinese gentleman, who had worked with our missionaries in China and was now retired in the US, to work with me in going through these documents to see what might be important. I could think of very little more appealing than to help with a bit of old China mission history. I got really excited when coming across some deeds of our mission property in Zhenjiang, and learned that during the civil war in the 1920s, when our missionaries had evacuated, Chinese troops had taken the houses and even stabled horses in them. Looking at those old deeds was like holding history in my hands. These were the houses where Aunt Grace had lived, and, later, our family.

The biggest thrill of that Richmond trip was the night I spent with Eloise Cauthen. She, too, was a China MK, and she had been a loving hostess to a little eight-year-old who had arrived in her house in Shanghai on Christmas Eve of 1946. Her daughter Carolyn had been my friend in Shanghai forty years earlier, and now Eloise was excited that I was going to China to live. Dr. Cauthen, already retired as president of the Foreign Mission Board, had died some years earlier, and Eloise was quite lonely. That evening of reminiscing, Eloise said to me, "When I learned that you and Bob were going to China, I decided I wanted to make a request of you." I assured her, "Anything. You just tell me what I can do." Leaving the room, she soon returned with a heavy black coat hanging over her arm. Eloise smiled as she sat down, rubbing her hand over the thick collar of the coat. "This was Baker J.'s overcoat," she told me. "He had this made by a tailor in Shanghai, and it kept him warm many a cold winter there." She gave a nostalgic sigh and continued, "I would be so happy if you would take his coat home to China, and you and Bob use it to keep warm. I think that would please Baker so much." I looked down at that coat and gave an inward smile, thinking how Elisha must have felt when Elijah's mantel fell on him. "You know we would be honored, Eloise, to wear this special coat." We did that very thing, and it helped so much when those deadly winds from the Gobi swept through Tianjin.

Yet another serendipity developed. We would actually have a family member also living in China: Jody. He was in the process of applying to numerous law schools, even as he continued working in student affairs at Samford. One morning late in 1985, he received a call from Harlan Spurgeon, vice president of the Foreign Mission Board. "Uncle Harlan" had a proposal to make. The newly established Amity Foundation in China, headed by Bishop Ting, leader of the 3-Self Church in China, was looking for foreign philanthropic institutions interested in cooperating with China in its efforts to begin some joint projects with the Western world. Amity needed a teacher for six months at the graduate School of Agriculture in Nanjing. Did the Foreign Mission Board have an interest in this? Harlan was checking to see if Jody would be interested in exercising his Mandarin language skills in China. He would indeed.

There followed six months in Nanjing for our son, teaching some eighty-five graduate students from every province of China, and we had numerous opportunities to see him during our year in Tianjin. Arranging our flights accordingly, we first flew to Nanjing and saw Jody in his setting and met those students. It was a rare treat, and they treated him with the honor the Chinese have traditionally awarded their respected teachers. It was a refreshing change from the typical American classroom. The young men and women were thrilled to be learning English from a native speaker who could also speak their own language.

Bob and I arrived in Tianjin in March, two days after the government turned off the heat available to citizens. Somehow, the weather didn't understand, and we were met with snow. It was an extremely chilly welcome to our new home, and we should have been prepared for the usual delays and miscommunications — our entire year was full of them. We sometimes felt like it was a wasted year — but, then, we are not the ones to judge. Our part was to be found faithful. The entire time, Bob had an uneasy feeling, because we were missionaries, yet not permitted to say we were. We could mention Christianity only if someone specifically asked us. Bob commented, "I feel a bit like Abraham must have felt, telling the pharaoh that Sarah was his sister." Shortly after our arrival was the day of Mama's birthday, and it was a bitter-sweet day of wonderful memories mixed with a deep sense of loss. It had just been two years; how I wished I could sit with her right now and talk through this strange new experience.

Not being able to openly (say nothing of freely) share our faith was the greatest strain of a highly unusual year. Progress on the building slowed to a halt, and then barely started up again. Delay after delay came as the government would renege on promises and then suggest something different. Visas and permits became nearly impossible to get. In spite of all the hassle, however, we had bright spots and learned a lot (probably too much) about human nature, including our own. Tianjin is one of the windiest cities in the world, and then when spring and autumn winds get started, the amount of dust and grit from the Gobi Desert that reaches Tianjin is incredible. Our transportation was by bicycle, and by the time we pedaled into the center of the city, we would take our glasses off and stare in a mirror at the rim of white all around our eyes. The taste of the grit was indescribable and unavoidable.

There was one nice hotel, the Astor, resurrected from colonial days and run by a Hong Kong consortium. Bob began teaching English to the staff and loved the contact and opportunity to interact. I loved going with him, for his "pay" was a free meal in the relaxing atmosphere of the Astor, and I could go along and do my correspondence and lesson plans, have delightful food with real butter to put on bread, and lovely surroundings in which to work. One student in particular, Alex (named changed) came to Bob with his interest in knowing about God. Such bright moments of opportunity got us through a number of challenging months.

Bob and I also began teaching some of the university professors who were planning to study abroad and needed English instruction. Had we waited on the project building to be completed, the teaching would never have happened. We were able to help several apply to graduate schools in the States, and, as we did so, we prayed that there would be open opportunities in

America for them to hear the gospel from believers who crossed their paths.

We lived in a four-room walk-up apartment with Henry, the other staff member in the vanguard. Privacy is a word that is unknown in China, so we got a personal taste of that. Jody declared that "privacy" is not in the nation's vocabulary. Talk about feeling paranoid; this was real. All our letters were opened and read, all phone calls were monitored, and the places in the walls that had been plastered over were listening devices. So, even in the so-called privacy of our bedroom — there *was* no privacy. Nor was there hot water. The apartment had a bathtub, but unless you heated kettle after kettle of water to fill it, there were no hot baths. We laughed about how something you have always taken for granted, but no longer have, can become the thing you most covet. Anytime we had to travel to a meeting and stay in a hotel, the first priority was a hot bath. Luxury.

The three of us lived in what was known as an "expensive" neighborhood, and a number of professionals lived nearby. There were even a few elderly residents who were survivors of Mao Tse Dong's "Long March." We were likely viewed with suspicion by most. That was understandable. However, the neighborhood children loved talking with the *waigwo ren* (foreigners). One afternoon, three adorable little children came to our door and wanted to visit. We had a rare old time, and they loved eating cookies and trying their two or three words of English. My heart wept that I could not even teach them the song that was "China's hymn" and much loved by Lottie Moon, "Jesus Loves Me." I ached to say to them, "Little ones, Jesus loves you, too!" There was also a special attraction in our neighborhood. A couple, in this country with a one-child-only regulation, had the rare good fortune of giving birth to twin sons. They were adorable, chubby little cherubs that came to recognize us when we would stop to play and coo with them. I've wondered many a night what would happen to those little fellows. Would they have an opportunity to learn that God loved them in a special way?

I loved the touches of history that Tianjin afforded. The German concession had been large and influential, and it showed in the architecture of the old city, as well as in the little antique shops. A bit of Christian history intrigued us. We often passed an old church that had been stripped of anything appearing "Christian" but was obviously a former place of worship. This was the church where Eric Liddell, "the flying Scotsman" of Olympic fame, had worshipped and worked. In fact, he was born in Tianjin, and after his Olympic glory, came back as a missionary, just like his parents before him. Liddell died a hero in a Japanese internment camp.

Food was an incredible challenge. We never found chickens in Tianjin. Occasionally, I could take the train to Beijing and lug back a couple of frozen chickens from their Friendship Store. Ice was a luxury. We had a tiny little fridge and two ice trays. All water had to be boiled, and when we went to the market, we had to have the beef ground up, bones and all, for hamburger meat. The taste and texture soon convinced us of the truth: This was water buffalo, and it had put in years of labor in order to toughen its meat prior to getting to the market. For much of the time, the only vegetable available was cabbage; I wished for a cookbook titled *One Hundred Ways to Cook Cabbage*. Our little kitchen also had the distinction of having just one gas burner for cooking. Bob and I tried to follow the three-second rule. However, in China it became the ten-second rule. If we accidentally dropped an imported goody like an M&M or a cookie, we allowed ourselves to dust it off and eat it if it had only been on the floor *ten* seconds. After all, imported treats were quite rare. We also developed another rule: We could only ask one "why" question per day. Early one morning, I caught myself asking a why, and said, "Oh, dear. It's only 8:30, and I've already used my *why* of the day!"

During our first weeks, the Chinese big bosses wanted to meet with Jordan and his team for a banquet. Since I was the only woman present, I was seated at the main table, between Jordan and the Chinese boss. He spoke no English, and Jordan, no Chinese, so I was the go-between, and it really kept me focused, trying to keep up with the technical terms. The slowness of progress on the building grew increasingly discouraging, and the Chinese project leaders were growing increasingly xenophobic.

Our apartment mate, Henry, had met a young man, Wesley, whose mother and grandmother had both been Christians. The message they had left with him bore fruit, and he came to faith. Wesley would come after dark, and we would worship together. Then a friend of his also came, then a professor, and they were able to worship with other believers, either for the first time ever or for the first time in thirty years. Our visitors never came together, but always quietly and separately, late in the evening, so as not to attract attention. It was a day of rejoicing when Bob led us in a service and had communion. Wesley's first-ever Lord's Supper brought us all to happy tears. I felt so ashamed of the many times I had just lightly taken for granted the privilege of communion.

The original plan was that the project building would be completed by August. However, it was barely a skeleton outline by then, and we were increasingly frustrated. Jordan, the project leader, was a brilliant man and a true visionary. Failure didn't bother him. If something didn't work, he would simply move on to something else he had going on. For the some twenty-six families who had committed to come to Tianjin, however, this was more than just a simple failure; it affected all their families. Bob and I spent much time orienting the couples who began to arrive and arranging language teachers for them — no simple task in such a bureaucratic system. Meanwhile, we were teaching professors as well as staff and trying to be circumspect in all we said and did. It was like walking on eggshells every day. I felt too clumsy to do that very well.

Nevertheless, there were bright spots, like when a student "got it" and we could see a light come on in their thinking, or when someone asked us if we were Christians, and we could tell them what that meant. Furthermore, Jody was able to come several times, and that was pure delight. The second time he arrived, a cabbie picked him up, and Jody said, "I'll give you the address where to take me." The cabbie grinned, "Not necessary; you are the son of the foreign teachers." (I ask you, have you ever seen a grapevine like that?)

A year earlier, Jody and a friend had taken the Trans-Siberian Rail from Beijing to Moscow, and on the train, they had met a young Chinese-Russian lab technician and her little son. They were going to Moscow, where her father lived. Natasha spoke Chinese and Russian, and Jody spoke English and Chinese. They set up quite an interpreting business. The first days of the trip, they were among a Chinese crew. Then that soon changed to a Russian crew. Therefore, people who spoke only one of those three languages needed translation help. Jody said it was sometimes like a three-ring circus. Some Englishman would tell Jody what he needed. Jody would tell Natasha in Chinese, and she, in turn, would tell the conductor in Russian. Natasha was from Tianjin, where her Chinese/Russian mother still lived. We had the privilege of meeting all of them and of introducing Natasha's adorable little boy to one of the sons of our project team from America. They hit it off instantly. Natasha's husband, a doctor, was highly connected, and when Jody visited the beautiful city of Hangzhou, Natasha and her in-laws had Jody to their palatial residence. Some of the family were government officials, including an uncle who had just returned from America, where he had been China's ambassador to the United States.

Jody and I had one bonus weekend — a trip like no other. We spent three days in Xian, China's ancient capital, and reveled in history to our hearts' content — from the fabulous old city wall, more than 1,000 years old, to the incredible Terracotta Soldiers, thousands of them built for and buried with the despotic Emperor Chin Shr 2,000 years earlier. This had to be one of the wonders of the ancient world. And it never failed; everywhere Jody and I went, the people were amazed at foreigners speaking Chinese. Of course, in those years, foreigners were not thick on the ground in China, especially those speaking colloquial Chinese.

Sickness played no favorites. It could happen anywhere. In Hong Kong, we had been blessed with great medical care, including missionary doctors. Tianjin was a different story. In August, however, a doctor arrived to be part of the joint venture and lived in an apartment near us with his wife and two little ones. Tom made his first visit to local hospitals and came back shaking his head, "Just don't get sick here. You don't want to go to the hospitals I've been in!" However, sickness isn't selective. Bob had a terrible bout with Ménière's disease, but our doctor was able to medicate him. Then I grew ill, and Tom was able to refer me to an Australian embassy doctor in Beijing. That doctor sent me to Hong Kong for surgery, and once more I gave thanks for our wonderful Baptist hospital in Kowloon.

Alice became the go-between that year for Jody and his communications with various law schools. He ended up with a scholarship to Columbia in New York. Alice, the new bride, spent a lot of time not only with her work at Redstone, but also helping Jody with information — and all the while helping care for her aging grandparents. We always knew when anyone called us from America that there were listening ears. We had to let the phone ring twice. That way, the "ears" had time to get on the line. One night, when Alice called, we heard the voice in Chinese say, "She got through this time." It put a bit of a damper on our conversations, and we tried to talk in "family code."

About this time, we learned that one of our own missionaries had talked unwisely and implicated us as missionaries, not as teachers. It was a shock and a blow. Being angry did no good. What we felt most was an infinite sadness. Bob and I were due to go to the US for two months, and it was a period of deep uncertainty. Nothing was clear. What should we do? Our presence in Tianjin had been compromised, and we certainly didn't want to jeopardize the rest of the Tianjin team. We prayed a lot, wept a good bit, and upon advice from the Foreign Mission Board, realized we should not return to north China. It was a bitter pill to swallow. Had it really been just a *year* since we had dreamed of sinking our roots in Chinese soil for the foreseeable future? It wasn't going to happen, and we earnestly looked to God for the next step.

I wonder how many times in our lives we have seen God true to His promises? He might not signal us ahead of time about the next step, but He is always on time. At just this juncture, there was an urgent need in Manila for a pastor at International Baptist Church, made up of Filipinos, Chinese, and numerous other nationalities. Our area director felt Bob would be a perfect fit for their need, and the timing was just right. We returned to Hong Kong to pack up there and then decide what to do about our furnishings and belongings in Tianjin. The Foreign Mission Board felt the best move would be for me to go back, depose of things, and quietly leave. Consequently, Bob headed to Manila, and I for Tianjin for the final time. From a distance of several decades, I look back on those last two days in Tianjin and vividly remember the sorrow and pain my heart felt. It still brings me to tears to remember the quick packing, selling, giving away, and telling friends on the staff and precious friends from our small Bible studies a last goodbye.

I could only pray that God had brought something of lasting worth out of this Tianjin year. My last act in our little apartment was to put on Dr. Cauthen's heavy Chinese overcoat. There was no space to pack it, so I would simply wear it. That coat felt as heavy as my heart. I took one last long look around our little place, closed the door, and let the tears have their way as they trickled down my face. At the airport, my stomach was in a tight knot as I stood by and watched customs officials dig through every suitcase, even examining one of them twice.

Within a short time, the Tianjin project did indeed come to an end. James Jordan, the leader, was arrested for Christian proselyting and then expelled from the country. The hope in our hearts was that there remained some positive outcomes of an experience that did not develop as anyone had expected. My mind so frequently recalled the old adage: Man proposes, but God disposes. And now our eyes were focused ahead — on Manila and ministry in that great city of more than 13 million.

Our adorable neighbors in Tianjin

Nolyn Cabahug and Bob introduce a new church project to interested IBC members

Harold Hall (Rosalie's father) with us at Jody's graduation from Columbia Law School

TWENTY

MULTINATIONAL MANILA
1987-1989

What an astounding contrast! Moving from the freezing temperatures of Tianjin, China, to the warm tropical breezes of Manila, Philippines, was like going on a winter vacation. Well, not quite. We weren't in Manila to frolic, but to become part of a wonderful, ministering, diverse, and loving congregation of unique souls. Moves are never simple, but wouldn't you think it would get easier with practice? Afraid not. We did, however, realize after so much practice that a favorite Chinese proverb of ours really does ring true. Chinese philosophy declares: *Guh You Haw Chew* — Everything has its good points. As my little blue enamel cup was unpacked once more,

227

I thought, *Little cup, I don't know if you will be overflowing in this place once again, but I'm thinking you probably will.* I hoped so. I'll admit that we felt like we had just come through a dry spell.

First impressions bombarded our eyes, ears, noses, thoughts and emotions. Everywhere was contrast. In wintry Tianjin, all seemed colorless and drab. There had been no supermarkets, international restaurants, or special conveniences. Conversely, Manila was full of them — bursting with stores and with some of the best cuisine in the world. Manila was also a riot of colors — with flourishing flowers scenting the air all year. In contrast, noxious fumes constantly came from the colorful "jeepneys" that served as open-air taxis for thousands of citizens. Jostling crowds filled every sidewalk, but ubiquitous smiles accompanied the crowding. Manila was a cacophony of contrasts. The two of us were met at the airport by smiling, ebullient church leaders from the IBC (International Baptist Church). You would have thought we were a gift straight from God to bolster their spirits.

Our biggest shock was the contrast in atmosphere. We had just spent a year being cautious about every word — wondering *who* might be listening and *what* we might be doing wrong. For a whole year, we had not been free to openly share our faith or worship in community. Now, here we were with both fellow believers and eager seekers, able to freely share. Both of us were nearly overwhelmed. On our first Sunday at International Baptist Church, the auditorium was full, the music glorious and uplifting, and the response heartwarming. In fact, for our nearly three years in Manila, there was seldom a Sunday when there was no response. Our area director had figured that Bob would be a good fit here since he was a people person. He was right. We formed lifelong friendships from the earliest days in Manila.

What musical genius! Doctors Eli and Elma Sarmiento — he a surgeon, she an internist and cardiologist — both ministered to ailing bodies each week with their medical skills and every week inspired hearts with wonderful music. Eli directed congregational singing, and Elma played the organ. They were just the beginning. Nolyn Cabahug, son of a Baptist pastor in the provinces, was a choir director with an extraordinary voice. We quickly learned that Nolyn was the tenor soloist in the choral group that sang with the Manila Philharmonic Orchestra. The first Sunday, as he sang "Great Is Thy Faithfulness," we knew *why* he was the lead soloist. Never before or since have we been so moved by a voice. IBC's choir was also remarkable. In all those three years, I never once heard anyone sing off-key.

Hong Kong had already given us positive vibrations about Filipino hearts and personalities. There were thousands of young Filipino women who worked as domestics in Hong Kong in order to send money home to their needy families. Scores of them had been in the memberships of both international churches in Hong Kong where we worked.

We also quickly realized that Filipino time and American time were two different animals. We Americans, who considered promptness a virtue, were brought up short by the new normal in Manila. If you are on time, you are the exception. Bob learned right away that when asked to perform a wedding ceremony, to first inquire, "Is this Filipino time, or Western time?" At his first wedding, Bob arrived a full hour before any of the wedding party wandered in. This was also the case on Sunday mornings, at least for our first few weeks. The second Sunday Bob was to preach, he began the service right on time. Looking around the auditorium that seated some 350 to 400, there might have been two dozen people present. After waiting several minutes, Bob swallowed his disappointment and began the service. People slowly began to filter in. By the time Bob was halfway through his message, the auditorium was full. The next Sunday, the usual handful were in the sanctuary, but Bob started promptly. When the majority arrived, they were shocked to find the message nearly over. Within a few weeks, the members realized that ten o'clock meant ten o'clock, and most adjusted accordingly.

Bob began his IBC ministry with the serendipity of a competent staff, led by secretary and office manager Aurora Rullon. Committed, talented, faithful, Au became a lifelong friend and advocate. Numerous young IBC couples held responsible positions: the Sarcos, Castros, Hernandezes, Tumloses, and on the list went. They were vibrant witnesses always ready to share God's love with the many seekers who were present every Sunday. Bob loved being able to baptize new believers several times a month. IBC also sponsored two mission points, both of which were growing.

We soon learned that every business, school, office, or church hired an armed security guard. It was a way of life. Bob and I looked at each other that first Sunday at IBC, wondering what was going on: an armed guard standing near the entrance to the sanctuary? Robert, the church's armed guard, was there both on Sundays and every weekday, for IBC had a thriving preschool program. We soon adapted and didn't think about it again. The only time in our years there that Robert ever fired his gun was the day he was handling it and accidentally shot his own toe.

The preschool/kindergarten was terrific, filled with children from a dozen nations. IBC is located in the Makati district of Manila, with several embassies nearby. I loved watching the young United Nations parade each weekday as the little ones arrived. What fun to see the little two-year-old from America playing hand in hand with the small Russian boy who joined his class. I inwardly grinned to see the young Iranian mother, wearing her traditional *hijab,* bringing her little boy and staying to visit and drink tea. Along with her Muslim *hijab,* she wore tennis shoes and jeans beneath her flowing robe. Our hearts sang the Sunday a bright young preschooler from China and her mother visited our service and listened intently to the first sermon they had ever heard. Within a few months, I was asked to be principal of the preschool. My heart sank. *Oh, dear. Preschool? I teach high school, college, or seminary. Little ones intimidate me.* But, as always, when you attempt to do that for which you are unqualified, God undertakes to qualify you. I never quite understood *how* that worked, but I saw it happen time and again.

Another contrast with our previous field was housing. In Manila, we were first in a mission house in San Lorenzo Village, very close to Makati's conveniences and near the church. A few months later, a more convenient duplex in the same village became available, and we lived next door to fellow Alabamians Martha and Phillip Anderson. It was a perfect spot for us, because Martha and I were team teachers with IBC's International Women's Bible Study. We had regulars who were longtime believers, and others who had never heard the gospel. Each week stretched us. The group's mix of nationalities and English language levels was a challenge, as was preparing material that spoke to the differing needs of women from Japan,

Korea, Thailand, Brazil, Hong Kong, and China.

Weather was yet another difference between Tianjin and Manila. Tianjin was usually either very cold, very dusty, and/or very hot with dry winds blowing. In Manila, most of the year was tropical heat, varying between 80 percent and 100 percent humidity, with temperatures constantly in the high nineties, and occasionally higher. Many a week, we had what we dubbed "three shower days."

IBC also had another large women's Bible study group made up mostly of Americans, both businesswomen and US military, but also including a scattering of other nationalities. Several deep friendships developed with those women, including Soly. Soly was Filipino, well-traveled, fluent in English, and from a Catholic background. Her English was colloquial and her wit engaging. Soly was deeply curious about the concept of a personal relationship with Christ. As the months advanced, so did her understanding, and I wept with joy the Sunday that Soly openly professed her faith. Her baptism was a unique experience. Soly wanted to be baptized with her last pack of cigarettes in her pocket, signifying that she was being buried with Jesus in baptism and raised to walk in newness of life — and no longer smoking. The cigarettes were "buried" as well. It was a vow Soly never broke, and her joy was contagious as she led others to Christ.

Bob was amazed at how much of his day consisted of both witnessing and counseling. The needs were as diverse as the people who came seeking. I recall one evening after a trying day for both of us. I was upset about something trivial and on the brink of succumbing to tears. Bob gave a long and audible sigh as he shook his head, declaring, "Don't you dare cry. I have had people in my office crying all day!"

Saturday men's prayer breakfast was a weekly evangelistic opportunity, and our Woman's Missionary Union a downright delight. I loved to listen and learn and watch the women lead. I recall the first Luzon Island-wide meeting held at our church; I observed the women from city and province meet in love, sing like a giant choir, dance with joy in the aisles on lively numbers, and then pray eloquently for a needy world.

Within a semester, I was teaching psychology and counseling courses at the extension branch of the Philippine Baptist Seminary (headquartered in Baguio), which met in our church facilities. I loved the students and their eagerness. American pupils usually took their educational opportunities for granted. Not these graduate students. I approached each session with zest, knowing the students were coming to really learn. Our first December in the Philippines, a deadly typhoon (like a hurricane in America) struck in another part of Luzon Island. Tony, one of my seminary students, was from the hardest-hit province. His parents had no phone, so after the storm struck, Tony caught a bus to go check on them. They survived, but their little *nipa* hut and everything they possessed was destroyed. Tony gave them all the money he had — 200 pesos (about ten US dollars) — which was his food money for the month. Our class, as well as the church, was able to help.

Even more than the preschool, WMU, Bible studies and seminary classes, my favorite responsibility was the high school-college Sunday School class. Those young adults — ranging from MKs from our missionary Faith Academy to a Pakistani student who had never before heard of Jesus — kept me challenged. Each Sunday was a new opportunity that I realized might never come again.

We had not been in San Lorenzo Village many weeks when the doggy incident occurred. In the midst of so many positives, it was a discordant and potentially dangerous experience. Early each morning, I tried to do a slow jog around the various streets in the village. After all, it was a gated community and ostensibly safe. That particular morning, as I jogged past one house surrounded by a low wall, I heard ominous growling and then barking. Glancing over one shoulder, I watched with growing fear as a hefty bulldog and a menacing Doberman pinscher bounded over the wall and headed straight toward me. I kept running, and so did they — the bulldog reaching me first, planting his teeth prints on my left thigh. I gave a pretty primeval yell, upon which the Doberman pinscher took a piece out of my right leg. By this time, I was running on pure adrenaline, sobbing as I ran. Thankfully, the dogs, seemingly satisfied at having vanquished the foe, trotted back home. My right leg felt strange, and I reached down one shaky hand to feel it. The hand came back up with a piece of flesh in it. I was nearly home by this time and raced into the house. Bob joined me in panic mode and immediately took me to Makati Medical Center. Thank God, here was another contrast to our previous city. Skilled, efficient staff in the emergency room took immediate control, bound up the wounds, sanitized the injuries (not without pain and shots), and pampered me royally. However, on the wall right beside the examining table was a picture of a rabid dog, and a list of instructions about rabies shots. Small comfort.

Bob and I followed up with a visit to the "house of dogs" and found it took repeated visits to even get anyone to the gate. It turned out that this was the residence of the former Miss Universe, and I immediately decided that her beauty was in sharp contrast with the ugly nature of her pets. We were grateful those two canines had up-to-date shots, which meant I didn't have to undergo rabies treatment. I did make two jogging changes; I never again ran on that particular street, and ever after, carried mace for protection.

Thankfully, we had a lot of ministry in the Chinese community. Many in our congregation were ethnic Chinese, and I often spoke at the Mandarin Baptist Church as well. Being able to speak their language gave us an instant inroad with the Chinese families that attended IBC. When one prominent patriarch died, the family asked Bob to make the funeral service an evangelistic one. Several friends and family professed their faith that day, and Bob had more than one baptism service resulting from the funeral. It was a touch of home for us to be able to speak Chinese occasionally, and our church treasurer even shared our Chinese surname.

Our large Philippine mission occasionally met in Baguio at the seminary for business and inspiration, and it was a treat to go to that higher elevation and feel some cool breeze even in the middle of a tropical summer. Baguio was also the location of at least one internment camp during World War II, and a number of our Baptist missionaries had been interned there. It was where Marian Gray (later Marian Cowherd, our neighbor in Taipei) and her husband, Rufus, had been imprisoned, and where he died at the hands of his captors.

Bob loved the Filipino custom of men wearing *barongs* as dress shirts. They often had intricate patterns on the front and were worn untucked, and, of course, no tie. So, naturally, Bob delighted in performing wedding ceremonies and preaching on Sundays in one of his comfortable *barongs*. And weddings there were — several dozen of them during our years in Manila. One favorite wedding custom delighted everyone attending, for many celebrations featured a releasing of doves.

One of our most exciting moments came in November 1987, when Alice called to tell us we were going to be grandparents. She, Jay, and Jody were able to come for about ten days in January, and the coming baby was our main topic of conversation. IBC members were thrilled to meet the family and welcomed them into the fold, with everyone pampering Alice. Our children, in turn, were able to meet our neighbor Susie, who lived just down the street from our house. Abel, who owned Susie, brought her for a visit when we first moved in. Susie was a ten-foot python, and I tried not to hyperventilate around her. Eventually, I came to the place where I could wrap her around my shoulders like a boa (!) and not noticeably shiver.

Exploring historic Old Town Manila with our children was a treat during their short visit. The presidential palace with its famous "Imelda Marcos" shoe collection was an eye-opener. There were more than a thousand shoes on display, and I wondered how many of them had actually ever been worn. A far more inspiring sight was the US Military Cemetery in Manila, with hundreds of rows of white crosses, tributes to the thousands of American lives lost during World War II.

In April, I was on "standby" to get a reservation to America when our grandson was to arrive. I had help in getting a quick reservation. Eli Sarmiento, our terrific congregational music director, was also founder and head of Medical Ambassadors, the organization that conducted medical clinics in some fifteen distant barrios in mountainous regions. In addition, Eli was the lead doctor for Philippine Airlines and was able to work some magic over my reservations. While winging my way to Virginia just days before the arrival, I thought about Mama in 1930s China, about to have her first baby and her mother some 10,000 miles away. What a privilege was now mine. I could be with our daughter, and I smiled to think of my little blue enamel cup again running over. To add to the joy of the occasion as

I arrived in DC, Jody was in Washington that same week for the international Jessup Moot Court competitions. Jody was nearly as excited about the impending arrival as was I. The baby arrived the middle of April, and the call to tell Bob was another special moment. My first sight of Carl John was through the window of the hospital nursery, where a competent young nurse was giving him his first bath. Jody and I stood watching and listening to those newborn screams of indignation. (Quite miraculously, I was later able to be present for the births of each of the subsequent four grands.) The little blue cup brimmed over again.

I was soon back in Manila, telling the brand-new grandfather about his grandson. When Alice was able to come in December to bring Carl, Jody came as well, and it was an exciting moment when Carl's "Papa" first held him in his arms. The next Sunday, Bob was beaming nonstop as he introduced his special visitor to the IBC family. I loved taking Alice and Jody to the various Bible study groups and also to meet the little ones at preschool. That actually took a good bit of time, because IBC had some fifteen various Bible studies and outreaches each week. IBC's founders some thirty years earlier had laid a strong foundation, and a small army of men and women were involved in daily ministry.

We lost an important part of our family in January 1989. Aunt Grace was nearly ninety-two when she died; it was like a piece of myself was gone. Aunt Grace was part of my earliest memories. I found in her papers a letter she had written to my grandparents the month before the Communists captured Shanghai, where she was working. She wrote, "I will go on in my regular work as long as possible; I'll keep you posted." Then she concluded, "I am surprised at my calmness of heart, so I know you are praying. I trust the Lord will keep you equally assured." My little blue cup was filled with sadness mixed with gratitude for her legacy of faith. I was able to go to the memorial service in South Carolina and spend a few days with Aunt Rhett. It was during those three days that she made a request of me. In all the years I had known Aunt Rhett, she had never asked me for anything, so when she took my hand and said, "Would you do something for me?" my immediate response was, "Of course, Aunt Rhett, you just ask me, and I will do it." She gave that endearing little half-smile as she responded, "When I die, would you come be with me, too?" I couldn't hold back the tears, and immediately reassured her, "Aunt Rhett, you have it. God being my helper, I'll be here for you, too." It was a vow I intended to keep. Mama and Daddy had not had the privilege of making a quick trip to the States when they were needed. We could do that, and I was grateful.

Josie, our young Filipino friend from Hong Kong days, came home to the Philippines and married her sweetheart, Ding Regacho, a young seminary graduate. They began pastoring a tiny little church in the province not far from Baguio. Whenever they were able to come to Manila, Ding and Josie would stay with us, and we watched them begin ministry from nothing and with nothing, and watched God at work. We were able to help them build a small *nipa* dwelling, and a year after the church began, Jedidiah, their little girl, was born. I remember one occasion, when JD (as they called her) was about eighteen months old, they brought her to Manila, and she had her first visit to a McDonald's. We took pictures of a big-eyed little toddler staring into the smiling face of the Ronald McDonald statue. (Ding and Josie became lifelong friends.)

Bob and I encountered a disease in Manila that was new to us. We learned about it up close and personal when Bob came down with several of the symptoms of dengue fever: severe headache, unremitting fever, and muscle exhaustion. A mosquito was the culprit, and the cure came via Dr. Eli Sarmiento. Never had we experienced more speedy care right at home. Dr. Eli set up a drip with medication and fluid right in our bedroom, conveniently bending a wire coat hanger to help hang the drip. Dengue fever was an experience Bob hoped never to repeat.

Our Bible study groups never became a chore. Each week brought its new challenges, and, often, a new member. The international flavor of one group was especially appealing. Along with our Bible study, we were able to sample all sorts of exotic recipes from various countries on several continents. Some were a smashing success, others not so much. I never learned to like Korean *kimchee* but watched in wonder as our Korean classmates ate repeated bites of the fiery mix and never even took a cooling sip of water.

Our group had varying levels of English, and I loved the willingness of the women to learn a new concept and to ask probing questions about what faith really was. They couldn't see it. They couldn't touch it. How could they *have* it? Our group members from Japan had come with very little previous contact with Christians or any understanding of what a personal relationship with Christ meant. My heart leapt with joy the morning Akiyo from Tokyo haltingly prayed aloud for the first time. Her face was radiant.

Mixed in with our three wonderful years in Manila were encounters with history, something of which I never tired. How could anyone *not* like history, I always wondered. A visit to Bataan, where the long death march had occurred in World War II, was chillingly shocking. Some nearly 80,000 American and Filipino prisoners of war in April 1942 were forced to march to the prison camp, and thousands died along the way of beating and starvation. Just as memorable was a trip to the little island bastion of Corregidor, where some 11,000 troops held out under siege in 1942 before being forced to surrender. The troops had lived underground in the Malinta Tunnel, and as we visited, our minds imagined what must have gone on in that eerie place more than four decades earlier. When Douglas MacArthur was forced to leave the Philippines in 1942, his famous words were: "I shall return." Return he did, and in 1945, the Philippines were once more breathing free air.

There came for us, as well, a day when we had to leave Manila and IBC, and we left with a swirl of mixed emotions. It had been an amazing three years during which we had seen God work in unusual ways. Bob and I had been blessed to be a small bit of it, and our IBC friends were forever in our hearts. The Foreign Mission Board determined that international churches must become self-sufficient, and missionaries could no longer remain as pastors. That was a blow. There were tears shed both at church and home, where we sometimes gave vent to our sorrow. IBC folk were a part of our DNA by this time. I repeatedly thought, *God being our helper, we will return.* (Unexpectedly, just a few years later, that happened.) Meantime, a request had come from the Baptist Union of Western Australia to the FMB to supply a couple to role model planting a church in WA. Our

area director asked us to consider this request. I recall my initial response.
Western Australia? The Land Down Under? Kangaroos and cockatoos? It
sounded like something exotic. Sure enough, it was — and WA was an
unusual, exciting, and challenging place to put down roots again. Who
would have ever thought — a China MK in Western Australia?

Carl and Rosalie enjoy meeting a koala at Cohuna Nature Park, Perth, WA, 1989

The family in Washington, DC, 1989

TWENTY-ONE

DOWN UNDER
1989-1991

Sparkling crystal-clear blue skies, clear, invigorating air, and smiles on nearly
every face: that's what we discovered in Perth, Western Australia (WA), the
Foreign Mission Board's most remote outpost. It is also undoubtedly one of
the most beautiful spots on God's earth. In just a matter of days, we moved
from the tropical heat of a Manila September to the beginning of spring in
Perth, discovering a countryside sprinkled with miles of wildflower fields
— enough to refresh the soul with every glimpse. Landing at midnight,
we were met at the airport by Bob Clark, director of Western Australia's
Baptist Union. (He became a terrific coworker and friend.) Gerry and Bob
Covington were there, the only Baptist missionaries in WA (teachers at the
Baptist seminary and destined to become our special friends). Bob Platt,
head of the union's home missions committee, was also there to welcome us

with his strong handshake and the huge smile that emanated from his heart. (The three "Bobs" met "my" Bob, and all the Bobs bonded. Bob Platt's wife, Anne, became my soul sister.) Bob and I took a deep breath (of amazingly clear and refreshing air) and both had the same thought: *And thus begins our new challenge — just two years to plant a church on Australian soil.*

Jogging that next bright morning, I breathed deeply the fresh, and a bit nippy, Australian air. I looked up in amazement to see beautiful pink and gray galahs (cockatoos) flying overhead; nearby were several green parrots with beautiful yellow necklaces around their throats. Never had I seen a more vividly blue expanse of sky, and I thought immediately of Mama and her love for "October's bright blue skies." The Perth neighborhood looked much like an American suburb, yet so very different — from the profusion of unusual flowers like kangaroo paws and banksia to the different large and little creatures on this continent. America and WA alike had plenty of dogs and cats, but never had I seen parrots, galahs, koalas, and kangaroos in Alabama or Oklahoma.

Bob and I quickly realized why Perth is known as the world's third windiest city, just behind Chicago and Auckland. More importantly, we quickly became aware of the lostness of the vast majority of Perth's people and their utter lack of understanding of a heart need for the security found only through faith in Christ. Bob and Gerry Covington helped orient us to Aussie life and patterns of thinking, especially its language differences. English was spoken everywhere, but we needed to learn "Australian English," a whole new variety. "G'day (dye), Mate" was the traditional hello. "Yes" sounded somewhere between "Yeh" and "Yeah." Instead of someone "getting under my skin," it was someone "up my nose." You didn't see it raining "cats and dogs," but rather "raining houses." If someone is "off their rocker," he is "out of his tree," and chickens were "chooks." If a person was a stranger, you might say, "I don't know him from a bar of soap." Then, there are the flies. Phillip, one of our new neighbors, grinned as he told us, "WA is great for upper-arm aerobics; you get a workout just waving away flies." How right he was. You could buy hats in any market prepared with little dangly bits of cork that shooed away the flies. The first day friends took us to see the Outback, the only unappetizing and shocking moment came when Bob accidentally swallowed a fly. He quickly discovered they are hard to cough up.

We visited a Perth church our first Sunday and observed both the familiar and not-so-familiar. At every church, however, there was one commonality: the after-service "cuppa" time, when everyone lingered and had tea and biscuits (cookies, in Australian) and visited together as they bonded. We loved it. Girrawheen Baptist Church, in the thriving suburb next to Ballajura (our target area), would be one of our sponsoring churches, and their two pastors, Rex and Fred (formerly a missionary in Papua, New Guinea) became our fast friends and steadfast encouragers. On several occasions we had baptismal services using their baptistry.

Where to start? First, we needed a house in Ballajura, a suburb with no Baptist church. Clipper Drive became our new address, and the neat little bungalow we rented had a small backyard carpeted with flowers. To a person, the neighbors were friendly and thought it fun to have "Yanks" in their neighborhood. Aussies got a kick out of our "foreign accents," and would frequently grin and say, "Just talk, Mate. We want to hear your accent." Anyone from America, even someone from Alabama in the Deep South, was a Yank. We adjusted quickly — and just as quickly learned that we were the "Grandma and Grandpa" on the block. Practically every day, we would have little visitors saying, "Hey, Bob, hey, Rosalie. We have come to visit." It took us all two years to get used to children addressing us by our first names. The titles "Mr." and "Mrs." were evidently foreign to their vocabularies — but then, nearly everything was casual and laid back in Australia. The most important time of year was "holidays," and the year progressed from one "hollie" to another. Clipper Drive was only ten minutes from a game reserve, so we felt doubly blessed to be surrounded by beauty. Our shipment from Manila took months to arrive, so we did a bit of camping out and making do in our new house. My faithful little blue enamel cup had negotiated yet another move; I wish I had kept track of how many moves it made.

Nearly everything had a shortened name. Truck drivers were truckies, postmen were posties, and on the list went. That first Christmas in Perth, Bob was startled when asked, "Well, how many prezzies did you get from your rellies this Chrissie?" Perth has to be one of the world's most beautiful cities, with a pristine skyline, the Swan River flowing nearby, and a quaint, old-world, downtown shopping area brimming with atmosphere. Restaurants and coffee/cappuccino bars abounded, and even the city's atmosphere gave off a laid-back ambiance. Restaurant names were fun and unique, like Gobble and Go, and Horsefeathers. We quickly learned that "tea" is the evening meal and "supper" is snacks, while "teatime" is having a "cuppa."

Bob and I began planning a church start even before settling in our Clipper Drive house. The home missions committee handed us a list of four families with Baptist ties who had moved into our area. This was our map for a beginning. Pastor Rex from Girrawheen Church introduced us to the administrator at the local elementary school; to our delight, we learned that when it came time to meet together for worship, we would be able to use the school's facilities. That solved one problem before it began. The first week of October, Bob and I visited each of the names on our list, introduced ourselves, and invited them to our house for a cuppa. Thus began what would become Ballajura Baptist Church. To be perfectly honest, we had little to do with its beginnings. It was just being in the right place at the right time in God's timing.

Coral and Ian Anderson, emigrants from England, were on the list, and instantly captivated our hearts with their interest and zeal. The Casses, Joneses, Barnetts, and others came. Most did not know any of the others. The first hour or so, our little core group seemed a bit reticent and hesitant, but that didn't last long. By the end of that first evening, you'd have thought everyone had been buddies for years. They also came with very divergent ideas of what "church" meant, so this new challenge was one we attempted to embrace and then glean from each a different idea of what might work in Ballajura. We weren't there to plant an American-style church; we wanted this to be uniquely theirs. The group agreed to meet in our home each week for Bible study and prayer, and to seek God's way for starting a church.

Our group agreed that the image of Christians wasn't exactly what we wished for in Australia. WA had affluence aplenty, but also apathy — as well as many who felt downright antipathy at what they freely called "Bible-bashers."

Bob and I had been some twenty years in five different countries, and never before had we felt any more keenly the need for prayer. Our own wisdom and discernment fell short of the task. We immediately wrote letters to build a prayer team, seeking twenty-five people who would commit themselves to prayer for a church beginning in Ballajura. Daddy was the first one on the list, the man who knew so much about prayer because it was so much a part of him. Within a few weeks, we had a small army of "pray-ers," a total of twenty-five who committed to pray. By November, our group consisted of seventeen adults and eleven children (who sounded like many more!) meeting in our small living room — studying, planning, and praying in earnest.

Each in our group headed out to survey Ballajura and meet our neighbors. Children gave an entrée to most of our neighbors. The little ones had come to visit us, and now we visited *their* homes and asked what they might think about a church in our community. The answers were about as varied as the people. This was not a homogeneous group to begin with. There were old-time Aussies, but our neighbors also included people from Russia, Italy, Ukraine and Burma. Ken and Pauline Roberts were seasoned Baptists from South Africa and a stable, steadying influence. (In addition, Pauline made the best curry I've ever tasted.) Perth was a bit of many nations, but there was one commonality that struck us: The heart needs were the same, and the lostness of the vast majority very apparent. Our little group continued to expand, and soon our house was simply not large enough. We first met for what we called "worship rehearsal" in one of the classrooms at Ballajura Elementary School, and the first Sunday was exciting. Two Bible classes were part of the beginning. I taught the children, and Bob the adults. Right from the beginning, we targeted officially birthing the church by April of the next year.

Christmas presented a wonderful community outreach opportunity, and we planned a Christmas by Candlelight to meet in the open area of the school, inviting the Ballajura community. Christmas carols, a candle-light service, the Christmas story, and refreshments were a hit with the community. Over 200 people attended. In fact, it became a Ballajura Christmas tradition. When I was putting a Christmas star wreath on our front door, four-year-old Allen, one of the neighbors, asked me about it. I told him this was for Christmas, when we celebrated the birth of Jesus the Savior. He looked puzzled and responded, "Rosalie, I don't know the Christmas story." Well, he heard it that day.

That first Christmas in WA was one we've never forgotten. December 3 was set as our first "worship rehearsal," and Alice, Jay and Carl came to spend Christmas with us. Carl fell in love with kangaroos and even got to feed a few. He learned to ask for Oat Bubbles (Australia's Cheerios), and we quickly realized Carl was the smartest little fellow who had ever been born. Each Christmas of our missionary career was unique, and this first one in Perth was certainly no exception. We sang "Jingle Bells" and saw Father Christmases on all the streets of Perth while enjoying ninety-degree weather Down Under. When we said goodbye to Alice and crew in early January, we could honestly echo the Australian expression for a rough time: "Me heart is in me heels."

There was no time to wallow in self-pity, however, for there was exciting work to be done. With our core group, we planned Sunday School and how we would officially "organize" as a church in 1990. Sunday School planning was a challenge to what diplomatic skills I wished I had. It was a foreign concept to many of them, so planning was really starting from scratch. Child discipline in Australia was certainly foreign to what I had always thought it to be. There were many times I had to bite my tongue (hard) and say nothing. Nevertheless, we slowly assembled a group of teachers and tried to work in teams. I brought out the old faithful flannelgraph stories, and, like children everywhere, the little ones loved them.

Our group had musical talent. Colleen Campione was wonderful playing guitar and singing, plus she had a winning personality that easily drew people's attention. The good Lord sent Warrick Platt (son of our friend Bob, the head of WA's home mission committee) to direct music. Our first Sunday, there were twenty-five adults and thirteen children; our little core group was excited. Amazingly, our numbers grew each Sunday, and more classes and more space were needed. The next step was to have worship service in the school library; it was a perfect setting. We visited, the people came, and friends told their friends.

Bob and I enjoyed the friendly greetings we began receiving as we visited in the neighborhood. One evening, we were walking home and saw the parents of a little fellow who had visited our house. They recognized us and called out, "Hey, Mate, come in for a beer!" We went in and had a cuppa (tea) and two hours of great fellowship. Sometimes in WA, a little child would lead them. One little girl in Sunday School told me, "Nobody in my family believes in God, but I'll help them." Sharp young Jodi, badly handicapped and confined to a wheelchair, pulled me aside one day and said, "Rosalie, you are a lovely girl." That brave girl melted my heart.

The women seemed eager to have more fellowship, so we began a Bible study at our house. They enjoyed "American" snacks, but much more the time of growing in understanding of God's love. These ladies' backgrounds and nationalities were as different as their ages and interests, but all had heart needs that beat to the same rhythm. I learned so much about human nature and compassion just by being part of these remarkable ladies. Liz was older than I and lived up Clipper Drive from us. She told me, "When I grew up, people didn't talk about spiritual things. It was too personal. But now," and her blue eyes sparkled, "it's different since I know the Lord in my heart. It's like I've been shopping and found a bargain and want to tell my friends about it!" Liz and her husband, Fred, were two of the first people that we baptized.

Tony and Jenny Millman, our next-door neighbors, were always available for a cuppa or some advice for newcomers who needed to know how to get around. Leslie and Shaun, their young sons, became two of our earliest Sunday School kids. We went to our first neighborhood "barbie" at their house for a cookout. I also learned some cooking hints from Jenny, making me wish I had found a cookbook that gave 100 ways to prepare squash. Jenny and Tony were helping us with arranging some things in our house one afternoon, when Bob and I disagreed quite noticeably about where to put this or what room might work best for that. Jenny listened a bit and her face lighted up as she clapped her hands in delight, "Oh, super! The Hunts are having a domestic!" We grinned, and ever since have talked about how to have a domestic the Aussie way.

Our core group was mostly made up of young couples, and the Lord providentially arranged an array of talents from music, to finances, to teaching, to relating to people. Our post-service cuppa time was a super bonder, and young couples got to know each other when their children attended Sunday School together. The little group was growing every Sunday. I wrote frequent updates to our prayer team in America to let them know how God was answering their prayers. We found it a real serendipity to meet new Chinese friends Down Under and use Mandarin again. The Stephen Changs, in a sister church, were stalwart prayer supporters and told us of the some-8,000 Chinese students in Perth and of opportunities to share the gospel with them.

A significant bit of time was necessary each week to correspond with friends and new believers in other countries where we had served. Frequently, we would hear from former students and coworkers and especially loved news from Huan, as we followed his burgeoning career after completing college and graduate school. Huan began traveling in some of his work, and was involved in various government projects and learning yet another language as he spent much time in Mexico. And Gerald, our student whom Bob had baptized in the South China Sea, realized his dream of studying in America. He received a scholarship to Auburn and spent his first Christmas in America with Jody in Boaz, staying at the Faucetts' house and being welcomed like one of the family. Gerald wrote a letter that we still cherish. In it, he caught us up on his exciting new experiences in a free country and said, "I really don't know how to thank you enough. I always say that it's Lord's blessing for me to know Him. And it's Lord's blessing for me to know you who helped me to find the way to our Father." Gerald ended by adding, "I pray for you and your new church. God bless you!"

The women's Bible group grew and kept me busy preparing. I loved to hear them chatting, smiling to myself as I noted how much more alike we are than different — no matter race, background or ethnicity. Rita had a contagious personality and a deep, spontaneous laugh. She came from a Catholic background and seemed puzzled her first two or three times as several women spoke of their personal relationship with Christ and how they talked to Him. Then one Tuesday, she came bouncing in and said, "It finally dawned on me! I was standing at the kitchen sink the other day, just thinking about talking to God and knowing Him, and I thought, *Hey — I don't need to go through somebody else to pray for me. I can go straight to God and talk to Him myself!*" Rita gave her infectious grin and finished, "That's just what I did, right there at my sink!"

Revathy grabbed my heart the first day we stopped by her home to meet the family. Revathy and Rasoo were immigrants from India, and initially, she was very hesitant to talk to these strangers from America. I went back several times to assist her with English and help her feel comfortable. Her young sons, Alan and Julian, wanted to come to the new Sunday School, and Revathy agreed to bring them. Revathy told me about the rampant prejudice she had encountered at the factory where she found work, and her eyes filled with tears when telling about her first interview at a Perth factory. When she walked into the office of the one in charge of hiring, the woman took one look at her and snarled, "Get out of here, you black bitch. We don't want the likes of you here." Those words cut Revathy to the core. She had no choice, however; she must keep applying. She had to work. A factory job was located, but Revathy felt isolated and rejected. Thank God, when she began bringing the boys to Sunday School, she found herself warmly and openly welcomed, and it was balm applied to her wounded heart. Revathy told me of the witch doctor her mother had paid in the village in India to protect her from evil spirits. As we studied and prayed together, she came to understand that a loving God accepted her without reservation and without bribes. Bob had the wonderful privilege of baptizing her during a service at one of our member's backyard pools.

To our own surprise, we were able to have the official opening of Ballajura Baptist Church about six months after the first gathering of a handful of interested people in our living room. Bob and I were as excited as children the night prior to our March 11 opening; it made us remember the long ago (*very* long ago) anticipation on Christmas Eve when we thought morning would never get there. That Sunday, we prepared our cuppa time, anticipating maybe 120 people. However, first one new face arrived, and then still another family walked in. All our regulars were there, and they were joined by families we had never seen before. Colleen and I welcomed a double number of little ones for our children's time. She played the guitar and I the Autoharp as we taught the children our little theme song: "I am special, there's just one me, God has a special plan for me." We were only seven people shy of 200 that opening service of Ballajura Baptist, and Bob and I were as happy as chickens with a beautiful new brood of chicks (chooks).

Ballajura Sunday School quickly grew to eight classes, and just before our two years were complete, the Baptist Union reported that Ballajura had Western Australia's largest Sunday School. We could scarcely believe our ears; it certainly wasn't because of anything we had accomplished. God was at work in the suburbs, and we were there to see what He did.

Each baptismal Sunday was a treasured moment, and when elderly Ern and Meg Avery were baptized, I knew my little blue enamel cup was flowing over the rim. This couple, in their eighties, had emigrated from England and found Christ in Australia. I could not watch without happy tears as Bob found a way to baptize Ern without endangering the hole in his neck that allowed him to operate his mechanical speech box. (Ern was a cancer survivor with no vocal chords.) Ballajura had a wealth of "firsts" for us, and our next letter to the team of "pray-ers" was filled with gratitude for what God had accomplished through the prayers of His people.

We basically spent our final year consolidating the gains the Lord had provided and continuing to grow. Russell, one of our core group, brought a young nineteen-year-old who was seriously considering suicide. His father was violently opposed to "Bible-bashers," but so desperate was this young man that he wanted to find hope anywhere he could. He came, and then he came again. Realizing the answer for him was Christ, he invited the Lord into his heart. The church rallied round the new believer and became a solid support base for him.

Bob and I had begun early in our months in Perth with what we dubiously named "casserole evangelism." I know for sure that God has a sense of humor. I have lots of interests and hobbies, and even some things I do pretty well. Cooking is not one of them. Nonetheless, we quickly realized that our best way to get to know families was through one-on-one contact and visiting. After all, what better way than over food? We began having a different family three nights each week, and I wore out those three casserole recipes: chicken, lasagna, and turkey spaghetti.

We were amazed at how well everyone ate and how appreciative they were. Not only appreciative — they were never in a hurry to leave. Bob liked to go to bed quite early, but he learned to adapt a bit, because his early was not the usual Aussie early. Arthur from England was a delightful elderly man who loved the fellowship he discovered at Ballajura Baptist. Arthur told us, "My word, I have never known such a feeling of belonging since I found Christ. Why, now," he beamed, "His love is in here," and patted his heart.

Several Burmese believers began attending. To a person, they loved to explain that they were spiritual descendants of Adoniram Judson, and I marveled to realize how much more these lovely people knew about their missions heritage than did most Americans. Sunday School was a special challenge for me each week — for most of the children had never been in Sunday School before and knew very little about the Bible, even the simplest and most familiar of stories. When I was telling about Jesus and His disciples 2,000 years ago as they traveled and learned about helping others, one little girl asked in amazement, "How old is Jesus *now?!*"

Jody visited during our second September in Perth, and he, too, fell in love with the Aussies. We were thrilled to be able to go to the southern tip of Western Australia and stand at the spot where the Indian Ocean and Southern Ocean converge. On the way, we visited a dolphin research center set up next to the Indian Ocean. It was not a busy day, and the scientist in charge let us put on waders and go out into the water to feed fish to the dolphins. It gave me a special thrill to see that smiling face right up close, just a foot or so from my face. It felt like the dolphin was smiling his thanks for the tasty fish I gave him. He gamboled around a bit, then came back for more.

Ministry in Perth was a bit of "whatever thy hand findeth to do, do it with thy might." Some days our house felt like the Hunt Counseling Center, and we set aside a special little room where people could come and share their problems and hearts. I began giving piano lessons again after about a ten-year hiatus, simply because there were so few teachers. Then the school allowed me to come once a week and have "Scripture Class," teaching the Bible as literature, and I jumped at the opportunity. Who would have ever thought to be able to do this in such a secular society?

As our two years were drawing to an end, our hearts started hurting all over again. We had loved every rich experience that had landed on our doorstep for these two years and had lasting friendships with so many special people. (We were thrilled to have several of them later visit us in America, and we still maintain contact with a number. One of "our" young Aussie kids is now a missionary in Bulgaria.) During the final months in Ballajura, our church had a weekend camp, and it was a spiritual high point that left indelible imprints on many hearts — including our own. We had mixed emotions as we helped the church select a pastor search committee and make plans to buy property in order to build. Our last service in Ballajura was a "laying on of hands," as our Aussie friends gathered around us to pray and send us off to be *their* missionaries in South Asia and the Pacific. My little blue enamel cup could not hold all the overflow. Here we were once more, leaving a piece of our hearts in yet another land. Bob and I decided that hearts must be like livers, which can reproduce — for pieces of our hearts were now in many places.

A baptism in Manila, 1989

A baptism in Manila, 1989

TWENTY-TWO

DOWN UNDER TO OVER THERE
1991-1993

During the turbulent years in pre-Communist China, Mama often commented that things were "consistently inconsistent." That was still true, for we were embarking on yet another adventure in a new setting. My dear little blue enamel cup was on the move again. We spent the month of April getting "oriented" to India, which would be a major part of our work with South Asia Pacific Itinerant Mission (SAPIM). Bob and I joined five other couples, who also lived out of a couple of suitcases and were likewise headquartered in Singapore. We had a room and a closet there, where we kept whatever earthly goods had gone with us to our new assignment. Now we were missionary nomads. This was a huge change but an exciting challenge. A year's furlough was due, but the month in India made us eager to get involved in opportunities there.

Bob and I arrived in Madras in southern India to discover it was like stepping into a story about the third world. We landed at two in the morning, dead-tired, only to find that the hotel had given our room to another traveler. Our introduction to India was a three-hour night on cots in the business office, where we were rousted from sleep at 5:30 so the staff could use the machine. Leaving that morning, Bob and I headed to Bangalore Baptist Hospital and our mission guest house to begin learning about life and ministry in exotic India.

India presented a whole new set of customs and mores to learn, one of which was to never point your feet in the direction of another person — a deadly insult. I suffered from severe edema in the feet and legs, and propping up my feet was one of the only ways to relieve it. That first morning in the airport, I automatically propped them up with a sigh of relief. A man seated nearby saw those feet pointing in his direction, and if looks could kill, I would have been gone on the spot. I put my feet down with alacrity.

In India, food was often served on a large leaf or a simple plate, with no utensils other than your hands. It was considered terribly rude to eat with your left hand. For we lefties, it was a lifelong habit that was difficult to break. Bob elbowed me time and again, or cleared his throat portentously if he saw me eating with my left hand. It took a lot of throat clearing. However, there was nothing either of us could change about the level of spice in most dishes. To call them hot and spicy was a vast understatement.

First stop was Bangalore, the *cooler* city, where the stifling heat and humidity were down one or two degrees — maybe to 102. Coming from wintertime in Perth to India was a shock. Nonetheless, the mission guest house was comfortable and located right next to Bangalore Baptist Hospital, where Dr. Rebekah Naylor had been making a huge difference in lives for long years. Rebekah and I loved recalling stories her father (many years president of Southwestern Baptist Theological Seminary) and mine used to tell us about their seminary years. The two seminarians drove together on weekends from Fort Worth to their church fields in

Oklahoma, and now their daughters were together half a world away in India, reminiscing about those weekends.

I found a tailor to make several *saris* to wear when speaking and working in churches or villages. Actually, it was two tailors — elderly identical twins who worked together and were fascinating to watch at their trade. Nonetheless, I found that wearing a *Punjabi*, with its pants and tunic top, was more comfortable for an occidental in a hurry. Our first assignment was in the mega city of Hyderabad, working at the city's largest church with Pastor G. Samuel and his redoubtable wife, Eve. We worked in tandem with Marge and Von Worten, South Asia Pacific Itinerant Mission veterans who kindly showed us the ropes. Marge "draped" me in a new *sari* that first Sunday morning, an endeavor that had me dripping wet with perspiration before she was half finished.

As soon as we arrived at the church, Eve Samuel took one look at me and imperiously motioned with her hand, "Come!" I obediently went, and Eve quickly re-wrapped me to her satisfaction. All of us went to the vast new sanctuary, still open at the back where construction was not complete. Eve calmly informed me: "You are to do the morning prayer." I looked startled, and she motioned me forward, "Just go with G. Samuel. He will tell you when to pray." With scant warning, I was propelled to the platform to pray. The building held at least 1,500 people, and bright spotlights focused on those seated on the platform. By this time, I was already soaked with perspiration, but what do you do? Grin and bear it. In spite of the heat and the language barrier, it was an incredible service, one of those where you feel the presence of the Spirit of God. I could not understand the language, yet I was moved to tears more than once. Immediately after the service, several university students came to Bob and me. One of them served as spokesman, asking Bob, "Sahib, you are a holy man. Will you pray for us, that God will bless us?" Bob attempted to explain that *he* was not holy. Not deterred, the students all removed their sandals, for they wanted to come to prayer in humility, standing before a holy man who would intercede for them. The two of us wept with them as Bob prayed that God would bless and direct their lives.

This particular day in Hyderabad remains vividly imprinted on my mind — not just because of the remarkable church and believers, but also due to a phone call from Jody to our hotel room that evening. We sat down to catch our breaths after a jam-packed day of meetings and fellowship. Opening our copy of "The Sunday Times of India," an English newspaper, we had a relaxing break looking through the "matrimonials" that filled about four pages. The various castes of India were listed in groups, seeking possible mates among others of the same caste. I looked at Bob and inquired, "Guess we ought to save this for Jody? He can't seem to find the right one." Bob grinned and replied, "Why not?" About that time, the phone rang. It was Jody. As soon as we got caught up on the latest news from America, I told him, "We are saving the Hyderabad newspaper's matrimonial ads for you." He laughed and responded, "Well, I *may* not need it; let me tell you about the girl I met last night at the Miss Maryland pageant. She was the emcee and a former Miss Maryland." It was Lori Windsor — and, sure enough, Lori was to become our treasured daughter-in-law. (I wish there was room to tell their story, but that's for another time.)

For a week, we taught pastors and church leaders at a conference at the Hyderabad church. Bob taught the Book of Romans and other topics, while I led groups in self-esteem and speech. The pastors particularly enjoyed learning about preparing and delivering messages. Never in any country had I found such attentive listeners. At "break" time, we did exercises. Everyone enjoyed "Head, Shoulders, Knees and Toes." Try that wearing a *sari* and working in 100-degree weather. (Several days the electricity went off, which meant the electric fans couldn't work.) One morning, I spoke to the group about China; one elderly man was so touched that he wept when he told me, "I didn't know until today that an *American* could be sentimental."

G. Samuel was a man who loved impossible goals. "It is with such goals," he said, "that we can truly see God at work." The Hyderabad church — which had a ten-year goal of 100 new plants — had already organized thirty-two daughter churches, and 100 church planters held an all-night prayer meeting once a month. The pastors attended the whole night from

6 p.m. to 6 a.m. — herein lay their source of power. We were in awe of this remarkable leader and his vision.

One day, we reached the church at 6 a.m. and returned to the hotel at 10:30 that night. Bob and I visited homes in several villages and met recent converts and others who were eager inquirers. We were amazed at similarities we were seeing to the actual New Testament church. We first held a service in the home of Hindu converts who were new believers. Their four beautiful children captured our hearts with their soulful brown eyes. Bob preached on "Blessings Bring Responsibilities," and everyone sat around on the packed dirt floor with their eyes glued on his face. Some of the hottest food I've ever eaten anywhere was in that little home. The only beverage to cool off the palate was un-chilled Pepsi. (Just picture the sizzle going down the throat.) Okra was a conflagration. We then went to the little home next door, where only the young wife was a Christian. She was eager for us to "pray a blessing on our home."

Our impression of the little roads in the village remains crystal clear. The pollution was so appalling that it made Manila look clean. Furthermore, the density of population put China's crowding to shame. Passing along by a river, we could see people bathing in the muddy water, right next to submerged water buffaloes. Then, next to them were women washing clothes and spreading them out on grass to dry. We were deep in a different world, one that stepped back in time.

In the various village services, everyone sits cross-legged on the floor. My poor occidental body couldn't handle long periods sitting like that, nor could I point my feet in the direction of anyone and thus insult them. I still remember the body aches after repeated days in the villages. Hyderabad Church not only conducted many of these village ministries, but also worked each week with slum children. There were thousands of them in Hyderabad, with no one else to give them any attention.

Bob and I next spent an unforgettable week out of Bombay on the Arabian Sea at a tent conference for pastors and leaders. My mind's eye can still see those tents and the beauty of the sun glistening on the waters of the sea. Our tent was fairly large — the only lighting a single 25-watt bulb hanging down on a cord. The public baths/restrooms were about a half block away, and we definitely needed our torches (flashlights) to walk along the path. Bob and I had been warned of the prevalence of cobras — and it was an eerie feeling, wondering what we might encounter on our next step. We also slept under mosquito nets out of necessity, and there were no fans to stir the air. Those nights linger in memory.

Two wonderful recollections revolve around our evening meal on the beach each night and the loving pastors and church leaders in our classes. Each evening meal was served in a tent on the beach, and the highlight was *naan* (baked round bread) from an open oven. For the first time in our lives, we could get all the fresh *naan* we wanted, piping hot from an oven. An even brighter memory is the faces of the people in our classes, drinking in every session. I've never encountered more appreciative, eager listeners; they blessed *us*. They were pure in heart, their faith both simple and deep.

Bombay assaulted our eyes and noses. Shacks lined long blocks of sidewalk in the city. People were bathing in little tin pans on the walkways. When the car would stop for a light, beggar children came to the windows, pleading, "Mem Sahib, one rupee, just one rupee." Our hearts were wrenched each time. At the conference in the city that week, there were more attentive listeners. Two of the pastors' wives asked me on the last night to tell them how to be a support of their husbands. They worked six days a week as nurses and wanted to learn how to be effective witnesses. Next, they asked me to tell them how to reach people and start a church. Ask *me?* I felt ashamed. They were thrilled that I would pray for them. Their deference humbled me.

Our furlough in the States was another period out of time. We lived in Huntsville, Alabama, in the missionary house of Weatherly Heights Baptist Church, Alice and Jay's church. There couldn't have been a better spot: We were able at a moment's notice to hop in the car and, in two minutes, be with our two grandchildren and spoil them all we wished. I thrived on hugs from three-year-old Carl and chances to spoil five-month-old Eric. Granny Ora and Ho Shien Sun were less than an hour away. Both were eighty-six, but in quite good health. We loved spending quality time with them, fitting it in around all the conferences, camps, and world missions gatherings. Meantime, Jody was working all hours with his law firm in DC, but we still had opportunities to visit with him and get to know his lovely new friend, Lori. For her part, Lori got to know Alabama pretty well that year. Sure enough, just prior to our return to Singapore, Jody and Lori announced their engagement, looking toward a December wedding.

Soon, it was back to the Far East, doing itinerant missions in Singapore, Malaysia, and India. We lived out of our suitcases, never really in control of our schedules or circumstances, but headquartered in Singapore. We loved that city/state, so clean and beautiful. Mixed with all the other languages and dialects, we heard a lot of Mandarin, making us feel right at home. Bob and I began with a week of meetings with area missionaries in Pattaya, Thailand. It was *déjà vu* for Bob, because that was where, twenty-two years earlier, he had met Ken Marak, the young pastor from Assam that we loved and prayed for. We tried to keep up our exercising, no matter what country we were in. Cultural contrasts hit our eyes every day. In Penang, they ranged from women in shorts to Muslim ladies wearing full covering, all black and even their eyes covered. They had to be led around by their husbands. Each time I saw one, I thought yet again, *Life isn't fair.*

We spent several months in Alor Setar, in northern Malaysia, attempting to establish a collegiate ministry with students at the university just out of the city. The university's Muslim leadership was extremely rigid, and we were only allowed on campus two times, both times accompanied by campus officials. Any work with students, meeting and developing relation-ships, had to be off-campus. Time was the greatest obstacle. We were able to meet several interested students and have meetings near campus, but their time was at a premium. We loved each meeting and the opportunity of pouring into these young adults. Inevitably, about the time Bob would get in the middle of a message, just across the road would come the loud and somber Muslim call to prayer. The Muslim call to prayer, broadcast everywhere five times each day, was pervasive — and depressing. This was the first culture we had experienced where Sunday was just like every other day of the week. Hindu and Muslim influences were strong.

There was also a strong Buddhist influence. Even in the parking lot of our apartment complex, there was a Buddhist shrine. A young Christian couple, Soon and Hwee, were wonderful in helping us get oriented to Alor Setar and occasionally translating when we were communicating with those who could not speak Mandarin. Each morning, our downstairs neighbor burned incense to her ancestors before her little shrine. The lingering odor of incense wafted me back to my childhood in China and the ever-present sense of hopelessness that odor evoked. We were thrilled, however, with the response to the gospel of our landlord's daughter, Sherece. She knocked at our door one morning to tell us she had been reading her Bible and saw God's hand in her life. Sherece was radiant as she told us, "Your coming here was no accident. I am telling my parents what I am learning, and I'm praying with them." She was like a bright ray of light in a land with so much darkness.

During our entire time with SAPIM, back home in Alabama, Catherine, our sister-in-law, was our angel of mercy. She helped Daddy in so many ways, assisting with shopping, running errands, welcoming him for meals, and, in general, making it possible for us to do our work. Knowing both of our parents were well cared for, thanks to Catherine and Joe right there helping, allowed us to remain on the field.

Our time in Malaysia had more bright spots than we had first discerned. We occasionally drove to Penang to speak at the Baptist seminary and loved passing long miles of rubber trees, with cunning little pots hung on the sides of each tree, catching the latex as it dripped from the trunk into the pots. I had one unusual translation experience at the seminary. A young professor translated my English into Malay, but I frequently had to explain to her in Mandarin what I had said in English, so she could then translate into Malay. It was something of a three-ring circus.

There were other opportunities to speak in Mandarin in the handful of Baptist churches in the Alor Setar area. Often the meetings were on Saturday, so Saturday seemed like our former Sundays. One Saturday morning, there were six professions of faith in one of the churches, a highly unusual number for ministry in that area. Then an opportunity opened for

Bob to go into northern India for a period of training local pastors. His letters were full of unusual and rich experiences.

Bob and the Wortens were conducting seminars in northern India for most of the fall, and I thrived on news from the letters Bob wrote when he could find a way to mail them. Most of the seminars/training conferences for pastors and leaders were in remote villages; Bob's descriptions were graphic, as he wrote of no running water, no electricity, no bathroom or bathing facilities. In one October letter, he recounted, "My bath this week has been a bucket of water and a hole in the floor. But … that's better than most of them have." On October 13, he wrote, "Living with the people is something else! I've already been sick with a stomach bug twice, so my stomach feels real flat!" One morning's letter recounted, "Out walking to the seminary spot, we saw a body laid in front of a little store by the path. It was wrapped in dingy white cloth, with two patties of cow dung at the head holding sticks of burning incense. Passersby were putting coins and small bills beside the body to help pay for the funeral." He concluded, "Our hearts were wrung with pity at such hopelessness." Another letter revealed a different kind of worry as Bob explained, "Never, NEVER have I seen so many mosquitoes. Even when we are covered with spray, they still bite! I must sleep under a net, which makes it even hotter."

Difficult as the conditions were, Bob's joy in his experiences just popped out of his letters. One day he wrote, "Von and I went to a slum area to preach. The tiny little hut held twelve men, six women, and a dozen children. What a unique time of worship. They have nothing but are just radiant." He ended by explaining, "Our messages were translated into both Tamil and Hindi." Bob was next at a seminary in a slightly cooler area and reported that for a change, he was not having daily headaches. He wrote, "Fifty percent of the people are Sikhs up here and wear colorful turbans. And," he remarked, "you can get a haircut for sixty-five cents!"

Bob and the Wortens flew from Chandigarh to Delhi. Marge and Von were going on to a separate assignment, so Jim and Carolyn McAtee met Bob in Delhi, and the three of them made the fourteen-hour train trip to Gorakhpur. Upon arrival, they checked into the city's only hotel, which

Bob described as, "Dirty, dirty, with lots of bugs!" The three of them next traveled several more hours into the interior of northern India and stayed in a pastor's home on the mission compound. In actual fact, the McAtees had the only spare room in the house, and Bob slept on the semblance of a cot in a nearby shed. He didn't mince many words in his description of the shed, writing, "Seeing is believing. Mosquitoes are serious up here — no choice but to use a net." There followed details of his first night: "I was thankful for my torch. There was a single dangling light bulb, faint light even when it was on. Turn it off, and the blackness is thicker than a thousand midnights down in the cypress swamp. I had no more than settled down on the low cot when I heard a bit of a rustling sound and then felt a faint movement against one of my feet. Visions of the cobras I had both seen and heard about popped into my mind, and I grabbed the torch and shined its light on my toes. There, gleaming in the darkness, were two sets of eyes belonging to a pair of tiny mice, each attempting to nibble my toes through the mosquito net. Heaving a sigh of relief, I simply turned off the torch and told the mice, 'Sweet dreams.' "

Bob loved the Gorakhpur experience, mice notwithstanding, and fell in love with the faithful pastor and his four teenaged children. From this assignment, he and the McAtees headed back to Bangalore. By comparison, our Baptist compound there was like a Ritz Carlton. In November, he wrote of preaching to a particularly responsive group in the area, followed by seminars in four different locations, teaching during the day and preaching at night. It was exhausting and exhilarating all at the same time. He later wrote, "I'm sleeping in bed #13 since October 1. I guess you could call it sleeping." He described his current location, "We are having classes out in the countryside. The villages have tiny houses made of cow dung and with palm branches on top." He went on, "I just saw a cow with its head in a front door. Cows here are everywhere and do whatever they *want* to do."

Their next assignment was the city of Hubli, some 400 kilometers northwest of Bangalore. He was matter-of-fact about conditions by this point, saying, "Just as we started the service, the electricity went off, so we preached with a few candles flickering." Next stop was a campground where they taught and preached several more days, and Bob sadly wrote, "Never in my life have I seen such destitute conditions, or poverty of this magnitude." In his final letter of the India trip, he concluded, "During this one India itinerant time, I've slept in seventeen beds. Enough." My greatest regret was not being able to go with him because of teaching responsibilities. However, I didn't regret missing the mice and mosquitoes.

What a change — from India to America, and Jody and Lori's wedding. It was a wonderful December family affair in Mt. Airy, Maryland. It was also highly unusual, with the groom fainting three times during the ceremony — but that, too, is a story for another time. Even the paramedics ended up arriving on the scene. After their honeymoon, Jody and Lori came to Alabama, and in their wedding gear, Jody introduced Lori to his Alabama church family at a reception at First Baptist of Boaz. Bob and I returned to Singapore and SAPIM with a wealth of new experiences and stories to share.

January 1993 found us in a new assignment in Singapore. The only Mandarin-speaking couple in the Singapore mission was on furlough, so we were assigned to their Jurong Chapel — preaching, teaching and reveling in being able to use Mandarin all the time. Simon and Dawn were a young couple who took us in hand, paving our way to student contacts and also ministry with Mandarin-speaking sailors who came to port in Singapore. There were a number who had recently come out of mainland China, and it refreshed our hearts to be able to minister to them.

During our months there, the board requested that I be part of a missionary team to help the Indonesian Mission with long-range planning. Over a two-year period, I was able to go to Indonesia and meet with both missionaries and national leadership, assisting with information and ideas for long-range plans. The assignment was especially meaningful because I was finally able to meet people in Indonesia who knew and loved Aunt Grace, many of whom had worked with her. Ibu Mia had been eighteen years old when she began helping Aunt Grace with the beginnings of Baptist publications in Indonesia. Now she was an elder stateswoman, doing church evangelism in villages and working with Woman's Missionary

Union missions organizations for children.

As per usual, the consistency of inconsistency that Mama used to talk about appeared again. There was an emergency at International Baptist Church in Manila. Circumstances there had swiftly changed, and church leadership turned to the Foreign Mission Board for help, requesting, "Could you possibly send the Hunts back to IBC?" Here it came again. Change.

Founders Day at Ballajura Baptist Church, Western Australia

With Aunty Doctor and Pastor Sam at a village service near Bangalore, India

TWENTY-THREE

MANILA

1993-1994

This was something new — a change that involved the familiar. We knew and loved the people of IBC (International Baptist Church) and were grateful to be back, even if briefly. IBC had experienced a period of transition after we left in 1989, and the Foreign Mission Board had temporarily assigned a missionary to serve until the church could work out details for self-support. A problem suddenly developed that meant this missionary was asked to leave the field immediately. The church desperately wanted to regain stability and momentum. We were happy to step in and pick up the reins, helping the membership do damage control.

Our first Sunday back was the Easter Cantata; it was exhilarating to hear those magnificent voices again, concluding with Nolyn Cabahug singing "We Shall Behold Him." IBC had progressed in self-support efforts and purchased a pastor's residence, so a furnished house awaited us, along with resident cockroaches and other odd and sundry little creatures. Philippine cockroaches could hold their own anywhere in the world. As one skittered across the terrazzo floor, I wondered if it was a small mouse. I grinned upon recalling Mama's description of our house in Zhenjiang when we moved in back in 1947. Writing home, she reported, "I'm trying to get rid of the pesky bed bugs left over from when the Japanese soldiers occupied our house during the war." *OK, I reasoned, cockroaches are a big improvement over bed bugs.*

What a refreshing move this time — a move where we were able to start at full steam, already knowing our setting and the needs about us. From the beginning of this tenure, the working of God's Spirit in hearts was so evident that we could only thank Him for letting us be part of it. Of the new ones coming into the membership, the great majority came for baptism. Scarcely a Sunday passed without professions of faith. I stepped back in to lead at the preschool, although the actual leading was done by our wonderful head teacher, Rosie Rico, a young pastor's wife. My role was basically a figurehead to serve as a mentor/encourager to our staff and help put at ease the hearts of mamas from many countries who were wanting to provide the best for their little ones. Rosie was magical with the children, and I learned so much from her. Several times a week, I had music with each class, sometimes using the piano and often the Autoharp when singing with them. They loved "Our God Is So Great" and thrived on doing the motions. Another favorite was "Old MacDonald," and they chose animals for his "farm." I laughed the morning one bright little four-year-old suggested, "And on this farm he had a zebra — with a stripe stripe here, and a stripe stripe there!" Not to be outdone, another child piped up, "And on this farm he had a giraffe — with a long neck here, and a long neck there!"

Bob and I loved being able to pick up several former ministries and to renew friendships with Filipino coworkers in other parts of the Philippines. Ding and Josie Regacho had two little girls now, and when the family came to Manila for meetings, they would stay with us and we could spoil Jedidiah (JD) and Debbie, their adorable toddlers. Ding had already established a second church in their area near Baguio and was helping train a young pastor to work alongside him. Josie was active in the area WMU association. (Ding went on to found nine churches and mentor countless younger pastors.)

Bob and I endeavored to keep up exercise routines in spite of daunting heat and humidity. I jogged early in the mornings, and Bob worked out regularly at the gym of the Mandarin Hotel, just blocks from our house. He never met a stranger and had all sorts of interesting contacts there, including visitors he regularly invited to come worship at IBC. One evening, he met a blond-haired guy who looked like working out was part of his everyday routine. Bob smiled and stuck out his hand, saying, "Hi, I'm Bob. Are you visiting here?" The well-muscled gentleman smiled in return, "Yes, and I'm Chuck." When asked why he was in Manila, Chuck told him, "Oh, I'm here working with a film company." Accompanying Chuck was another beefy man who came every time Chuck worked out. Since we seldom saw a movie, the name "Chuck" didn't register with Bob. A few days later, Bob mentioned to a young coworker at IBC that he had met a new friend at the gym — a guy named Chuck. The coworker's eyes got big, and he quickly asked, "What's his last name?" Bob looked puzzled, then replied, "I think it's Norris." Bob's young friend looked amazed, "Oh, my! You've been working out with Chuck Norris. He's here in the Philippines making a movie!" (Sure enough, the well-muscled man who always accompanied Norris was the actor's bodyguard.) Bob and Chuck had a picture made together, and for years Bob has had fun showing it to young people in America. To a person, they said, "*You* know Chuck Norris?!"

Our family's newlyweds came to Manila in May, and we loved showing the sights and history of the Philippines to both of them. This was Lori's first time in Asia. The temperature was another revelation. Lori knew what hot meant, but never such intense heat and humidity all at once. We loved introducing them to our IBC family, and they, in turn, felt an instant rapport with the folk we called "the lovingest people in the Philippines." Jody also declared the international cuisine for which Manila was famous to be some of the best food he'd discovered anywhere. As for his mother (someone who only cooks when it is necessary), having access to reasonable and delicious food on every hand was a luxury indeed. From Japanese delicacies to Filipino *adobo* to exquisite green mango shakes, the choices were infinite and available. Thirty-five years later, our family conversations frequently allude to "the food of Manila." We managed a short trip to Hong Kong with Jody and Lori, and she quickly picked up on the allure of that one-of-a-kind city. In 1993, it was still a shopper's paradise, and our feet could have told a long story after just three days of exploring Hong Kong's treasures.

Back in Manila, Bob and I often had unexpected opportunities popping up. I met a number of young mothers whose children were in preschool. Some were connected with one of the many embassies in Manila, and others were there with their husbands who worked with businesses and various companies in the city. Milka from Japan came to church, bringing her two little ones to Sunday School. It was her first time ever in a worship service. She spoke very little English but was eagerly learning, telling us her two children came home from school talking about God and the Bible, and she wanted to learn as well. I was likewise thrilled the Sunday a young mother from mainland China walked through the door with her little girl who had told her about God. IBC's preschool had a unique ministry, and the teachers were winsome Christian women who shared their faith.

I was back teaching the high school-college Bible class again, and I loved those youth. Many were MKs (missionaries' kids) from Faith Academy, the school sponsored by several missions with boarding students from across the Philippines and other Asian countries. Several of the MKs discussed their issues about going places where they often felt different, looked different, and were bothered by people staring at them. I was thankful to be able to call on my own MK experiences as a child in China. We shared a common bond, and they knew it was safe to express their frustrations in the safety of our class.

In August, IBC held a special service we called a Solemn Assembly — a Sunday where the church family came together as one to confess, repent, worship, and dedicate ourselves individually and corporately. For several

Sundays, we studied about the elements of worship and commitment. On Solemn Assembly morning, the church was so crowded, we had to line the aisles with chairs and add more chairs outside in the narthex. The presence of God's Spirit was a palpable thing, and we concluded with Nolyn Cabahug and that powerful, resonant voice singing "Great Is Thy Faithfulness." From that day forward, this became IBC's theme song.

Members of our IBC congregation continually inspired and encouraged us. Pastor Elicanal, now retired and in ill health, loved relating stories. One evening at their home, he recounted, "Over sixty-two years ago, a young boy flying a kite followed his kite by its string and finally found it in a Bible school. He was invited in, and, for the first time in his life, heard the gospel. That changed his life." Pastor smiled as he concluded, "I was that little boy. Never underestimate the importance of Vacation Bible School."

There was a strong Chinese component in IBC's membership, and we formed close bonds with these people. Remedios Ng and her son, David, faithfully attended. Remedios came to Bob one day, quite concerned about an elderly relative of hers who was dying of cancer and already confined to a hospital. He had never trusted Christ, and Mrs. Ng feared he would die soon. "Please, Pastor," she asked, "would you come talk with him? He speaks no English, but I know he would at least listen to you if you spoke Mandarin with him." Bob quickly accompanied Remedios to the hospital and found Mr. Ahng in his private room, connected to all sorts of tubes and machines. Taking his hand, and speaking to him in Mandarin, Bob talked to him about the condition of his soul and presented the plan of salvation in straightforward terms. Bob prayed, and then Mr. Ahng, weak though he was, indicated that he wanted to trust Christ in the forgiveness of sins. The following day, Bob returned and found Mr. Ahng somewhat stronger. He asked, "Mr. Ahng, do you have peace in your heart?" The man nodded. "Yes!" came the unequivocal response. Bob continued, "You have trusted Christ as your Savior, and He lives in your heart?" Mr. Ahng quickly reiterated, "Oh, yes!"

The following Monday, Mr. Ahng died. His family asked that Bob conduct his memorial service as an occasion to present the gospel. Bob did exactly that, and three family members professed faith. That family, and the entire clan, became very supportive of IBC. Bob had the unusual experience that year of being able to baptize ten members of the same family at one service. It reminded us of the times in the New Testament where we had read of someone coming to Christ: "And his whole household," the passage would say. Now we actually saw this happen, and it was a revelation.

In August, Alice and Jody both called to tell us that Aunt Rhett was failing fast. They were at Bethea Home in Darlington where she was in the infirmary. "Mom," the children said, "Aunt Rhett will not be here long. She wanted us to call you." Immediately, I recalled the day Aunt Rhett had taken my hand and made of me the only request she ever voiced: "When I die, would you come be with me?" I told the children, "I'll be there quickly." Eli Sarmiento, our wonderful music director and the physician for Philippine Airlines, was able to get an emergency reservation. Two days later, I was walking into Aunt Rhett's room in the infirmary. She grasped my hand, and, giving her gentle little smile, said, "I knew you'd come."

Fortunately, the other bed in the semi-private room was vacant and the infirmary staff, who to a person adored Aunt Rhett, allowed me to sleep there so I wouldn't have to leave her side. Thursday morning, I was seated by Aunt Rhett's bed when she opened her eyes. She looked intently at me, then asked, "Have I died yet?" I smiled into her eyes, "No, Aunt Rhett. You are still right here with me." She took a deep breath and seemed to relax. Aunt Rhett spoke very little that day, but everything she said was clear and lucid. There was nothing frail about her mind. Mid-afternoon, she suddenly opened her eyes, looked at me and spoke, "I see the spaces." A chill of recognition raced through me. Those were the exact words Mama had spoken to me the day before she died. "What do you mean?" I asked quite gently, but she simply smiled and gave no answer. Aunt Rhett peacefully fell asleep early that evening, not seeming to be in pain.

I had called my cousin, Herb Wells, who was so attentive to Aunt Rhett and often came from North Carolina to talk family history with her. I needed to let him know she was failing rapidly. As we talked, I told him of the strange statement she had made about "spaces," and remarked how puzzled I was.

Herb immediately responded, "I think I may know the answer to that!" and he sounded excited. "Just last week when I was there, she was telling me how she had had repeated dreams about heaven and had seen the whole family sitting around the old dining table at their farmhouse at Tindal." Herb repeated Aunt Rhett's words to him, "I see the spaces, Herb, and all are taken, except the last one. That's for me." I finished that phone call weeping, for now I knew what Mama had seen those nearly ten years before.

I was holding Aunt Rhett's hand the next morning when she slipped into eternity. The children returned the following day, and all of us felt privileged to be at the service honoring this one who, though she never traveled outside the country even one time, did indeed travel around the world through her praying and giving. This remarkable woman, who never had more than a state pension, but who daily did handwork to raise money for missions, left $30,000 to the Lottie Moon Christmas Offering.

The following November, Bob and I had an unusual opportunity to observe some Baptist history when we attended the William Carey Bicentennial in Calcutta. We then spent much of the month working in various areas, especially around Bangalore in Karnataka state. We were amazed at the many ministries of Bangalore Hospital. Our missionary doctor, Rebekah Naylor, was quite a legend in her leadership, and her skills and compassion were inspiring. That hospital treated nearly 6,000 patients a month, and for those hospitalized, there was a daily visit from a chaplain. When they returned home, there were also follow-up visits by chaplains. It was a personal and remarkable means of evangelism.

Bob and I fell in love with Prakash, a young Christian pharmacist and his aunt, Aunty Doctor (as the villagers called Lakshmi), and her husband, Pastor Sam. This family invested their time and energy in village evangelism, working all around Bangalore — villages where intense poverty and lack of education were the norm, and where Aunty Doctor was their sole source of medical care. Those three were also their spiritual resource, as the three of them reached out to villagers steeped in darkness. Witchcraft and belief in demons were everywhere, leaving a trail of darkness in their wake. Many villagers had the concept of pastors and preachers as "holy men" and pled for them to pray and bless them. We went into the villages with Prakash and his family, and Aunty Doctor translated for Bob when he preached. As many as could crowd in would fill a little hut, and dozens more stood around outside. One ancient couple came with their three-year-old great-grandson. Both were more than ninety years old. We found it amazing that they had survived so long while living in such conditions. Their precious only great-grandchild had been dying of fever when Aunty Doctor got to the village the previous month. She had managed to treat the little boy, and his life was spared. Now the great-grandparents wanted to understand how they could personally know a God who was that strong and powerful. Bob and I sat in amazement to see God at work in that little hut. It was a sacred experience.

In each village, we met hundreds of children, many of them malnourished, all of them with large, brown, beautiful eyes. I can still recall the look of those eyes some thirty years later. I used flannelgraph to tell the story from creation to the cross, and scores of children flocked around, amazed to see little people sticking to a piece of cloth as I told the stories. (We were later able to send the whole Bible in flannelgraph to Aunty Doctor to use in the villages.)

All of us participated in a baptismal service in the muddy waters of the river that ran through one of the villages, noting the contrast of a baptismal service just yards away from a Hindu idol sitting next to the riverbank. The power of God was far greater than that of the darkness evident all around. None of the children in the villages where we visited and worked were able to attend school, and our hearts ached with the realization of how much we have in our own land, and how we simply take those blessings for granted.

From the villages, Bob and I headed to Calcutta for the Carey Bicentennial. Once seen, Calcutta is never forgotten. Even walking on the sidewalks, you are confronted on every hand by beggars, the crippled and lame, and entire families sleeping on strips of cardboard placed on the walk. The sights and smells and sorrows of that great city are forever stamped on our minds. On the other hand, the time of worship — as Baptists from all over the world gathered to commemorate the arrival of William Carey 200 years earlier — was a high point. All my "history bones" were activated, and my little blue enamel cup overflowed with the joy of seeing singular sights in special places. I took a deep breath before entering Carey Baptist Church in the heart of Calcutta and viewing the pulpit where Carey had stood 200 years earlier to share the good news. I took a picture of Bob at that pulpit and marveled at how short the pulpit stand was, for William Carey was very slight of stature. It is hard to realize he stood just over five feet when he was such a giant of a soul.

I was doubly excited to be able to stand on the board covering the baptistry in the floor of that historic church. It was on that spot that William Ward, one of the famous "Serampore Three" (missionary pioneers), had baptized Ann and Adoniram Judson on September 6, 1812. Bob and I were even able to go to Serampore and see the building where Carey did his translating and visit the cemetery that held the graves of Carey, his wives, and many missionaries who had died in service. My heart skipped a beat in sorrow at the sight of so many graves, the little ones whose parents had come to serve and who had ended up losing so many in infancy.

The bicentennial celebration itself was thrilling, with thousands of Baptists from around the world. Bob saw pastor friends from his seminary classes from earlier years, and friends from our time in Hyderabad came as well. G. Samuel and Eve were there, and we sat with them for most of the sessions. When Eve first saw me, she grinned and again gestured, "Come." Sure enough, she wanted to re-drape my *sari*. I had never really gotten the knack.

One of the most joyous times was seeing Ken Marak, Bob's young pastor friend from more than two decades earlier, whom he had met in Thailand at the BWA Youth Congress. Ken, now a professor at the Baptist Seminary in Assam, traveled long hours by train from Assam to reach Calcutta; he and Bob had a glorious reunion. Bob was astounded to see Ken wearing the same shirt Bob had given him twenty-something years earlier, threadbare now but treasured by Ken. We were delighted to be able to send most of our clothing and shoes home with Ken for his wife, children, and other family members. I knew Ken's wife would have far more use for my *saris* than did I. She certainly wouldn't have problems with draping them. (Until the time Ken died some twenty years later, we were thankful to be able to send regular support to the Assam seminary in north India.) Ken had long wanted Bob to be able to visit Assam; that never happened, but Bob would have loved seeing Baptists at work firsthand in that land.

We headed back to Manila with India permanently on our hearts, its people in our prayers. Even with vast needs and many problems, life in Manila was easy by comparison with India. Praying that we would never take our privileges for granted, Bob and I gave renewed thanks for being able to work among people who were responsive and eager to learn about God. The work continued to grow and thrive. Time for our final furlough was coming, and both of us approached it with mixed feelings. We were tired. On the hottest afternoons, I would daydream about "retirement" and picture leisurely going to an air-conditioned library, reading all the books I wanted to, and eating all the chocolate available. Even as I daydreamed, I didn't really expect that to happen. Knowing the frail condition of our two remaining parents, Bob and I both realized they needed us just now. On the other hand, our work here was such a pleasure and challenge, it would be crushingly difficult to say goodbye. Why are the goodbyes of life so hard? I've never figured that out. Nonetheless, I had no doubt that my little blue enamel cup, wherever it might end up traveling, would continue filling up.

Teaching at a pastors' seminar, Hyderabad Church, India, 1993

Alice and Jody at Alice's graduation from Vanderbilt Divinity School

TWENTY-FOUR

YEARS OF CHANGE
1995-2000

Several weeks before our furlough, Bob received an unexpected call from Aaron Johnson, pastor of First Baptist Church of Guntersville, Alabama. Aaron had been one of Bob's students the years he worked with youth ministries in Boaz. Hearing that we were coming on furlough, Aaron asked, "Brother Bob, would you consider being senior associate pastor and working with me in Guntersville?" Bob was shocked. Such a possibility had not occurred to him. Agreeing to pray it through, Bob and I were now looking at a new type of ministry. Would this be a means whereby we could continue to minister and also be on hand to help our parents? The thought of not returning to International Baptist Church brought a pang; we loved these people. They were like home. Realizing we might not be back made saying goodbye doubly hard.

Within weeks, we were in Alabama and taking our final furlough, which meant much traveling with conferences, retreats, and conventions. It also meant family time and being close enough to be involved in our grandsons' lives, watching them grow and change by the week. Ho Shien Sun and Granny Ora were thankful we were nearby. She was living in an apartment at the Boaz retirement complex, and Daddy moved to the retirement village just about two blocks from our Guntersville house. Both were close to ninety-one, frail, but holding their own. Daddy discovered a real serendipity, for living in another apartment just yards from his was Clarabel Isdell McDonald. Clarabel had been our missionary neighbor in Yangzhou, China, when I was just two years old. Those two nonagenarians loved talking over old times. Though frail, his mind was sharp and clear. He might not be able to recall what he ate for lunch that day, but he could tell you what occurred on that same day in Yangzhou sixty years earlier.

We quickly came to love our Guntersville church family and had the added serendipity of being just twenty minutes away from Boaz, which meant the Faucetts and many other longtime friends were nearby. Jody and Lori were now living in Atlanta, and Alice and Jay in Huntsville, about forty minutes away. Alice was earning a master's degree in theology at Vanderbilt, then planning to pursue a PhD. Bob and I managed to see Carl and Eric every chance that came our way. They kept us on our toes with their antics and questions, often weighty theological ones like, "How is God everywhere at one time?"

By 1996, we were officially considered emeritus missionaries, but retirement was just a word. Our Guntersville church surprised us with a retirement/reception. We didn't have a clue. That January Sunday night, I was a bit disgruntled because Alice insisted that I wear my best dress to the evening service. With an inward sigh, I agreed and was shocked upon reaching the church to see so many cars. *Hmm.* This was unusual for a regular Sunday night service. We soon discovered why. Jody and Lori, Alice, Jay and the boys all went with us into the large fellowship hall, and there were Daddy and Granny Ora standing near the door. That was strange. Then we walked into the hall and were shocked to see it full of people, some of whom we had not seen in many years. It was impossible not to shed tears upon unexpectedly coming upon friends from all over the country gathered to wish us a happy retirement. We saw Harlan and Joann Spurgeon from Missouri — our erstwhile next-door neighbors in Taiwan. We turned around and there were Mike and Kitty Wilson from Georgia, more Taiwan next-door neighbors. By this time, I was bawling.

Then we spotted Bill and Maxine Vandry (now in Kentucky), our heart friends from Taichung days — those days when Maxine had blessed everyone with her creative cakes and constant love. Standing near them were Gerry and Bob Covington, our superb coworkers from the Perth, Australia, years. Virginia Smith and daughter Lynda from Mississippi were there; we couldn't believe our eyes. Then, in walked Alma Hunt, retired executive director of WMU, and her dear friend and ours, Helen Fling, past national president. Through our tears and laughter, Bob and I let them know that this was similar to the general and the admiral coming to bring wishes to the privates in military service.

All around were our new friends from Guntersville and dozens from the Boaz church. It was like our two favorite church families meeting together. We were further stunned when the church announced the establishment of the Hunt Mission Fund — a fund that would allow us to travel all over the world and teach and preach as invitations were extended. (Since that date, Bob and I have been able to make twenty-nine such trips — and, in the process, research and write nine books, thanks to the generosity of our church family.) We discovered "after the fact" that our close friend Frank Duckett was the mastermind behind the reception *and* the mission fund; he was clearly talented at keeping secrets.

By this time, the pastor who originally asked Bob to come on staff had left and a new minister was on the field. Bob and Joel Samuels worked together for a number of years. The beauty of this position was being able to be involved with the local church and also have opportunities to serve periodically in first one country and then another. Later that year, a church in Perth, Australia, had some big challenges and requested our help and encouragement. We filled in until the church was able to call a new minister.

Six days after returning from Australia, I left for a three-week trip to Lottie Moon country in China. Ten years earlier, I could never have imagined being able to experience such a journey. In addition, three friends from our Alabama area joined the group led by Dellanna O'Brien, director of national WMU. It was thrilling to stand in Lottie's Monument Street Church in Penglai (Dengzhou) and picture Lottie herself worshipping there a century ago. Pastor Qin and his wife were delighted to be able to tell me their experiences during the Cultural Revolution and use Mandarin to fully express what was in their hearts. They escorted me to the little house next to the church to meet Mrs. Qin's mother. She was in her mid-nineties but alert and thrilled to be able to tell me her story. She and I shared the same Chinese surname and decided we really were kin.

Our itinerary next took us to Lottie's home in Pingdu, further into the interior. I was awed to stand in Lottie's room and look around at the brick *kang* (bed) and desk that had been hers. She used to sit on that *kang* as the visitors came each day to hear the "heavenly book visitor" (as they dubbed Lottie) tell them how to obtain eternal life.

In 1997, our number of grandsons doubled in a short time span. Aidan and Gannon, Jody and Lori's twins, were born fifteen minutes apart, and our hearts immediately enlarged and fell in love with those two. Hearing them jabber to each other in "twin-ese" was more fun than going to the movies. Shortly after their births, Bob spent a wonderful month in Burma, helping train pastors in the highlands of Chin state. That same year, Daddy was the first resident to move into Branchwater Assisted Living in Boaz. He loved the fellowship with so many members of the church he had attended in Boaz years earlier who now lived there as well. I picked him up each Sunday morning for services with us in Guntersville, because he had formed deep ties with this church as well. Granny Ora was quite frail, and we were thankful to be able to spend time with her several days each week.

The next year, Alice and her family moved to Florida, and Alice completed course work for her PhD in Hebrew Bible. We were scattering, and it was harder to have time with grandchildren. Nonetheless, we learned not to complain too much. I always remembered how far Mama and Daddy had been from their families — and then, in turn, when we were overseas, they could seldom see *their* only two grandchildren. That has to be one of the toughest problems for missionaries scattered anywhere in the world. It is part of the calling, but that doesn't make it any easier. Jody and Lori moved to Washington, DC, and Jody joined the staff of the US Department of Justice. Florida? Washington? Now we really were scattered, and we put many miles on the car.

A real serendipity occurred for us that year. Bob and I went at the invitation of Hawaii WMU to speak at WMU conferences and in churches on four of Hawaii's islands. It was a terrific homecoming for me, because I had previously been able to spend so little time in the place where I had been born. The women of Hawaii WMU captured a big piece of my heart, and I have loved being able to return again and again to spend time with them and take part in their state meetings. I was honored to meet Sue Saito, the state WMU director, who had been a teenager in the Wahiawa chapel when Daddy and Mama had ministered there fifty years earlier.

The year 1999 brought vast change for all of us. We lost both Daddy and Granny Ora. Daddy had survived a broken hip and learned to walk and exercise again; in general, he was in better health than Bob's mother. However, both were close to ninety-four — and we consequently spent as much time as possible with both, storing up precious moments. In February, just a couple of weeks prior to his ninety-fourth birthday, Daddy's body began to shut down. He was in no pain and was quite comfortable but stayed in his chair or in bed. Within a week, he was no longer eating, just sipping water. I stayed at his side each day, and at night had someone right there with him.

However, the last few days prior to Valentine's Day, I stayed with him around the clock, sleeping on the couch in Daddy's studio apartment. Saturday night, he was no longer talking, content for me to simply sit at his bedside and hold his hand, talking about memories and friends near and far. I secured a lady to stay there that night as well, in case I needed help. About midnight, I lay down on the couch, and the sitter remained by Daddy's bed. About an hour later, I experienced what seemed like an "out of body" moment. I was asleep, but suddenly roused, for I distinctly heard a voice. It was Mama's voice, so clear I thought she was in the room. Mama had been gone fifteen years, but in that moment, I distinctly heard her softly say, "Rosalie. Rosalie." My eyes popped open. She spoke again, "Rosalie, go to Harold." Immediately, I got up and went to Daddy's side. Taking his hand, I checked his pulse. It was there but faint. As I monitored it, the beats became slower and slower. Then quietly, gently, Daddy slipped into eternity. It was Valentine's Day. Mama had known. Thank God she could alert me in the moment of passing. It was strangely comforting to my heart. *Oh God, how can I thank You for letting me be here when You called him home.* (Sitting here recounting that experience over two decades later still brings me to tears.) The chapel was packed for Daddy's memorial service. First one spoke, and then another. Bob led the service, and as Daddy's special song request was sung, we knew he was literally in that Holy City, standing in the presence of God.

We were not through with loss, however. Just thirty days later, Granny Ora passed away and left a huge hole in our hearts. It was a privilege to be around this time. When Bob's father died so suddenly, we were 10,000 miles away. Bob led his mother's memorial service, and we were so grateful to be present, even as we wept when the soloist sang "Finally Home."

In July, Bob and I boarded a flight to Yangon (Rangoon), Burma. Bob was an old hand; this was his third trip, but the first for me. It felt like I was stepping into the pages of a book about Burma and our first missionaries. Forty years earlier, while a student at Oklahoma Baptist University, I read Courtney Anderson's *To the Golden Shore,* an account of the lives of Ann and Adoniram Judson. My heart leapt a bit when I began reading their story. This felt like looking into family history, for my Grandmother Wells (Mama's mother) had been named for Ann Judson. Grandmama was born Ann Judson Fogle, and I was given her name as my middle name. Prior to going to Burma, I reread the book so it would be fresh on my mind. Bob and I were to teach for a month at the Gospel Baptist Seminary in Yangon, and, essentially, we would have our weekends free to explore. This sounded like a special adventure ahead of us. Little did I know how *much* of a life-changer it would be.

We arrived the same month that Ann and Adoniram Judson had reached Burma some 186 years earlier. Burma — lush, tropical, decaying, beautiful. Our senses were assaulted with a great mix of impressions. Grissom, principal of the seminary, met our flight and introduced us to his world. Grissom quickly became a special friend; the Burmese people as a whole were not "high smile" like the Filipinos, but Grissom was an exception. His smile was as winsome as his spirit. Grissom was a fifth-generation Christian, and, like others with a similar legacy, considered himself a spiritual descendant of the Judsons. Our first Sunday, Bob preached at one of the larger churches that made up their convention (one of several Baptist conventions in the country).

We stayed at a little inn on the outskirts of Yangon, and a driver picked us up each weekday. En route to the seminary, we passed a giant garbage heap, with people foraging for food. Each day we saw flooded yards (a mosquito-breeding paradise) and rows of monks with their begging bowls, going from house to house begging for rice. Housewives earned merit by putting rice in the bowls, trying to earn a way into heaven. The concept of grace was unknown. Many carried loads on their heads, and everywhere you looked, people were chewing and spitting out red *betel* juice. Use it long enough, and the teeth rot out. I watched the many who were chewing and remembered that Ann and Adoniram saw the same thing every day. Also familiar to their eyes was something else we saw daily, ubiquitous and ever-present — pagodas, large and small, an ever-present reminder of the hopelessness of Buddhism.

Our first sight of the seminary classrooms was another revelation. Set in a swampy area rich with mosquitoes, the rooms were ventilated by screenless open windows. We lavished on insect spray every morning and hoped it would help. There were not even electric fans. By the time we had been teaching an hour, every stitch we wore would be wet. Bob and I just learned to live with it. There were a few tables and some rickety chairs, but those chairs were filled with students eager to learn and grateful for the opportunity. We needed a translator, which meant everything took twice as long to teach. If the students had been graded on attentiveness, each one would have received an A+. They shamed us with their eagerness. Ninety-nine percent of their books were in English, which increased the difficulty of their learning process. We taught there a month: Bob concentrating on biblical studies and theology; I on counseling, speech, and missions history. Our students particularly loved learning the history of missions, excited to learn in-depth about Ann and Adoniram Judson and how the gospel had reached their shores 200 years earlier.

Bob and I visited the headquarters of the Myanmar Baptist Convention (the largest of the various Baptist conventions), and I started the search for the Judsons' story. Several convention officers knew certain pieces of Judson history, but it was frustrating that some of their information was contradictory; however, that didn't deter me from plowing on. Here we were, right where the Judsons had lived and worked, and I was determined to follow their trail. Late one afternoon, Bob and I were walking down the sidewalks of old Yangon when we discovered a small bookstore. Stepping in, we found the proprietor to be an elderly scholar with very few teeth but with excellent English. He was a storehouse of knowledge about the Judsons. The first thing my eye fell on was a large dictionary titled: *Burmese-English Dictionary.* Under the title was the author's name: Adoniram Judson. My heart skipped a beat. I began asking the proprietor questions, and we spent long minutes talking about the Judsons.

The following Sunday, Bob and I visited Immanuel Church — the largest and one of the country's two oldest houses of worship. It is located about a block from Sule Pagoda, the first spot Ann and Adoniram passed when they set foot on Burmese soil July 13, 1813. Even in 100-degree weather, I had chill bumps thinking about that monumental moment in Baptist missions history happening right where we now stood. The timing was perfect. We were worshipping on Judson Day 1999, commemorating the arrival of the

Judsons 186 years before. There were hundreds in the service as Pastor Paul Johns told the Judson story and closed with the statement, "Judson has passed the torch. Now it is up to us to pass it on again."

After the service, we met Dr. Johns, and he volunteered to be our "Yangon Judson guide" when we had free time. He was a godsend, and took us around Yangon, showing us where the Judsons had first lived, where the former Baptist hospital was located, and various buildings that had been Baptist schools. Most exciting was to pinpoint the place where the Judsons' house had stood. It is now part of the central rail station in downtown Yangon, and only about two blocks from Immanuel Church. Paul also took us to a couple of his favorite tea rooms, and we sat at little tables sipping tea while experiencing life in Yangon much as it had been lived two centuries earlier. (Every time we went to Burma, Paul Johns was an important part of our research, a fountain of information and provider of local flavor.) He was a fifth-generation Christian, with Indian, English, and Burmese heritage. His mother had been a faithful deacon in Immanuel Church.

The evening of Judson Day, we visited Judson Baptist Church on the campus of Yangon University (formerly Judson College). The service was led by different ethnic (tribal) groups, wearing their unique dress and singing hymns from their tribal traditions. Several of the ethnic groups are ninety percent or more Christian, and their songs and testimonies were inspiring. As we sat listening, I had the recurring thought, *Had not the Judsons stepped out in faith and come to Burma, none of these people would have been able to hear the good news from their ancestors.*

At that point, there was no thought in my mind about writing a book. I loved to talk — not write. However, the seed of an idea was born that month in Burma, and I never got away from it. It went from interest to compulsion; I felt like I was on the precipice of discovery and began using spare time to search for information. We returned to the convention headquarters to talk with several leaders there, asking who and what to see. One helpful spot was Myanmar Institute of Theology, the largest and best-known of the Baptist seminaries in the country. Their librarian was gracious and helpful, allowing me to copy material. The research began.

Bob and I also absorbed some local flavor. Seeing the massive Shwe Dagon pagoda, one of the first sights that greeted the Judsons' eyes, was simultaneously impressive and depressive. Shwe Dagon contained thousands of gems and more than sixty tons of gold, yet the great masses lived in poverty. Catching the wafting odor of incense burned to please the idols always left my heart hurting. I never smelled that scent without remembering the many in China who spent money and energy bowing to idols.

The third weekend, we were able to visit Mandalay and Ava, the ancient capital, where Adoniram had been in prison nearly two years. Sixty percent of the country's many thousands of monks lived in Mandalay. They were ubiquitous, and we were constantly reminded of these thousands who lived their lives trying to earn enough merit to get to heaven. The Judsons must have felt the same urgency as they invested their lives in telling those around them the *only* way to heaven.

No experience was quite like that of going to old Ava — and to Let Ma Yoon. For nearly a year, Adoniram had lain in the death prison there, fettered in fourteen pounds of chains. Ann literally kept him alive. (In the book *Bless God and Take Courage,* I recount the story of that incredible visit.) The first day I visited Let Ma Yoon, Bob wasn't with me. A local cart driver obligingly took me to the spot out in a former corn field where the infamous prison had stood, right in the shadow of the emperor's palace. There were two large marble slabs lying in the field, and I later learned more about them. Noticing several pieces of bricks lying around, I asked the cart driver (through an interpreter) what those were for. He replied, "Oh, they are bits and pieces of the old palace/city wall that surrounded this area." My mind immediately leaped to the thought, *These are pieces of Baptist history! Judson was in prison right here.* I put one small brick in my satchel and later, upon reaching our hotel room, showed it to Bob. His eyes got big and he exclaimed, "You stole a brick!" "Oh, no," I responded. "This brick is a piece of Baptist history. I *appropriated* it." Bob fretted that we would be arrested, but thankfully that didn't happen — and I've had the joy of sharing that brick with hundreds of Baptists in many states, all of them interested in missions history.

While in Mandalay, we went to its outskirts to explore the village of Aungbinle, the location of the second prison that held Adoniram. On that land, there is now an active Baptist church with a devoted pastor. Saw Seelah was deeply interested in and knowledgeable about Judson history. He showed me Edward Judson's biography of his father and kindly trusted me with his only copy. I took it to a stationer's in Mandalay and had it copied. Pastor Saw came into the city the following morning to retrieve the book. We bonded over Judson history, and every time Bob and I have been back to Burma, we've spent time with Saw and his engaging family.

Our last full weekend, I went with two missionary wives far south to Moulmein, where Ann and Adoniram had lived after the Burmese-English war. That story (and exhausting and exhilarating trip) is recounted in *Bless God and Take Courage*. I just wish there was some way to adequately explain the sensation of stepping *into* missions history and recalling how God used two remarkable missionaries to change a nation. Carolyn McAtee, Carrie Chappell and I then traveled still further south to the spot originally known as Amherst and visited Ann Judson's grave. Ann only lived to be thirty-six but left her imprint on Burma and paved the way for all women since who have followed God's call to missions service. It was impossible to stand by Ann's grave, remember her sacrifice, and not weep.

By now, the history bug had bitten. I was determined to learn more. It felt like I had just seen the tip of the iceberg. Bob and I reluctantly left Burma but with the intent of returning. As soon as we got home, we called both of the children. I told each of them how exciting it was, and how amazing to think that the people of Burma knew more about the Judsons than did the average Baptist in America. Someone needed to tell the story. I called the name of a well-known Baptist historian, saying that this writer would be perfect to share the message. Both children responded the same way: "Mom, you tell the story. You are the one who's been there." Explaining that I loved talking, not writing, they persisted in remaining insistent. Somehow the idea wouldn't let me go. Nor would the people of Burma leave our thoughts or hearts.

With Sue Saito Nishikawa and WMU leaders at annual meeting, 1998. (Sue was a young teen at Wahiawa church when Harold and Alice Hall were there in 1938.) The Hawaii Pacific Missions Offering is named for her.

Ho Shien Sun (Harold Hall) poses with his four great-grandsons

Carl and Eric meet Pastor Wu in Yangzhou

TWENTY-FIVE

FROM BURMA TO CHINA
2000-2004

God's not through with you yet was a frequent thought most mornings as I woke up. Life was never dull, for there was always more to do than time to do it in. Another frequent thought always brought a smile to my face. *Had I really thought we would retire and return to America, where I could spend leisurely days reading in well-stocked libraries, eating tasty chocolates?* I visited scores of libraries (and ate way too many chocolates), but the leisure and relaxation never happened.

I became a woman with a mission: dig into the Judsons' story. Archivists became some of my favorite people, starting with Betty Layton at the Valley Forge archives of American Baptists. That was a depository of history located right next to America's fabled Valley Forge. Research began when I was able to purchase a first edition of James Knowles' 1829 memoir of Ann Judson. I was hooked from chapter one; thus began six years of research and writing. I was way too naïve, having no idea how hard it was to get published. However, at the end of the publishing trail awaited Providence with the answer.

Other than the children's mission study book in 1975, I had only written articles. Three years of research were exciting. At some point, however, you have to *write* to produce a book. I would frequently come across a previously unknown fact, and experience another "aha" moment. Bob would patiently listen to one tale after another.

In 2000, he retired as senior minister at First Baptist, Guntersville, and we moved to DC for a year. Both children and their families were there for that year, and it was a treasured number of months when we actually lived just short miles from children and grandchildren. Washington was also a perfect spot for research, with all the riches of the Library of Congress right at our doorstep. Furthermore, Lori was a marvelous navigator and went with me several times to Massachusetts and Rhode Island, exploring what we called the Judson history trail. I tend to get hopelessly lost with directions, but Lori had a built-in antenna and could unerringly find her way to the very spot I needed. I got goosebumps galore every trip, as I discovered Ann's birthplace in Bradford, Massachusetts, then Adoniram's in Malden. After the first year's visits, I managed to return and find a way to go inside their homes and look around as well as visit other spots important in the Judsons' lives.

Bob and I began the year with history, spending a month in Burma, teaching at another seminary and spending weekends doing Judson research. Research was addictive. I ended up making over fifty pages of notes just about what we saw, heard, learned, and felt. We still found a few living links to the Judsons' time some 200 years earlier, but those links would soon be gone. Through Paul Johns' Immanuel Church and members of the Judson Church on the Yangon University grounds, our contacts began to grow.

The pastor of Judson Church went each month to visit the Nyein sisters, four remarkable sisters who were living links to Judson history (see *Bless God and Take Courage)*. We were awed to meet those venerable saints. This was the beginning of our relationship with the family of Ah Vong, the young Chinese/Burmese who in 1841 printed Judson's epochal first edition of the Burmese Bible. When we met Daw Tin, Daw Dwe, Daw May, and Daw Nge, they ranged in age from 93 to 104. Sheila, their great-niece, lovingly cared for her aunts, and they all were obviously frail and just as obviously sharp and keen of mind. Daw Nge, age 104, told us that their grandmother, Daw Lone Ma (Ah Vong's widow), lived with them in Moulmein when they were young. Daw Lone Ma was actually baptized by Adoniram Judson, and she helped raise her grandchildren on stories of the Judsons and the early years in Moulmein. It was through these unique sisters that we met *their* great-great nieces, whose father, U Hla Bu, the first Burmese president of Judson College, had yet another fascinating legacy. Joan Myint (a university economics professor in Yangon) and her sister Harriet Bain (a WMU leader in Missouri) became treasured friends and later visited us in Alabama.

By this point, I was completely immersed in the Judson story. Several visits to Burma produced compelling new information that I was deter-mined to get on paper. The following year, the four Nyein sisters looked at the old map I had found of Moulmein and the Judson sites there, identi-fying them and explaining how to find various places when we went south to explore. They were a treasure trove of help and recalled little incidents of daily life in the nineteenth century that their grandmother had shared with them. Ah Vong and Daw Lone Ma, their grandparents, had twelve children — all of whom became early Baptist leaders. We were astounded at the beautiful English of this quartet of sisters.

Our weekend in Mandalay was another fun adventure. Bob went with me this time to Ava, to the site of the death prison. I took along a tape measure, and he and I walked around the ancient tree still standing, just as it had stood right outside the stockade wall. Measuring over twenty-six feet in circumference, the tree provided a bit of shade for Judson in 1824.

We next went across the Irrawaddy River to the Sagaing area and the church that stood on land there, just across the river from the death prison. Judson's great-grandson was born in the mission house we found next to the church — and, even better, we met the daughter of the man who had been pastor of the Sagaing Church decades earlier. Daw Khin Nu, retired principal of Mandalay Baptist High School, had been a little girl when Stanley Hanna was born in 1920. Daw Nu smiled as she recalled, "He was such a tiny little fellow, and I found him adorable." Daw Nu and her pastor father gave their priceless copy of the first Judson Bible to the Aungbinle Church nearby, built on the site of the second Judson prison.

Bob loved meeting Saw Seelah (Silas), pastor of the Aungbinle Church. He graciously allowed us to hold the massive first edition Bible while he told of his memories of Judson history. He called Daw Khin Nu "our church mother." Silas told us that years earlier, some of the original fetters that had bound Judson when he lay in prison were housed in the church. However, when the Japanese overran the country, the fetters disappeared, never to be found again. The Judson history was vastly important to the Baptists of Burma, and I longed for Baptists in our own country to know and love their heritage.

Bob ended up spending that year on several continents. International Baptist Church in Manila was still without a pastor, and Bob spent several months helping them. I was there for a period and then spent much of the time in the New England area, doing Judson research. Our Guntersville church literally made the research (and all those miles) possible because of the Hunt mission fund. This was also a year of change for our children. Alice completed her master's degree and became the academic dean of Vanderbilt Divinity School in Nashville. Meanwhile, Jody became counsel to the deputy attorney general, and both children became even busier than before.

I made several trips to California to meet with Adoniram Judson's closest living descendant, great-grandson Dr. Stanley Hanna, retired professor of physics at Stanford University. This prince of a man clearly inherited Judson's brilliant intellect, and I learned so much from him. Dr. Hanna shared with me over 700 family letters and documents, and I was awed by his knowledge of his family and its legacy, and his generosity of spirit in sharing with me. He made it possible for me to base much of my research on primary sources; I could never have done it without Dr. Hanna. He actually entrusted me with primary materials from the Judson family trunk, and I was able to get them safely housed in various university archives.

Among the intriguing contents of the trunk were bound fragments of what appeared to be portions of writing in some language we did not recognize. Having Alice at Vanderbilt was a wonderful boon. I scanned a page of the ancient document and emailed it to Alice. Sixty seconds later, the phone rang. It was Alice. "Mom," her voice sounded excited, "where did you get this?!" I explained, "It's from the Judson family trunk. The printing is pretty clear, isn't it?" "Mom," she retorted, "that's not printing; that is handwritten and it's *old, old.*" By this point, I was just as excited. Alice and the Hebrew language faculty then examined the documents and determined them to be portions of Genesis and the Psalms, evidently somehow transported (possibly by Middle Eastern traders on the Silk Road) to the Far East. They were medieval and Hebrew. It was likely that these had somehow gotten into the possession of William Carey, who had been most generous with giving encouragement and materials to Judson for his translation work. In the margins of the fragments were personal notes in Hebrew, evidently transcribed there by Judson himself. It was a thrill to just stand and hold one of those fragments and think, *This is something used by Adoniram Judson himself.*

Bob and I sometimes met ourselves coming back and wondered where we would go next. He went twice to Burma in 2002 to teach in various seminaries, and my cherished friend, Stuart Calvert, and I traveled to South America for the first time. She and I were on the Alabama WMU board of trustees and represented Alabama WMU at the Venezuelan WMU annual meeting. Events on the home front were even more exciting, however, for our one and only granddaughter, McKenna, was born. Alice received her PhD in Hebrew Bible that year, and Jody was named director of federal programs for the Civil Division of the Justice Department.

The year 2002 was a banner year in Judson legacy and lore. I had the

immense pleasure and honor of going to Burma with my cousin Iva Jewel
Tucker (retired from national WMU staff and as managing editor of *The
Alabama Baptist*) and stalwart friend Kaye Carlisle, accompanying Dr.
Hanna and his family. Born and raised in Burma, Dr. Hanna was going
home (I remembered that wonderful feeling from going home to China).
This was the first time to Burma for his wife, Jane; daughter, Sue; and son
and daughter-in-law, David and Robin. Dr. Hanna was excited to be able
to introduce them to his Burma roots, and it was my thrill to be part of the
experience and look on as wide-eyed Burman Baptists would say, "*This* is
Yood-a-than's (Judson's) great-grandson? His closest living descendant?"
More than one timidly asked me, "May I just touch him?" Such was the
respect with which Judson is remembered in that land 200 years after his
arrival there.

We had a special purpose in this trip. It was the 175th anniversary
of the Judson Baptist Church in Moulmein, the oldest continually active
Baptist church on any mission field. The whole trip became a missions
odyssey, as we visited the various cities and sites that were key in the
Judsons' years in Burma. I particularly loved watching Dr. Hanna introducing his children to their Burma roots, beginning with showing them
the house where he was born in Sagaing. Next, we hired a little boat to take
us across the Irrawaddy to see the spot where the death prison had stood.
I again got that eerie feeling of stepping into history as I heard Dr. Hanna
tell it from his family's perspective and listened as he told his children how
their great-great-grandfather had lain in fetters for months on that spot.

I never had a simple trip to Moulmein and Amherst, and this time
around was no exception. Our hired minibus broke down four times on the
journey south, and the nine-hour trip became a fourteen-hour endurance
test. An extra joy in Moulmein was being there with Harriet and Joan,
the daughters of U Hla Bu, first Burmese president of Judson College. The
two were, through and through, a part of Baptist legacy as the great-great-
granddaughters of Ah Vong, the Chinese/Burmese printer who produced
the Bible. All of us took part in the heart-warming service at Moulmein's
Judson Church. Dr. Hanna was the highlight (and the hero) of the

anniversary celebration, as hundreds of Baptists crowded into the church to listen raptly while he spoke about the Judson family and its legacy. Of course, as he and I spoke, we needed an interpreter; consequently, it was no short service, but it *was* a memorable one.

To top it off, we went still further south to Amherst, where Ann was buried. She had founded the little church there in 1826 while Judson was away in the capital translating a peace treaty. The church stood just yards from where her grave is now located, the earliest church ever built in the ancient kingdom. Three months after its 1826 organization, Ann died of cerebral spinal meningitis. The little church lived on. However, it was destroyed by Japanese bombs in World War II. Now move forward fifty years, and on December 9, 2002, Stanley Hanna, closest living descendant of Adoniram Judson, laid the cornerstone for the rebuilding of Ann Judson Memorial Chapel.

The marble tablet of dedication was unveiled, reading: "The plinth stones are laid by the leaders of the Myanmar Baptist Convention and the descendants of Rev. Dr. A. Judson, Baptist missionary to Burma, (1813-1850) on 9th Dec. 2002." All in our group were thrilled to be allowed to lay a stone at the spot. Meanwhile, my fast-beating heart was thinking: *Studying history is enthralling, but getting to be* in *history is even more thrilling.*

Just months later, Bob and I were on yet another continent, having a reunion at Easter with the church we had helped plant fourteen years earlier in Australia. Our time with Bob and Anne Platt and with Meg and Ern Avery was like a gift. This was yet another family reunion; it felt like we had family on at least three continents.

The two of us were never happier, however, than when we had time with the grandchildren. Carl was in high school, Eric in junior high, and Alice completed her PhD in Hebrew Bible. Aidan and Gannon were kinder-garteners, and one day while riding in the car with them, I asked, "Boys, what do you want to be when you grow up?" One immediately piped up to say he was going to be a dentist, and his brother declared his determi-nation to be a lawyer. McKenna was only a year and a half, so I asked her big brothers, "Well, what will your sister be?" Immediately, one of them matter-of-factly answered, "Oh, she will be a princess."

The following year found Bob and me back in Burma. He taught in two seminaries, and I had the fun part by being able to help the Myanmar Baptist Convention set up a Judson museum. Even more rewarding was being able to share the Judson legacy at several seminaries and churches. One particular afternoon when speaking at a seminary in Yangon, one of the professors, an elderly man with beautiful English, translated for me. He had known of Yood-a-than (Judson) all his life, but quietly told me after the meeting that he had learned new nuggets that day. At one point, as I was describing Judson's years of suffering in prison and then Ann's death, he suddenly stopped translating. Tears overcame him. Taking a deep breath, he haltingly explained, "I am just overwhelmed to think they loved us enough that they sacrificed their very lives so we could know of God's love." *His* tears brought mine on, as all of us remembered what God had done in this place 200 years earlier.

We were soon back in the United States, but Burma was never absent from our hearts, nor was China. I found it incredible how each opportunity to revisit my heart's home in China brought fresh joy and insight. None was greater than the sheer joy of taking our two oldest grandchildren to China that May and June of 2004. For the first time ever, I celebrated my birthday in China's capital. Carl was sixteen and Eric thirteen; they, too, will never forget those weeks on the other side of the world. Beijing was our first stop, and the boys were in awe of the Forbidden City and its fabled history of more than 700 years. Of all things, we found a Starbucks inside the grounds; I drank the most historic drink of my life. The next day, the Great Wall rivaled Beijing for what the boys labeled "awesomeness." Standing on the 2,000-year-old wall and looking out into the infinite distance would make the mightiest person feel tiny.

There was more to come, and Carl and Eric were astounded at the Terracotta Army unearthed in Xian, China's ancient capital. America's history felt awfully recent by comparison as we stood looking at terracotta soldiers that been buried more than two millennia earlier. We weren't finished with history, though, for next we flew to Nanjing, China's capital until it fell to the Communists in 1949. Here in Nanjing, nearly 100 years earlier, Aunt Grace had studied Mandarin. As a child, I had climbed the ancient Ming Wall that had surrounded the city for 700 years. Best of all, our wonderful friends, Faye Pearson and Gwen Crotts, were living and teaching in Nanjing, and we had a heartfelt reunion. Faye had arranged for Carl and Eric to teach two of her classes while we were there, and the university students were excited to meet two American boys and asked them endless questions about America. It was a great opportunity for the students to hear "native" English, but an even greater opportunity for our grandsons to get an authentic taste of real China and its people.

Taking the boys to Zhenjiang and my childhood home was a deeply emotional time. I could not help but weep as we stood with the boys on the place where the beggar had knelt, and I recalled the Christmas morning that had altered the trajectory of my life. The house had been both restored and "upgraded," but the place was the exact spot of my memory.

The next day, Carl and I hired a car to take us to Dan Yang, the small city in the countryside where Aunt Grace had pioneered a work. I had been fascinated as a child by the Ming Tombs of ancient emperors buried there, with their giant stone animals still standing nearby. Carl hitched a "ride" on a Ming Dynasty stone horse and temporarily found himself in history.

Yet nothing matched the following day when we went to Yangzhou, my first home in China, and worshiped again in the Syi Lyang Jye (West Gate Street) Church. Ladies who remembered me from previous visits clustered around after the service in the crowded sanctuary to welcome me back. Inquiring about the absent Pastor Wu, we learned that he had at long last retired (at the venerable age of ninety-two). However, he was still helping with a small country church, and the ladies graciously explained how we could get there.

After visiting the compound where I had lived as a tiny little girl, we drove to the countryside to see Pastor Wu. Ever since we planned this trip, my greatest wish was for our grandsons to meet this dear friend of their own grandparents and thus link the generations. The service at the little country church had not yet begun when we arrived — and, clearly, the members here in the countryside had seldom seen any foreigner, say nothing of teenaged foreigners. We were a curiosity but graciously welcomed as Bob and I strained to understand the local dialect. Then an incident occurred that remains seared into my memory. An elderly man slowly struggled to push a heavy wheelbarrow into the entry of the little building. Small wonder the man was struggling; the wheelbarrow contained an even older man, one so bent he could not stand straight. Nonetheless, he slowly climbed out of the wheelbarrow and painstakingly made his way to a small offering box hanging on the nearby wall. Slowly reaching into his jacket pocket, he pulled out a well-worn piece of money and tucked it into the slit on the box. The four of us stood, silently watching. I noticed Eric's heart in his eyes, his focus set on the old man's face. Turning to me, he whispered, "Nana, can I put some money in that little box, too?" My eyes glistened with tears as I assured him, "Of course you can. Just slip back there and put it in."

Then Pastor Wu arrived, and we had the matchless opportunity of introducing our grandsons to a veritable saint who was part of the fabric of our family's legacy. That glowing face, etched with deep lines, was just as radiant as it had been twenty years earlier when we had first reunited at the Yangzhou church. The boys marveled at his colloquial English. "Pastor Wu," Carl declared, "your English is the most amazing I have heard in China." Pastor Wu gave that winning smile as he responded, "Your grand-mother, Alice Wells Hall, was my English teacher." (Two years later, Pastor Wu went to his heavenly reward, and I often ponder on the extraordinary reunion that must have taken place the day he arrived in Glory.) Those two grandsons sensed, even as we had done each time we saw Pastor Wu, that we were in the presence of a man who was after God's own heart. We rarely have such glimpses. That moment was one of those signal times.

Indeed, there are a few choice moments that occur in life when we think, *Oh, it can't get better than this.* But then, God provides yet another evidence of His great providence and loving heart, and more blessings arrive. I don't know why I continue to be surprised by grace and joy. God is famous for those very things.

With Aidan, Gannon and McKenna, visiting Helen Keller's birthplace

TWENTY-SIX

FAST FORWARD

2005-2010

The births of our two children were two of the most marvelous memories of my life — those moments when I first held them in my arms. On a different level, but highly rewarding, were the moments when I first held the book I had labored to bring to life. The path to the birth of *Bless God and Take Courage* was a long one that took six years to walk. The morning the author's copy arrived, I got a silly grin on my face and couldn't seem to wipe it off. This was like holding six years and 100,000 miles in two hands. These miles had an assortment of adventures; along the way, I met all sorts of special people. Jerry Cain was one of them. Dr. Cain, president of Judson University in Elgin, Illinois, was also a member of the national board of American

Baptists. He had heard of a person researching the Judsons' history and gave me a call, inviting me to come to Judson to speak about the Judson legacy.

That visit marked the beginning of a special friendship. Jerry Cain was steeped in Judson history and loved to share his excitement with his student body. At Judson, I found faculty and students who loved and appreciated their Baptist missions heritage. Before I left, Dr. Cain asked, "Who is going to publish your book?" I must have looked startled, and taking a deep breath, admitted, "I don't really know — I don't have a publisher." Jerry gave that winning smile of his and responded, "May I be your advocate?" I mean, what more could a person wish for? I immediately responded, "Yes, please!"

Just two weeks later, I had a phone call from the managing editor of Judson Press (named for Adoniram Judson) in Valley Forge. Within a week, the press had decided to publish the book. I was purely ignorant of the publishing world, having no idea how hard it was to get published. In the previous year, however, I had made contact with several publishing companies and was beginning to understand that this was a tortuous road. Dr. Cain's advocacy had been a gift of Providence, and I immediately recognized it as such. Consequently, in April 2005, I held that first copy in my hands. That same spring, a couple in our Guntersville church said they wanted to buy 2,000 copies of *Bless God and Take Courage,* and, as Bob and I traveled and spoke, the proceeds could go to missions. That sounded like a perfect plan and has become one of the rich blessings of our lives. (Who would have thought that sixteen years and eight books later, Bob and I would have had the privilege of contributing over $275,000 to missions causes around the world?)

The year showered us with further serendipities, for we attended the Baptist World Alliance in Birmingham, England, traveling with Denton Lotz, general secretary of the BWA. Dr. Lotz had written the foreword for my book. Like Jerry Cain, he was a true "Judsonophile" and knew and loved missions history. Our group visited various Baptist points of interest in England, concentrating on the life of William Carey. Bob and I were doubly appreciative of this opportunity, understanding as we did how Carey had personally befriended the Judsons and made the beginnings of their work in Burma possible.

Back in the States, grabbing what time we could with any or all of the grandchildren was important, and we loved watching them grow and develop. By the time McKenna was four, it no longer worked to spell in front of her. Spelling was her forte. The five grands ranged from preschool to university, and family time was fairly rare but doubly precious. Bob had the matchless privilege, over a several-year time span, of baptizing each of our grandchildren; those were red-letter days that remain vivid in our memories.

In 2005, I began serving as Alabama state WMU president, and it was a fabulous opportunity to travel the state and get to personally know a host of terrific women who enriched my understanding of grassroots missions fervor in Alabama. More than ever, I realized that, from the very beginning, it was women who had set alight the flame of missions zeal and were continuing to keep the torch blazing.

During research on the Judsons, I visited New England and the "Judson Trail" repeated times — but in 2007, I experienced an exciting twist to the trip. In April, a group of some twenty people, mostly WMU women from Alabama, did a New England tour of Judson history. Ann Hasseltine Judson's 1781 birthplace was in the process of renovation, and we were actually able to go inside and watch the work in progress. Two men were chipping 200-year-old horsehair plaster off the walls and removing centuries-old wallpaper, piling it all in buckets. I looked into one of those buckets, and, picking up a piece of 1780s wallpaper and plaster, asked, "What are you going to do with this?" The men looked at each other quizzically and, shaking their heads, answered, "Nothing, lady. We'll just throw it away." I quickly asked, "Would it be OK if we kept a little of it?" The two looked genuinely puzzled, as if to say, *Who on earth would want dusty old plaster?* Aloud, they replied, "Sure, we don't have any use for it." So it was that I obtained some historical Baptist plaster and have it framed in a shadow box — a piece of missions history. The most sentimental moment was standing in front of the mantel in the west parlor, where Ann and Adoniram had exchanged their wedding vows in 1812.

Malden, Massachusetts — Adoniram's birthplace — was about twenty miles away, and I wished we'd had a whole day for this one town. Malden

First Baptist Church was like a memorial to Judson. The famed commemorative plaque on the wall read: "Rev. Adoniram Judson, born August 9, 1788, Died April 12, 1850. Malden, His Birthplace, The Ocean, His Sepulchre, Converted Burmans and the Burman Bible, His Monument. His Record is On High." I knew about the tablet, of course, but literally gazing up at those words brought on tears. (The memorial tablet was written by another Andover graduate, Samuel F. Smith, who wrote "My Country 'Tis of Thee.")

Nonetheless, visiting the house where Adoniram was born had to be the brightest jewel of all in that day's crown. The doctor now renting the historic 1651 house, the oldest in Malden, welcomed us to explore the place. Dr. Tabrizi conducted us from the top (where we saw the room in which Adoniram was born in 1788) literally down to the basement, where we gazed wide-eyed at the dark opening in the cellar corner. It was used as part of the Underground Railroad during the Civil War and connected to a tunnel leading to a nearby road that was another step closer to freedom. We were intrigued to learn that the tunnel was originally designed for use in case of an Indian attack.

Our next day was spent exploring Salem, going from First Baptist Church, circa 1804, with its priceless stained-glass window depicting the Judsons' sailing to the Far East, to Tabernacle Church across the road, where Adoniram was ordained in 1812. Only a couple of blocks away was the wharf from which their ship, the *Caravan*, sailed in February of that year. But then, Plymouth was every bit as wonderfully rich in Judson lore, for Adoniram's 1801 boyhood home was there. A Mrs. Sproles lived in the house and had a personal interest in American history, for one of her ancestors had arrived on the *Mayflower* in 1620. I particularly loved seeing the beautiful original banister that had been in place when young Adoniram walked those stairs. Our Judson pilgrimage ended most fittingly at Providence, Rhode Island, worshipping in the First Baptist Church in America, founded in 1638 by Roger Williams. The pastor knew of our impending visit and kindly asked me to have a small part in the service by reading the morning Scripture. I found it deeply moving that Sunday to stand in the very place where Judson had stood in 1807 to deliver his valedictory address. I used Mama's well-worn Bible to read the Great Commission from Matthew 28, and I vividly remember the deep emotion of that short moment.

The next May, Bob had a dream fulfilled when he and Gerald, the young believer he had baptized more than twenty-five years earlier, returned to south China for two wonderful weeks with the "boys" Bob had taught in the 1980s. All were now successful businessmen. Each evening they celebrated with their honored teacher, giving him the opportunity to fellowship and witness to them yet another time. It was hard to tell who enjoyed the weeks the most: those boys-now-men, or the teacher who had the privilege of time with them once more.

The following June found me headed back to the Orient — this time home to China, although for this trip I wasn't able to include time for a stop in Yangzhou and Zhenjiang. Candace McIntosh, Alabama WMU director, and I took a group of Acteen "graduates" (now college women) and WMU ladies from our state to Lottie Moon's China. The most astounding part of the trip for me was the blessing of our in-country tour guide. (To be cautious, I'm changing names.) We had requested a guide that could accompany us the whole trip, and Lillian was terrific. Her beautiful Mandarin was a joy to listen to, and her English was a boon for all the group. I knew that Lillian had been the guide for my friend Alice Newman, director of Hawaii's WMU. Alice had raved about her guide, Lillian, just the year before. I now learned that Alice had also intrigued Lillian as she told her about what a personal relationship with the God of the universe was all about. She had planted live seeds in Lillian's mind. Alice's tour group had also gone to Lottie Moon's part of China, and that meant Lillian had visited in Lottie's church the year before. She spoke very honestly with me about her concept of God. "Until I met Alice," she explained, "I thought stories from the Bible were just that, interesting stories, rather like fairy tales." Her father was a devout Buddhist, and her mother a member of the Communist party, so Lillian had no basis for believing Christian "fairy tales."

The fabulous Forbidden City was like an old friend to Lillian, and she mesmerized the group as she told stories of intrigue that had happened in this piece of history hundreds of years earlier. The same was true of the Great Wall, and the college students in our group were particularly amazed with that Wonder of the World. The ancient capital of Xian was another favorite, and our college coeds couldn't decide if their favorite site was the fabulous old city wall or the army of terracotta warriors, standing eternally in their solemn line in the pit where they had been buried 2,000 years earlier. The highlight of Xian for me was a reunion with Janet Hicks and her daughters. Janet was a missionary doctor and had gone to college with Jody some twenty years earlier. Her lovely little blond MK daughters spoke Mandarin like they were born to it, which they were. Janet surprised me with a gift when we left the next day, a scroll with Mama's favorite verse on it in Chinese calligraphy, Deuteronomy 34:27: "The eternal God is our refuge and underneath are the everlasting arms." Of course, I cried again. (It now hangs on our dining room wall, a daily reminder of both the everlasting arms and Mama who first told me about them.)

We arranged to be in Dengzhou (now called Penglai) on Sunday so we could worship in Lottie's church. Since my previous visit twelve years earlier, a large new sanctuary had been constructed right beside the original building, and it was crowded with more than 1,300 worshippers that morning. Pastor Qin graciously welcomed us and insisted we sit on the front rows reserved for visitors. Our young college women had the opportunity to bring greetings to the congregation from their churches in Alabama, and then they sang a hymn in English. Pastor Qin's message that morning was astounding. I took careful notes so I could translate it for the group when we were back on the bus.

I had actually prayed prior to our arrival that his message would be the one God had in mind for Lillian to hear — and was it ever. He preached over an hour — but to me, it seemed mere minutes. He asked the congregation, "Are you ready to meet God?" Pastor Qin next made a remark that stuck in my mind and, just a few years later, took on a new significance, as he said to the more than a thousand listeners, "Every night before sleeping, I learn a new verse. And then I consider," he told us, "Is this my last day?

I know I am not promised tomorrow." This elderly man who had endured so much made the point, "Today becomes yesterday tomorrow. You can't take it back. Live it for Him. Today is yesterday tomorrow. Yesterday is history. Tomorrow is the future. Make today something that makes great history tomorrow." I was enthralled as he continued by outlining in simple, clear, and compelling terms, the way of salvation. Pastor Qin ended with a beautiful assurance, "My friends, Emmanuel (God with us) is for *you,* the people of China."

Several times during his message, I glanced at Lillian out of the corner of my eye. *Her* eyes were absolutely transfixed on Pastor Qin, as she drank in every word. It was much later, when we finally departed from that remarkable service, that I was able to talk with Lillian about her impressions as we continued to our next spot. She was radiant as she began explaining what was in her heart. "Last year when Newman Alice (in Chinese style, she used the surname first) was here, it was like she was laying the foundation. You know," and she shook her head a bit, "I wanted to believe in my head, but I just couldn't quite understand. I think it's like this," and she motioned with her hands, "as if I have been standing at the gate looking in. And now," she was glowing, "I have just gone in!" Our tour group was excited to learn of Lillian's story. She assured them, "If all the pastors in China were like Pastor Qin, no one would be bored at church!"

Following the service, our group was given a reception/visiting time with church leaders, and it reminded me of the beauty of "cuppas" together after worship in Australia. Now I had such an opportunity in the land I claimed as my own. Pastor Qin took us to see the remains of the school that Lottie Moon had founded and kindly gave me a brick from the original structure. (It's now a special part of my "bits of Baptist history" collection.) Only two years later, we were shocked to hear the news that early one morning, Pastor and Mrs. Qin had been in his study preparing for the daily morning devotions service when a crazed former member burst into the office and cruelly murdered the two octogenarians. The church family was in disbelief. Elder Matthew of the congregation later wrote me that just a couple of weeks before his death, Pastor Qin had said to him, "You know, I feel like I will soon be with the Lord." What a legacy that remarkable couple left. The church had averaged over 300 baptisms per year for the past several years, and the church now had more than 3,600 members. Immediately upon hearing the tragic news, I recalled what Pastor Qin had preached two years earlier, about asking himself each day, "Is this my last day?"

Not only was 2008 the year of the memorable Lottie Moon trip, it was also the year Alice became president of Chicago Theological Seminary, and all our family had one of those rare and treasured Thanksgivings together. Alice was already an ordained minister of the National Baptist Convention and now received dual ordination, this time with the Church of Christ, whose seminary she led. The campus of CTS was on the grounds of the University of Chicago and was a piece of history, with amazing stained-glass windows and an intriguing cloister that was reminiscent of Europe. All of us were in Chicago for Alice's inauguration. The reception following the service was at Chicago's famous Adler's Planetarium and capped off an amazing day. As I watched Alice in her academic regalia that day, my mind harked back to the little girl starting Chinese kindergarten in Taipei, Taiwan, and wondering, "When am I going to look like everyone else?" I gave an inward smile (which likely showed on my face as well) as I reflected on how much she was now uniquely herself, just as God intended.

I still kept looking for the meaning of retirement and wondering if Bob and I would ever realistically attain that status. Where was the "extra time" that was supposed to be a feature of the "golden years"? I was beginning to have an understanding of the meaning behind the phrase "Old age isn't for sissies." As a college student, Robert Browning had been among the poets we studied in English literature. One of his phrases stuck in my mind: "Come along, grow old with me; the best is yet to be." I checked his biography and learned that he had died at the age of fifty-seven. Old age?! What does a fifty-seven-year-old know of old age? My understanding of the meaning of "old" started to change when I regularly began waking up with a new ache in some body part I didn't even know I had. Nonetheless, there was too much to do and too many places to go to spend time dwelling on "old." More adventures and reunions were just ahead. There was no accounting for the speed of the years flying by. Had something pressed the fast-forward button — and left it running?

Reading the Great Commission at morning worship — First Baptist Church, Providence, Rhode Island, from the lectern where Judson gave his valedictory address

At national WMU in Birmingham with director Wanda Lee; Harriet Bain of Rolla, Missouri; and her sister, Joann Myint, Yangon, Burma. They are the great-great-granddaughters of the Chinese-Burmese leader who printed the first Judson Bible, 1836.

Bob has a reunion with Alma Hunt, 2005

Introducing the grandchildren to the congregation of Syi Lyang Jye Church in Yangzhou, where their great-grandparents ministered in the previous century

TWENTY-SEVEN

CHINA REUNION
2009-2010

Nearly a decade into the new millennium, and we were still on the go. Nonetheless, we still had places to go and things that needed doing. June 2009 was memorable for the family, for we had the rare experience of having the whole family together the Sunday morning Bob baptized McKenna. Spanning two decades, he had been able to share in that sacred experience with each grandchild.

My four years as Alabama WMU president ended, but the same year marked the beginning of a five-year term as national recording secretary of WMU. When asked to be secretary, I laughed in disbelief. Me? A secretary? Surely not. My secretarial skills were non-existent. This was another of those times when personal ability fails, the Lord comes along and "picks up the slack." Several months later, I became part of the board of the national WMU Foundation. Working with an organization whose total focus was guaranteeing the future of WMU and missions education was immensely satisfying. Simultaneously, being on the board of *The Alabama Baptist* made me newly aware of how our state had the most vibrant state publication in the Southern Baptist Convention, and the one most focused on missions.

However, none of these were more rewarding than beginning to teach first through third graders in Sunday School. Those lively girls taught me so much. I confess that one motivation for teaching this age was to share missions with them. Our church no longer had GAs and RAs, and I wanted those children to catch a vision of world needs and how God could use them. Each Sunday, we did intense Bible study, memory work and Bible drills — and still made time for GAs. Watching the missions "light bulb" go off in one young mind after another was more than worth the time and effort that the preparations took.

The year 2009 also included an exciting week in Manila, celebrating the fiftieth anniversary of International Baptist Church. Our IBC friends were the kind where, even if you haven't seen them in years, it feels like it was just last week since you caught up. Bob and I decided it would have been worth the whole trip just to hear Nolyn Cabahug again as he sang "Great Is Thy Faithfulness."

Molly Marshall, president of Central Baptist Seminary, asked me to join her trip with nine seminarians for a "Judson Journey" to Burma the next March. I relived the magic of seeing one historic Judson site after another through the eyes of brilliant young students just embarking on their own journeys. To make it feel even more personal, one of them was the granddaughter of the Spurgeons, our next-door neighbors in Taiwan. Two moments stand out vividly in my mind from that journey. The seminarians also visited all sorts of spots sacred to the Buddhists, as well as places significant in Baptist missions. Our side trip to Bagan with its literally thousands of pagodas dotting the landscape immediately brought to mind Adoniram Judson's declaration that, one day, the spires of churches pointing toward heaven would also be piercing the skies over Burma. (He was right.) In Bagan, as in so many of the places sacred to the Buddhists, pilgrims removed their shoes as a sign of respect in the presence of something holy. I wept the morning, several days later, when our little group gathered in the church at Aungbinle, one of the spots where Adoniram had lain in prison. We had a time of devotion with Pastor Saw Seelah, and each student was able to briefly hold the rare first-edition Judson Bible. One young seminarian spoke into the quietness of the moment, saying, "*This* is the place where we need to take off our shoes."

Dr. Marshall spoke at the graduation exercises of Burma's MIT, Myanmar Institute of Theology. The heat was sweltering, but the warmth of communion with MIT's students and faculty left a glowing feeling that lingered in the heart. I had an unexpected surprise when Dr. Saw Hlaing Bwa, director of the institute's Judson Center, came up, bowed low, and introduced himself as "the one who had the privilege of translating *Bless God and Take Courage*." I had not known who the translator was, and immediately assured Dr. Saw, "Believe me, sir, the privilege is *mine* to meet you." Dr. Saw began relating his translation experience, "I thought I knew all there was to know about Yood-a-than (Judson). I learned so very much more, though. You see, I began translating with my head." Saw paused, choked up, then finished, "But I ended up translating with my heart." He began to weep; I did the same, and we shared a unique heart-to-heart moment, remembering the magnificence of the faith and courage of Judson, the man who changed a nation.

The year 2010 marked a special milestone in all our years of traveling — we took our family "home" to China. It was the most emotionally draining *and* simultaneously uplifting journey of all. Thankfully, we had been able at one time or another to take each family member to China to experience my childhood home and memories. Unfortunately, there was never one time when *all* of us could get together for a combined journey, but this time around, all except Alice and Eric were able to come. I was especially grateful to have been able to show both of them, at different times, our family's China roots, but deeply regretted they could not be part of this family pilgrimage. Considering our ages, and our realization that the older the "grands" got, the more scattered we would be, Bob and I determined to go while we could.

I still get choked up recalling so many signal moments of that 2010 trip. The nine of us, ranging in age from eight to seventy-seven, began our adventure in Beijing. Jet lag had to take a back seat to the excitement of starting at the Great Wall of China. It boggled the mind to think that over 5,000 miles of wall were still standing, parts of it over 2,000 years old. My seventy-something-year-old legs had to stretch it to keep pace with active twelve-year-old twins as we climbed the magnificent structure and gazed into the hazy distance of that ancient land. The wall was crowded with hundreds of Chinese tourists. They not only reveled (as did we) in the sights from one of the world's wonders, but also loved staring at these unusual young foreigners. Scores of Chinese tourists tried chatting with the young Americans standing on the wall with them. "*Ni Hau Ma?*" (How are you?) our grands would greet the friendly faces wanting to engage them. Our grandchildren came bearing little gifts. Norma, a talented friend in our WMU group at home, had made cunning little felt teddy bears, and our GAs had stuffed them. Those teddy bears came along to serve as gifts for Chinese children. McKenna was an outgoing little eight-year-old sprite and became the giver of gifts as we encountered mothers with their young children. Those small teddy bears were beautiful ambassadors that cut across culture and language.

On the way back to Beijing, we stopped at the Ming Tombs, a valley of thirteen burial sites of various ancient emperors. I loved watching our crew walk down the Sacred Way, as the avenue leading to the tombs was called. I observed Jody and his two sons walking three abreast, the twins' arms around their dad, chatting as they gazed at the giant stone animals and carvings lining the way. Walking behind them, I smiled to myself, thinking, *It doesn't get any more satisfying than this.*

The next day tried to rival the previous one for moments to etch in the memory, beginning with Tian An Men Square, so crowded it felt like half the city was there. From the square, we entered the Forbidden City, and

Carl was quick to comment, "Oh, no. The Starbucks is gone!" Nonetheless, 500 years of history surrounding us was sufficient to make up for the loss of a Starbucks. Our family strolled those ancient cobblestones and looked in one building after another, wondering about the lives of the 100,000 people who had lived there long ago. History is so much more satisfying when we can share it with family. Next stop was the fabulous Temple of Heaven, that ancient structure built with no nails. I made a silent salute to Mama, recalling the many times she reminisced about her fascination with that fabulous building.

It wasn't just the wonderful sights we were experiencing, it was the fact that we could build family memories together. The ancient capital of Xian had to rival Beijing for exciting history. Nothing could be more amazing than the army of terracotta warriors buried over 2,000 year earlier to guard the tomb of the great emperor Chin Shr Hwang Di. The kids loved going to the terracotta factory and being allowed to mold a little terracotta soldier of their own. Also at the factory, there were massive terracotta figures in which tourists could pose and see what kind of a "warrior" they might make. Later, we flew to Nanjing, and Jody had a "moment of remembrance" as he showed their children the college where he had taught graduate students some twenty-five years earlier. (See Appendix: The Story of Harry.)

All of our eyes were wide with the sights of Shanghai. It had changed out of all recognition from the Shanghai of my childhood. The joy of introducing children and grandchildren to the friends of my childhood, however, was a changeless moment in time, like a special gift from God. Legacy loomed large in my mind all those weeks in China. We visited Grace Church, and had a priceless visit with eighty-something-year-old Pastor Chi. His father had been Aunt Grace's pastor in the early 1950s. Just the Wednesday night before, Chi and his fellow pastors had baptized 100 new believers. My dear friend, Wu Wang Ying Gwang, joined us at the church; the two of us felt like we had come full circle again.

On the train from Shanghai home to Zhenjiang, the countryside flashed by in double time, and I marveled, thinking of how it had taken more than four hours to make the trip in the 1940s. On this modern super-speed train, we covered the distance in slightly over an hour. Daddy and Mama would have been astonished. The Zhenjiang train station was completely changed, but my heart held the picture of that wintry day in 1948 when our family had fled the city from this same spot. Flashing into mind was my dear little blue enamel cup, overflowing yet again. I was actually *here,* and able to share "home" with all of our family.

Our wonderful tour guide from more than two decades earlier became our gracious host, showing us this city he loved and treating us to a fabulous feast. He also found for me my favorite condiment from sixty-five years earlier — *lwo bwo tudz* (pickled baby turnips). The grands looked at me with wide-open eyes, and one of the twins asked, "Nana, do you *really* like that?" I assured him it was wonderful but failed to get even one grandchild to take me at my word. However, each of them absorbed the sights they saw that day, and that made my heart swell with joy. We visited Pearl Buck's home, now a museum, and the children well knew the importance of this author who shared some China legacy with their own grandmother.

The family had heard us talk about the famous early missionary, Hudson Taylor, and appreciated being able to visit the small memorial room honoring him that stood next to Zhenjiang's open church. I told them the story of the tall gravestone that had disappeared from the cemetery during the Cultural Revolution and then turned up in the backyard of our house years later (see Appendix). On this visit, I noticed another gravestone leaning up against the wall. My heart skipped a beat when I read the inscription and realized this was the tombstone of Rev. Leonidas Pierce, who arrived in Yangzhou in 1891, and had drowned in the Yangtze River in 1922. This was the father of Dr. Ethel Pierce, the missionary doctor who had delivered my brother.

We next discovered how the ancient street near my home had changed. I was shocked. The old *dagoba* still stood sentinel over the cobblestoned street, but the city had gone to great lengths to preserve ancient history and restore centuries' old structures. This was a new thing — preserving the old for posterity and helping new generations appreciate their history.

After taking a family picture at the *dagoba*, I was more than ready to go to the place I had been wanting to show the grandchildren for long years — my childhood home. Change again! Since my first trip back in 1983, the former Baptist mission compound had undergone a massive facelift. Now it was not possible to just walk in and look around, for it was part of the city's museum. We had to buy a ticket for admission. I discovered that our two mission houses were now the business offices of the museum and not open to visitors. However, purchasing tickets would allow us to walk into the compound and see the exterior. The first thing I noticed was the front yard where my brother and I had pulled up so many old weeds. It was restored now and looked happily familiar. (Maybe someone had been put to work, pulling up weeds again.) This was the moment I had longed for ever since our children, and then grandchildren, had been born — that someday I could stand with them on the spot where the beggar had knelt over six decades earlier. All of them had heard me talk about the Christmas morning beggar, but I now stood with them on the place and relived with them the moment a nine-year-old child had felt God tugging at her heart. It had been *the* pivotal moment of my early spiritual journey. It didn't bother me that tears filled my eyes and overflowed as I recounted the Christmas morning of 1947.

A kind museum employee saw us and spoke a greeting. I explained to her how this had been my childhood home. Not one to let rules bother her, she invited us to come inside and look around. I'd have loved to hug that good-natured lady as we went inside, where I regaled the grands with happenings right here six decades earlier. We walked up the staircase. It was unchanged. The door to my bedroom was locked, but we posed for a family picture in front of it. I was amazed at how much the interior of our house resembled its 1948 appearance.

The next day, Sunday, however, was the culmination of my wishes and dreams for a China reunion as we crossed the Yangtze River to visit Yangzhou. This was my first home in China, and now was the golden opportunity to take the family home to see the city and attend services in Mama and Daddy's church. We hired a van for the day and began with a ride on a vehicular ferry across the Yangtze. Right next to our car was an unexpected sight — a truck piled high with hogs on their way to a slaughterhouse. I would swear those were tipsy hogs, each with a grin on its face. I laughed out loud and told the grands, "Hey, look — these *big* piggies are going to market!" One of them snapped a picture of our traveling companions, possibly the most unusual of all our time in China.

Yangzhou is a fabulous old city, redolent with history and atmosphere. We visited the hospital compound where our family had lived in the 1930s. Our house was gone now, but the Stamps' residence, where Mama and Daddy first met, was still there, as was the hospital clinic where Dad had lived his first year in China. Our driver took us past beautiful West Lake and the parkland surrounding it. I reminisced about my ninth birthday, when the highlight of the day was our family paddling on the West Lake in a little hired boat. On the way to the church, we passed the old stone Tang Dynasty pagoda, and I remembered this familiar childhood sight. It had stood there for over 1,500 years. Each time I saw that pagoda, I knew we were close to the church; sure enough, a block away, the church came into view.

There was the cornerstone with its etched characters: *Jin Shin Hwei* (Baptist church). Sweltering August heat and humidity engulfed us, but the parishioners packed into the sanctuary seemed oblivious to the ninety-five-degree temperature. All of us were perspiring, but simply being able to be in that place, worshipping with fellow believers, made it a beautiful experience.

As the grandchildren noticed, "Nana lost it" several times that memorable morning, including the moment when the congregation raised their voices to sing "I Love to Tell the Story," Mama's favorite hymn. Tears trickled down my cheeks as I recalled the many times I had heard Mama sing those timeless words, "I love to tell the story, for some have never heard the message of salvation from God's own holy Word." Pastor Ju Ming Hwa preached forty-five minutes, and, of course, it meant more to Bob and me because we could understand her message. I noticed how attentive and respectful our grandchildren were, in spite of the language barrier. The thought kept running through my mind, *Ah, Daddy, Mama, don't you rejoice to see your great-grandchildren here in this place where you planted your lives?*

As the service ended, Pastor Ju surprised me by telling the congregation about these visitors in their midst and spoke to me, saying, "Mrs. Hung,

won't you come speak to our congregation?" Here was an unexpected serendipity. I asked all the grands to come for a moment to the platform with
me. They looked a bit taken aback but politely did what Nana suggested.
I never even imagined having a privilege like this — to introduce Ho Se
Mo and Ho Shien Sun's (their Chinese names) great-grandchildren to the
membership of their church in China. I briefly related Mama and Daddy's
Yangzhou story and their love for this, their first church home in China,
nearly a century earlier. I got choked up when explaining how I recalled,
as a child, hearing my parents praying for their friends here in Yangzhou.
"Not a day passed, from the time they had to leave China, until the time
they reached heaven," I assured them, "that Mama and Daddy did not think
of you and love you and pray for you." I wasn't ashamed of my emotions,
for this was a pivotal moment of joy. "I am deeply thankful to be able to
represent them here today, in this place so special to their hearts. Please
know," and I swallowed hard, "that each day I will be remembering you and
asking God to touch and bless and strengthen your hearts."

The final "amen" had scarcely been uttered before church members
began to flock to the front where we stood. Those I had met in the 1980s
who had known and loved Daddy and Mama were gone to their heavenly
reward, but their descendants welcomed us royally. I also noticed a number
of people coming to the altar to kneel and pray, including an elderly man
who prostrated himself there in earnest supplication. Seeing the devotion
and unwavering faith of these who had endured so much was incredibly
stirring. An older woman holding a beautiful little chubby-cheeked baby
came up, broadly smiling and managing to grasp my hand in hers while
still holding her smiling little fellow. Her face was radiant as she introduced
herself, "I am the daughter-in-law of Pastor Wu, who loved your parents
so very much. This," nodding her head at the little one, "is his great-great-
grandson." I responded, "No wonder this child has such a luminous little
face. He has the same glow that his great-great-grandfather gave off." I
introduced McKenna, who was standing at my side, and she gave little Mr.
Wu a teddy bear. He solemnly grasped it, then broke into a big grin.

Standing behind Mrs. Wu was another woman who looked to be in her early sixties, patiently waiting her turn. I turned to talk with her, and the tears that had been lurking in her eyes spilled over. She appeared to be laboring under deep emotion as I grasped her hands in mine. "I am so happy to meet you today," the weeping lady assured me, introducing herself as Mrs. Li. "Let me explain my tears," she spoke. "I was born the year the missionaries all had to leave China, but my parents told me about their message and their love and how they left their homes and comforts and came far across the ocean so we here in Yangzhou could hear the good news." She hesitated as the tears continued trailing down her cheeks. Mrs. Li managed to finish, "My parents found God and His love for them because those missionaries came, and they, in turn, shared the message with me. But you," and she tremulously smiled as she looked directly into my eyes, "are the first missionary I have ever met or heard myself. I simply want to say 'thank you' for caring enough to come with the good news."

By this time, we were weeping together. My heart was too full for mere words, overcome with a wave of humility. To this precious woman, I represented something much more than what I was, receiving praise for nothing I had done. I simply personified for her the many who, long ago, had given up home and fortune to invest their lives in sharing the gospel. Grasping the dear woman's hands in mine, I spoke through my own tears, "I thank *you* for sharing your heart and family with me." Looking into her tearful eyes, I passed on to her the beautiful blessing from Numbers 6: "The Lord bless you and keep you, the Lord make His face shine upon you, and be gracious to you; The Lord lift up His countenance upon you, and give you peace." That singular moment is etched in memory, and I know we two will meet again in Glory.

Our family had come full circle. Mama. Daddy. Aunt Grace. God's guiding hand on their lives led them to this place, and they planted seeds that came to full bloom. Because of God's faithfulness, I now had the unique opportunity to see the harvest of my parents' ministry. My little blue enamel cup — so symbolic as it recalled the presence and power of God at work in our lives — was full and running over with joy. The great Shepherd who led their paths — and *our* paths — also guided us beside the still waters. And how many times, even in the valley of the shadow of death, had God led, comforted, anointed our heads with oil and then — *glorious* then — allowed our cups to run over.

With the grandchildren at the dagoba near Rosalie's childhood home, Zhenjiang, 2010

Standing with Pastor Qin and Candace McIntosh, Alabama WMU
Executive Director, at the Lottie Moon memorial, Penglai, China, 2008

AFTERWORD

Have you ever opened a long-forgotten book and found in its pages a pressed flower? It's like discovering a gift from the past. In reading through the hundreds of letters my parents and others in our family left behind, I came across a letter from my mother to *her* mother in 1933. It was written the fall after her wedding in Shanghai, and she had slipped in a delicate little spray of orange blossoms that had been in her bridal bouquet. I sat there holding that little spray and shedding nostalgic tears. Mama knew her mother would cherish this flower from the wedding bouquet. In turn, Grandmama had saved it, and now I could pass it on to our daughter, Alice, the bride's namesake.

Since our retirement nearly thirty years ago, we are frequently asked, "What is your best memory from all those years in international missions?" Or some will inquire, "What would you change about your service overseas?" Without hesitation, Bob responds, "I just wish we could do it all again." We are truly blessed with rich and deep memories, and I know we shall never pass this way again. However, this final volume has been more difficult to write than the first one, probably because many of the people in this book are still living. I want to tell the story, but do not want to tell it "amiss."

Through these many months of researching our family's missions journey, scores of letters and records have jogged my memory time and again. Sometimes it felt like I was reliving some event, and I would experience a sharp pain of loss, or a remembered grief, cutting and painful. Other times, I felt regret over something that I could have done so much better, or maybe left undone. Occasionally, I felt a pang of hurt when remembering something sad. Far more often, however, I experienced a jolt of joy. Some event would make me smile as I recalled the emotions of that long ago moment, and sometimes I would just laugh out loud. Sometimes in reading those letters, I recalled some occasion where I had felt wounded and reacted with anger or deep hurt. But time has revealed that in the mending of our "broken places," we can become stronger where wounded and healed. Many a time, when an unexpected adversity rears its head, a sudden physical affliction hits, or a relative or friend brings emotional grief, I can remember God's mercies in the past and look for them again. More than six decades ago, I first read a prayer by Amy Wilson Carmichael (author and noble missionary for half a century in India) as she wrote, "Lord, we would endure; sift us clear of weakness. Make us strong." I think of that every day, especially rough ones.

The joy of reunions in China have affected and enriched our entire family and remain forever a part of our collective history. In the intervening years, our grown children are now enjoying children and grandchildren of their own. After ten years as president of the Chicago seminary, Alice became executive director of the American Academy of Religion. Jody followed his nearly two decades as director of federal programs for the civil division of the Department of Justice by serving as chief of staff for Attorney General Jeff Sessions. The following year, he was named Assistant Attorney General, directing the civil division. Jody recently left government service and joined a law firm. Meanwhile, our children's children were finishing their educations and moving into the business world. They are now scattered from Dallas to Raleigh to Washington, with our granddaughter, McKenna, completing her university work in Alabama. My brother, Arthur, who for years was chief financial officer of a banking corporation headquartered in California, later switched to private financial consulting. True to our childhood passion for reading, Art gathered a fine collection of first-edition books. Arthur died in his sleep in 2018 and left a trust that continues missions involvement.

Beginning in 1999, I've been immersed in researching and recording our Baptist missions experience, with memorable trips to Burma — including escorting a group of Baptist historians and ministers on a Judson trip to honor the bicentennial of the Judsons' arrival in Burma in 2013. Delving deeply into the lives of WMU heroes has been another sweet-scented sprig of missions history "orange blossoms." In addition to writing the story of Ann and Adoniram Judson, I fell in love with Hephzibah Jenkins Townsend, Fannie Heck and Kathleen Mallory, and recorded their exploits for this new generation. The fragrance of their legacies still lingers in the air.

Bob and I have learned that opportunities do not stop; they simply change and evolve. Our bond of friendship with so many on several continents is not broken by distance. That cherished little blue enamel cup given to me as a baby has endured the miles and the vagaries of life. My blue cup brings a smile to my face each morning as I look at it perched on the bookcase right by the desk. At some unexpected moment, a chill will skid down my spine—like a thrill of recognition. It might be from that joy that came in a letter yesterday, the call from a long-ago friend this morning, or the thrilling news of a man's salvation, someone we had prayed for over many years. Then our cup overflows with joy; it overflows with grace. In those times — *Yes, my cup runneth over. Surely, goodness and mercy shall follow me all the days of my life, and I will dwell in the house of the Lord forever.*

The grandchildren with their grandmother, 2002 and 2017.
Lovingly known as "The Stack" in the family.

ACKNOWLEDGMENTS

Writing each book has been a new adventure — and now, more than ever, I realize how dependent I am on the memories of others and their generosity of time and energy in sharing those memories. No one has been more essential in this China journey than Kyndal Owens, archivist at IMB. She is a treasure-trove of research skills, providing priceless information from the archives of the board. Just as helpful and highly knowledgeable about China is historian Catherine Allen. Her research skills and memory of China Baptist missions history have been like a gold mine. Cindy Goodwin, volunteer at Woman's Missionary Union archives in Birmingham, has helped me with many hours of research and locating materials.

We are blessed with special relatives. Our nephew, Wayne Hunt, has shared his love of family history, along with providing little-known information that has kept the dates, places, and people in our family in proper order. My cousin, JoAnn Tucker Coleman, has assisted with a wealth of information from my father's side of the family — and both have been essential to accuracy.

During the many years overseas, each week I would write home several times and make copies for both sets of parents and a special friend in Boaz, Jamie Faucett. Mama saved all the letters I sent those first two terms, and they provided a weekly record of life on the field. Mama died in 1983, and Jamie faithfully kept all letters, making it possible for me to go back and recall what happened each month of all those subsequent years. *The Blue Enamel Cup: An MK's China Legacy* would not have been published without her help.

I run out of words to describe how valuable my editor, Ella Robinson, has become. She has assisted me by editing the last seven books and literally making them readable. Along the way, she has become an esteemed and appreciated friend. A sincere shout-out goes to Butch Blume and Denise Huffman of Courier Publishing. They are superb to work with.

Another special gift in publishing these books has been our grandson, Eric Hudiburg, a photographer and media person who has edited the pictures for these past five books and designed the covers. The little hand holding the blue enamel cup on this book cover is that of our first great-grandson, Bobby Hudiburg.

APPENDIX

THE STORY OF THE STONE

When Jody and I explored Zhenjiang in 1984, we visited the old European cemetery, looking for Hudson Taylor's grave. I had long regaled the family about how, during my growing-up years, we would take guests to our city to see a famous gravesite. Hudson Taylor, one of the earliest and most famous missionaries to China, had died and was buried in Zhenjiang. Jody and I discovered that near the end of the Cultural Revolution in the late 1960s, the vast majority of the cemetery's graves had been destroyed and the markers cast aside or hauled away.

As Jody and I walked through the area where the cemetery had been located, we realized it was now a sea of small squatter houses with a labyrinth of alleys and paths. Along the alleyways, we spotted tombstones and would stop to scan each one. Maybe *this* one would be that of Hudson Taylor. But no. Many were of British sailors who had died in the area, with an occasional American's gravestone. Occasionally, a friendly or curious resident would ask us what we were looking for. "I'm trying to find the grave of Dài Mushr," I would tell them, "the famous missionary who lived in this city many years ago." Each would shake their heads: no, they didn't know of a Dài Mushr.

About the time we decided to give up, we found an elderly little lady who seemed fascinated by these foreigners who could speak her language. "Do you possibly know where the tomb of Dài Mushr (Dr. Taylor) might have been?" The little lady beamed, "Ah yes!" and she grew excited. "You are looking for the grave of Dài Mushr Yang Gweidz Fuhn!" (Dr. Taylor, old foreign devil man!) Seems this very woman had been one of the caretakers of the cemetery. Her face grew solemn as she reported, "I'm sorry, but his gravestone is gone now. They came and took it away." We had no idea who "they" were, but that put an end to our search.

Seven years later, we miraculously discovered the story of the stone. Bob and I were planting a church some 4,500 miles away in Perth, Western

Australia, and learned that the great-grandson of Hudson Taylor himself was speaking at a conference in town. Eagerly seated near the front, we listened attentively as Dr. James Hudson Taylor recounted thrilling experiences from his personal missionary journey. Following the service, we found an opportunity to meet him and greet him in Mandarin. Dr. Taylor's face lighted up, and he replied in beautiful Chinese. (That was actually his first language, and English his second.) His Mandarin was flawless, and he was delighted to hear about my background in Zhenjiang, a city he knew well. I told him about what had transpired seven years earlier, when our son had gone with me to look for his ancestor's grave. I concluded, "So you see, we met with unsuccess." By this time, his face was alight with pleasure. "Let me tell you," he broke in, "the gravestone has been found and is safe."

His tale was fascinating. Like Jody and I, he and the pastor of the Methodist church — the city's only open church — went to the old cemetery to search for his ancestor's grave. His experience was much like ours. However, the Methodist pastor was able to locate the old cemetery caretaker who was very familiar with Taylor's grave. Sadly shaking his head, the caretaker told the visitors, "I'm sorry. They came and took the stone away. I don't know where it is, but," and his face looked pensive, "you might ask at the city museum." Immediately, Taylor and his pastor friend headed to the museum, which, at that time, was in the old British Consulate, located just at the back of the two Baptist mission houses (where I had lived nearly half a century earlier. Those houses, too, were now part of the museum complex.). Upon meeting the museum director, Dr. Taylor made inquiry about his ancestor's gravestone. The curator's eyes began darting around, and he became evasive. "Ah, well," he started, "I just don't know, but I will do some checking. We do have some markers stored out back." He concluded, "So, check back in a day or so."

Consequently, two days later, Dr. Taylor and his pastor friend returned. Upon inquiring again, the museum director replied that yes, that marker "had been located" out back with a few others they were "taking care of." He reluctantly led to the spot where the markers stood propped up against a wall. As soon as Dr. Taylor described that scene and that moment, I felt a chill slip down my spine. Hudson Taylor's tombstone had been propped against the back wall of our house in Zhenjiang.

Dr. Taylor explained to the director that the Christians of the city would like to have the marker back and place it at the church, thus preserving it for the many who would be interested in seeing the memorial stone. Immediately, the museum director again became evasive and repeated that they would "have to come back later." By the end of the week, the museum director informed Dr. Taylor that the church people would have to "promise to take good care of the marker." Furthermore, he would confer with city authorities and make a monetary determination.

Dr. Taylor left the matter in his pastor friend's hands. Several months later, the pastor wrote Dr. Taylor to report on the museum's decision. Christians in the city would need to "pay rent" for the years the museum had kept the stone "safe," and at $500 US a year rental fee, the charge would be US $13,000. Upon hearing this news, the pastor set his jaw, took a deep, calming breath, and told the museum director, "That is alright. You keep the stone. We have the message of the marker written on our hearts."

That might well have been the end of the story, but strangely, a handful of years later, and with no explanation, the museum gave Hudson Taylor's gravestone to the Christians of Zhenjiang. Now located in the courtyard of Zhenjiang's open church is the little memorial hall holding the 100-plus-year-old grave marker of Hudson Taylor, pioneer missionary to China. The stone is surrounded by information, photographs, and artifacts related to Taylor's remarkable ministry. There it stands, a tribute to a remarkable man of faith and courage, but even more, a tribute to the power and honor of the God he served.

(Years later, construction work in the area of the cemetery uncovered the actual graves of Hudson Taylor and his beloved Maria, and they were moved to the church where the gravestone now stands. Dr. James Hudson Taylor, Taylor's great-grandson, died in missions service in Hong Kong in 2009.)

*Bob and Rosalie stand with grandsons Carl and Eric at the tombstone and memorial
to Hudson Taylor, founder of the China Inland Mission, Zhenjiang, China, 1997*

Harry's Story

Note: Our son, Jody, spent a semester teaching in a graduate school in China and had an amazing experience with one of his students. He recounts it as follows:

I arrived at the Nanjing Agricultural University on the outskirts of Nanjing, the old southern capital, in February 1986, to teach English to Chinese graduate students. They had been selected from across the country for a special intensive language training program. Upon arrival, I was informed that I would be teaching five classes with varying levels of English ability — "low," "fair," and "good." One of the first things on the agenda was to give each student an English name, which they found exciting. To assess their level of English comprehension, I introduced myself and then called on students to identify something they had learned about me from this introduction. The first student to speak was Sam, who mentioned one or two things from my introduction and then added, "Mr. Hunt has studied in Taiwan for one year." I had not mentioned this when introducing myself. This caught the class by surprise, and it prompted a good laugh when I asked Sam how he *knew* that. (As our family knew from having lived many years in Taiwan and China, there is really very little that is private in the Chinese culture!)

I was not permitted to "proselytize" in class, of course, but I *was* permitted to talk about religion and Christianity to the extent that vocabulary and class discussion naturally drifted that way. And there were occasions for such discussions, particularly because the students discovered that I attended church on Sundays and often asked me questions about it. One week early on, five students asked if they could go to church with me, and not infrequently in the weeks that followed, several students joined me in attending worship services. These visits to church prompted some intriguing questions and sometimes led to interesting class discussions.

On one occasion, I explained to the class what a "Dear Abby" letter is, and, as a homework assignment, instructed each student to craft a "Dear Abby" letter that would present a dilemma or question for "Abby" to answer. Students took their assignments seriously, of course, sometimes spending hours poring over their worn dictionaries to find the right words to use. For this particular assignment, one of the students, Harry, wrote the following:

Dear Abby,

Yesterday morning we went to church with our English teacher. It's my first time to visit church. I was shocked by its splendid spectacle. We stand in the church and listening to Anthem. Such beautiful singing I never hear it before. I was moved so deeply by it's nice sacred tone that I could feel the tears coming to my eyes. I even could feel God being talking to me, but my problem is I am a member of Communist Party I don't believe in any religion. I am puzzle such feeling.

Harry

As it would turn out in the months that followed, this was not the only time Harry would make mention of God. When I assigned the students a speech on the topic "Something I Regret," Harry told the class that his younger brother had died fifteen years earlier, at the age of 8, from a tragic fall as his family was getting ready to go for an outing early one morning. Harry's regret had been that his younger brother had gone to bed angry the night before because Harry would not give him all of the candy he wanted. Harry lived every day with a feeling of guilt because he failed to fulfill his younger brother's last wish, and because his brother had died with anger directed at him. At the funeral, Harry placed an entire bag of candy in the coffin with his brother. The speech was haunting, and I so wanted to say to Harry that he should not feel guilty because in his heart his younger brother surely knew that what Harry was doing was for his own good. Perhaps providentially, the next day Harry and I happened to meet in passing in the dormitory staircase when no one else was around. Our minds both ran to the same place in that moment. Harry spoke first: "I want to tell you I'm sorry — you know, yesterday when I told about my little brother, I could almost not speak because I was about to cry." I assured him: "I know. I want you to know that you shouldn't feel guilty — your brother knew you loved him because you were doing what was best for him." And then Harry said: "That's why I hope what you say is true — that there is a God and my brother lives in heaven."

At the end of the semester, I gave Harry a copy of a dual Chinese/English Bible. Little did I realize at the time how that Bible would be used to transform Harry's life. After I returned to the States, and was attending law school at Columbia University, I received a letter from Harry. Following the intensive English language program in Nanjing, Harry had spent many months researching and studying yak breeding in an extremely remote region of western China, about 4,000 to 5,000 meters above sea level. In the letter, Harry described how he had traveled by truck, Land Rover, and on foot for a week to reach this cold and desolate location, and that he had slept those many cold months in a tent lit by lantern at night. Harry wrote that he only had two things there that cheered him up — one was a battery-operated shortwave radio on which he could sometimes listen to Voice of America. The other was:

"... (the) Bible that you gave me. I take it sacred and very special to me. I read and recite it with great loyalty. Of course, I cannot say I can recite the whole book but the valuable things I get from this book is countless. From it I find God with me and know for what and how to live under God. What can I say to show my thankness is that it is you guiding me believe in God. After reading it over and over again I deeply understand that God really does give me power for living. Now I put God first. I now recognize that my living goal and power for living come from a personal relationship with God. It is true that those who hope in the Lord will renew their strength. They will soar on wings like eagles. Now in everything I do, I put God number one. When I have a personal relationship with Jesus Christ, He give me peace of mind. There is great thrill that I am gradually becoming a research worker but there is no greater attainment than to know God in a personal way. After I give my life to Christ, I feel myself very special to God. I saw that the book was God's way of talking to me and try to seek God in what I do. Now I firmly believe that if I put God first and my family after that, along with my social existence and my job, I can withstand any attack. This is how I do it. I simply get alone somewhere and tell God that I believe in Him, that I can't go on living without Him, that I am now accepting Jesus Christ as my Lord. ..."

The Huu family in 1975, when they arrived in America

THE HUU STORY

The young student with the striking dark eyes sat solemnly on the far side of the front row, her eyes unwaveringly focused on her teacher. Winter quarter, 1974, was beginning, and the rather apprehensive-looking girl was noticeable, for she was the only Asian student in English 101. Snead College in Boaz, Alabama, had scores of students in their new international program, and I was learning on the job as English instructor and director of international students. Students were from a dozen countries, the majority from the Middle East or South America. My heart skipped a happy beat to find an Asian student at Snead — a small, long-established community college tucked into the corner of northeast Alabama.

When I introduced myself to the new coed, a smile transformed her face. Eighteen-year-old Thu Nyugen had arrived just days earlier from Thailand, where her Vietnamese parents were currently living. She explained that she arrived the night before Thanksgiving, not knowing a person. Anxiety was written on her face. Her large, close-knit family was 10,000 miles away, all of them in distress over their homeland, for Vietnam's very existence as a democracy was in immediate peril.

Within a week, the caliber of this new student was obvious. Her English was beautiful, a great relief to me. So many entering our young international program had far too few English skills, and I struggled to help them catch up. Not Thu. She excelled. During those early weeks, I became acquainted with the family's amazing story.

Nguyen Dinh Huu, Thu's father, was a colonel in the South Vietnamese army, serving since 1973 as South Vietnam's military attaché to Thailand. Meanwhile, the South Vietnamese army, along with American forces, were attempting to save Vietnam from the Communist Viet Cong forces sweeping down from the north. With Colonel Huu's colloquial English, he was a large part of the Vietnamese government's liaison with their American allies. Huu was highly educated, holding a master's degree in literature, and known as a man of unimpeachable integrity, just what his government needed to represent them in the strategic attaché role in Bangkok.

Thu and her siblings enrolled in an elite international school in Bangkok — and were driven to the school each day by a driver. They adapted quickly to a totally new environment. Hao, one of Thu's younger sisters, remained behind in South Vietnam to live with an aunt in Nha Thrang for a year or so. Meanwhile, Peter (her oldest brother) studied at a large university near Saigon. The rest of the eight siblings were in Bangkok. By April 1975, a tense military situation in South Vietnam was growing more dire each day. One city after another fell to the Viet Cong as the northern army relentlessly inched closer to Saigon. The Huus' home in Saigon was in the gated area reserved for high-ranking officers in the South Vietnamese army. As such, it would be one of the first targets of the Viet Cong when they entered the city. Now Colonel Huu faced another challenge. Peter, at his university outside of Saigon, and Hao, in Nha Trang with her aunt, were both in imminent danger. If Saigon fell, they would be lost to the family.

In America, and thousands of miles away, Thu's face grew more tense each day as she lived in fear for all of her family, especially Peter and Hao. Just days earlier, Hao's aunt tried to fly her to Saigon, where she could board a plane for Bangkok and safety. That didn't happen — the airport was closed. Hao's aunt somehow managed to secure a little boat and reach a small, nearby airport to fly her niece to Saigon. Thu's mother, Lien Anh, meanwhile, had flown to Saigon, hoping to rescue their daughter. The two fell into each other's arms at the airport and quickly boarded another flight taking them to Bangkok and freedom.

Simultaneously, Colonel Huu was able to get a message to Peter, "Go to Saigon. I will try to find a way to get you out." But there was a huge barrier: Peter was of the age that was legally liable to serve in the military. He would not be allowed to leave the country. By the brilliance that is born of desperation and through divine intervention, Colonel Huu was able to contact an American diplomat friend in Saigon, who, in turn, managed to "adopt" Peter, and flew out of the city with him just before the Viet Cong entered. On April 30, 1975, Saigon fell to the Communists.

Back in Alabama, Thu was distraught. Not knowing what was going on with Peter, she grew physically ill. We were able to get medical help, and then, through some miraculous contacts, discovered that Peter had been rescued and was on his way to America. When we heard this news, I got on the phone and called first one and then another, trying to locate Peter. Still vivid in my mind is that night when we were able to speak to a bilingual gentleman in Virginia and were given the phone number of Colonel Huu's diplomat friend. With trembling fingers, I dialed the number. A man answered. Identifying myself, I asked him, "Is Peter there? Could he come to the phone? His sister *really* needs to talk to him." In less than a minute, I heard a young male voice say, "Hello?" I responded, "Peter?" The male voice replied quickly, "Yes." My heart was full as I turned to Thu and handed her the phone. I'll never forget the blinding joy that flew across her face when she heard her brother's voice. I still get chill bumps remembering that moment.

Thu was now a woman with a mission. Her family needed help. She was the eldest daughter, and she must do her part. We discussed options for getting help. With South Vietnam in total chaos, the United States government faced the dilemma of hundreds of thousands of displaced

Vietnamese desperately needing help. At the time, there were no policies in place to aid Vietnam's refugees. Furthermore, the Huus were not technically considered refugees, because they were in Thailand when Saigon fell. Furthermore, there was no way they could return to Saigon; their house and all their earthly goods were gone. Had they returned, Colonel Huu would have spent his life in a labor camp, with no future for his eight children. They were literally people without a country. Searching for an avenue of help, Thu, the quiet young college coed, revealed her strong inner core. The hand of Providence in subsequent events was obvious. Thu and I talked to Snead's president and dean, then realized that Dr. Joe Brindley, also a Snead administrator, served concurrently as a state legislator. Introducing herself to Joe, Thu declared, "Dr. Brindley, I'm going to Montgomery with you to see the governor." And she did. Finding a friend to accompany her, Thu proceeded to the state capital on her mission to rescue her family.

Dr. Brindley later told me about that visit, grateful that Governor Wallace always lent his ear to his legislators. Joe phoned Wallace, explaining that a young international student urgently needed to speak with him. That June morning, eighteen-year-old Thu Nguyen bravely marched into the office of Alabama's governor and said, "Governor Wallace, you *must* help my father." I have often wondered if the fact that George Wallace had been shot and was paralyzed and confined to a wheelchair might have touched a personal chord, reminding the governor of how he knew what it felt like to be helpless and dependent on the good will of others. Wallace listened, and he acted. Within weeks, he had set into motion a path whereby the Huu family could legally come to Alabama and follow the citizenship path.

Things began to move quickly. Sometimes, it does "take a town" to help a family, and that is exactly what Boaz did. Our church, Boaz First Baptist, led the way, and St. Paul Methodist and Sardis Baptist Church willingly pitched in and were able to help these new citizens moving to our little town get started. The eight Huu children ranged in age from ten to twenty-one, each one solemn-eyed and in the midst of cataclysmic change, for their whole world had been turned upside down. From our first greeting at the airport on July 10, we fell in love with this unique family. I've tried for years to find an adequate way to describe Mr. Huu. It is difficult. My first impression upon seeing his open countenance and encountering that beaming smile was, *Here is a man in whom there is no guile.* Nearly fifty years later, that initial impression has been affirmed time and again. Unique in countless ways, his influence both then and now is far-reaching. He is literally a man who sheds bright beams of good will.

Of all the family, the adjustment was most difficult for his wife, Lien Anh. She did not speak English; here she was, a stranger in a strange land. Our friend, Jamie Faucett, became her English teacher, and they bonded. Then there was Mama. Mrs. Huu did not speak English, and my mother knew not a word of Vietnamese, but they were like kinfolk. Every time Mama and Lien Anh Huu saw each other, Lien Anh's face would light up, and she would tearfully say, "Ma!" as they hugged. Mama and Daddy were the ages of the Huus' own parents, now lost forever to their sight, so this bond was not surprising. (Decades later, when we were visiting the Huus in San Jose, they pointed proudly to the little dining table they had kept from their Boaz home. Beaming, Mr. Huu said, "This is the table your mother and father gave us in 1975.")

The local paper interviewed the Huu family. Huu told the reporter, "My heart hurts for loved ones left behind, but I think of the other side as well; I am more fortunate than they are; they are probably now in labor camps." Looking solemn, he continued, "My children have a future — at least we have freedom. In Vietnam now, we would live in a labor camp and be persecuted, but here we have plenty." This spirit of gratitude was apparent in the whole family. It was not just temporary. To this day, they remain grateful and appreciative, and thank God for His deliverance and protection.

The Huus were fiercely independent. Each child did his job, whether it was stellar schoolwork, chores around the house, or an afternoon job to help support the family. The family became active in our church as well. The Huus called their escape from Vietnam a miracle of God. Second son, Hung, attended Snead and was the same kind of outstanding student as was his sister Thu. The younger ones were all at the head of their classes in

Boaz schools. Huan, the next-to-youngest son, was multi-talented — from art, to academics, to tennis. Small in stature, his efforts and heart were giant. The first thing everyone noticed about him was his radiant smile. (I often thought to myself, *Huan smiles on the just and the unjust alike!)* Huan also found time to work part-time, serving as school janitor, cleaning at the high school every evening after classes. This allowed him to help the family financially.

We marveled at the Huus and how they coped. Mr. Huu told the reporter, "It's difficult to make ends meet, but these things have not discouraged me. I am very sentimental and very ambitious — I like to make things better." And that is exactly what he did, for his family and for the many lives he affected and influenced over the coming years. Nothing was too menial for him to do. Determined not to be a burden on his community, Mr. Huu — this erudite man with a master's degree, a leader of men — first worked on the city garbage truck and then became a gas station manager to earn money to support his large family. Through it all, he maintained his dignity and was highly regarded and admired by the entire town. All the family pitched in. Lien Anh worked as a seamstress for the Lee company. Hung worked at the gas station after classes. Peter came home from the university on weekends to work. Thu worked part-time at Snead, and on Saturdays she and Huan ran the gas station for eighteen hours at a stretch.

Mr. Huu decided the best way he could help others was by obtaining a master's degree in social work, and he set his face toward that goal. Acing the GRE, he enrolled at the University of Alabama, and all the family pulled together, working, struggling, studying. Nguyen Dinh Huu earned that master's degree and became the first Vietnamese social worker with such a degree to work in social services in California, the state with many thousands of Vietnamese refugees. Huu had spent his early years helping others, and neither time nor adversity kept him from continuing to do so.

The move to California was a special blessing for Mrs. Huu, because she was able to be in a community that spoke her heart language. However, the move was a loss to Boaz, the little town that had taken them to heart, and had been loved and appreciated in return. The younger children were fine with the move, and the older ones were already in college. However, Huan, a rising senior in high school, faced the largest dilemma. He had excelled all his years in the local high school and was loved and admired by the entire school. He wanted to graduate with his class, and we found a way to make it possible. The Huus allowed Huan to live with us his senior year. It was our blessing. Huan always carried his own weight, pitching in to help — that young man who was never without his flashing smile. Huan was remarkable. Honor after honor came to Huan his senior year, and we loved watching him receive the Eagle Scout award. He followed that by winning a state art contest as well as the county tennis championship. Huan also won a co-op scholarship to Auburn University in engineering and paid his own way through college, ending up with multiple job offers.

Meanwhile, Mr. Huu was making an impact in California. His work in social welfare for children earned him the title "Patron Saint of Orphans." Nguyen Dinh Huu went on to co-author two books chronicling the story of Vietnam's refugees, and to establish two foundations to aid Vietnamese orphans abroad. Mr. Huu took his own money and vacation time to visit Southeast Asia to see the plight of war orphans. He then enlisted the aid of hundreds of people in establishing an orphanage abroad as well as an agency to support and educate children without parents. The list of his accomplishments and honors literally covers a whole page.

Even in retirement, Mr. Huu continued ministering to others. We were occasionally able to visit them in San Jose. It rejoiced our hearts. Lien Anh had a backyard full of wonderful fruit trees — orange, lemon, persimmon, and pomelo — and a greenhouse full of beautiful orchids that was breathtaking. We also knew without doubt that she made the world's best spring rolls and egg custard pies.

The Huus had the joy of seeing each of their eight children excel. Three are accountants, the other five, engineers. Hoang, the youngest, has an accounting business in Honolulu. She has a room ready for us each time we are able to go to Hawaii to attend WMU conferences. Most of the children live in San Jose and tenderly care for their parents, now in their nineties. It doesn't surprise us a bit to see Thu right there as the chief caregiver. She mothers the whole family, including her parents.

When Vietnam fell, it was a rewarding thing that our church and community could help this family seeking asylum. Now, in an amazing reversal of care, they have ministered to us and contributed to our ministry in other countries. One of their great gifts was sharing their son Huan with us. That young man would do anybody proud. He is the son who looks most like his father, and we have found in him the same remarkable sweet, generous spirit that characterizes Mr. Huu. The list of Huan's accomplishments rivals his father's in number and depth. His first job after graduating from Auburn was with General Dynamics. That must have been an exciting experience for a brilliant young engineer, for he was given security clearance and applied both his art and engineering skills to helping design the revolutionary bubble canopy for America's famous F-16 Fighting Falcon. Huan kept being recruited by top firms. The world's largest automotive electronics company selected him as operations manager. In the course of his work, Huan spent significant time in Mexico, where he learned to speak and write his fourth language, Spanish. General Motors selected him for their management program and paid his expenses as he attained an MBA at the University of Texas, graduating with a 4.0 GPA.

Job offers continued, and Huan worked with Nortel's global supplies, until yet another firm hired him, and then another, each time with more responsibilities. Huan spent twelve years with Google, as their global supply chain manager, before being recruited by a burgeoning new corporation, Arista. In his work, Huan has traveled to more than twenty countries and put all of his language skills to work. At the same time, he somehow managed to involve himself in numerous charities at his home base in San Jose. Not forgetting the hand-up that was given him as a young student, Huan has endowed scholarships both at Auburn University and his high school alma mater.

A few years ago, Boaz High School recognized Huan Nguyen as an outstanding alumnus, inducting him into their Wall of Fame. At the luncheon honoring the occasion, Bob and I sat in for his parents and couldn't wipe the smiles off our faces the whole time we heard Huan's accomplishments recognized and honored. Huan has also become an important part of ministries Bob and I are able to continue supporting on three continents. In fact, he has made much of it possible. We are awed by his generous spirit and concern for others. He visited us a few years ago, and the first thing that struck me as he walked in the door was: *That glowing, infectious smile has not changed one iota in all the years we have known him.* I often smile to think how it all began in English 101. Beginning that November morning nearly half a century ago, we have seen God's remarkable love and care in rescuing a family in peril and molding and making them instruments of blessing to thousands of others.

The Huu Family in 2013

Huan receives Eagle Scout Award, 1980

THE TALE OF THE TAPESTRY

China was in turmoil in 1948. The Communists already controlled northern China and were fast taking more territory as they swept through the entire country. Simultaneously, President Chiang Kai-shek and his forces fled south ahead of the oncoming troops. Chiang and the Nationalist army next retreated to Taiwan, establishing "Free China" there — and taking with them many priceless artifacts from the national museum. Thousands of these treasures had been stored up and taken to safe spots during the Japanese occupation and most had not even been uncrated, making it possible for the Nationalist Chinese to retain and preserve countless works of art.

With China in such a state of uncertainty, our Baptist missionaries had been holding on and continuing to work as best they could in tense circumstances. Poverty, lawlessness, and even famine in several areas were a constant specter. Inflation was wild. When missionaries got their monthly paychecks, they would immediately buy supplies for the month — food, fuel, etc. — because, in a matter of days, their Chinese currency would be worthless. A few missionaries began to take any leftover funds and invest them in Chinese artifacts that desperate people were often selling for a song as they fled their homes with only the bare necessities.

Harold and Alice Hall, my parents, lived and worked in Zhenjiang, the capital of Jiangsu (Kiangsu) Province, just forty-three miles south of Nanking, what was then the capital of China. My parents weighed their choices. Should they try to stay and help their Chinese brothers and sisters, or was it coming to the point where their presence would endanger their Christian friends when the Communists swept through their city? My aunt, Grace Wells, lived in the mission residence next door and faced the same dilemma. As the remaining missionaries in our station met, prayed, and discussed all options, they decided that the Halls would leave with their children, and Aunt Grace and another single missionary colleague would remain a brief time and see what developed while they oversaw the work. The Foreign Mission Board strongly advised that all missionaries with children leave the country quickly.

Across the Yangtze River, fellow missionaries in Yangzhou were facing the same dilemma. Two missionary nurses from our Yangzhou Baptist hospital decided to evacuate with us. Nurse Thelma Williams, along with the rest of her personal luggage, brought a heavy footlocker loaded with everything she could possibly cram into it. All of us had first class tickets to depart Zhenjiang for Shanghai. (Believe me, you didn't want to ride a second or third class train in China in the 1940s.) The train usually took about four hours to make the trip, and all the missionaries figured this would be a doable thing. I was not quite eleven years old that November, and the day started early, seeming like quite a nifty adventure to a child. We were fleeing from danger and didn't know what would happen next. This sounded a lot more fun to an eleven-year-old than it did to her parents. Our train was scheduled to leave at 8:15 a.m. All of us settled in our passenger coach — a pretty tight fit, considering all the luggage everyone had brought. After all, this was all they had left from a houseful of furniture and family mementos. However, Thelma Williams had brought more than the rest of us, and it fell my lot as youngest of the group to ride all the way to Shanghai with my feet propped on *top* of her footlocker. The other luggage was stored in overhead racks, but there was no way to place a cumbersome footlocker up there. I was glaring balefully at that pesky trunk long ere we reached Shanghai.

And that was the next chapter of the adventure. 8:15 came — and went — as did 9:15 and 10. Finally at 10:15, an apologetic stationmaster came and asked us politely to get off — the Nationalist military had requisitioned the entire train for their troops. So, we were put on a third class train and told it would depart soon. The seats were solid wood — straight up and down — and the odor is best not described. By noon, the train was full — but not moving. Train after train from Nanking, to the north, came slowly through, but were so crowded that people were literally clambering up on top to get a spot to hold on — anything to get away from the advancing enemy. Aunt Grace brought lunch to the station, and it still seemed a bit like an adventure — but, by late afternoon, there was no fun left in it. There was, instead, a growing sense of fear. By nightfall, we still sat there, and several actually squeezed onto the train and climbed up in the luggage racks to escape. Finally (at midnight), the train pulled out of the station, and a nightmare of a night — eight hours of it — finally saw us in Shanghai and a step closer to safety.

I never saw that bulky old footlocker again, but many years later I learned what had ridden to safety under my feet that long-ago November night. In the 1980s, I first visited national WMU headquarters in Birmingham and was immediately captivated by the beautiful artifacts hanging on the walls, priceless Chinese mandarin official collars and robes that had belonged to China's elite. Most fascinating of all was the matchless antique tapestry hanging in the lobby, right next to the elevators. It was the most priceless artifact in the building. Surely there was a story behind these treasures. Loving history — and especially loving Chinese history — I began asking the librarian and archivist for some background information. The story was that a missionary from China named Thelma Williams had donated these treasures to WMU. Thelma Williams?! This rang a bell. I asked for information about her and learned that she was in an assisted living facility in Colorado. By getting in touch with a niece, I was able to obtain Miss Williams' phone number. She and I had a wonderful long-distance visit and a great time of remembering God's mercy and grace.

Miss Williams happily told me the story of the tapestry. Sure enough, she had taken her salary immediately upon receiving it, and, after purchasing necessities, had invested in treasures in order to preserve them. Guess how they got out of China? In a footlocker, as she evacuated from the Yangzhou hospital. The priceless tapestry of the eight immortals was a favorite of Miss Williams. She could have sold those artifacts at great profit. Instead, she wanted to pass her heirlooms on and see them preserved. I continue to love visiting national WMU and stopping right in front of the tapestry to reflect on God's protection and blessings. Our headquarters is full of treasures that have been shared by so many saints who have invested their lives in sharing the good news and want their legacies to pass on to the next generation. This is a call to each of us, in our own unique way, to give the gift of precious memories to those who follow.

[Note: Yangzhou, Thelma Williams' city, is one of the oldest and most historic cities in China. Yangzhou held many ancient Chinese treasures and pieces of art, and this likely made it easy for Thelma to locate such items. Yangzhou is the city of Marco Polo, who was governor there several years in the 1260s. Part of the ancient wall remains. This was my first home in China, and my brother, Arthur, was born there at Yangzhou Baptist Hospital. In fact, my mother and father actually met each other there on the compound of the hospital in 1932. It was the second Baptist hospital founded on any of our mission fields. The first was in Hwangshien (now called Lungkou) in Shantung Province (Lottie Moon territory). It was founded in 1902, and, later the same year, the Yangzhou hospital was built. One of the earliest doctors there was Dr. Richard Field, the grandfather of NAMB missionary Taylor Field, who founded Graffiti Ministries in New York City!]

Written in My Mother's Bible

On the flyleaf:

1) Life's greatest quest: to seek the will of God
2) Life's greatest discovery: to find the will of God
3) Life's greatest achievement: to Do the will of God

Also on the flyleaf:

Practice the Presence of the Lord

Poems found in my father's papers:

I live For those who love me
For those who know I'm true
For the future in the distance
For the wrong that needs resistance
For the right that needs assistance
For the good that I can do

— Harold Hall 1924

We stand before the swinging gate
the opening door
Let us not sigh and wish for more,
But reach that goal beyond the door
And in the coming days and years
Let us overcome our fears
By looking back over the past
And prioritizing by those
lots already cast.

— Harold Hall 1924

Alice, 11

Jody, 8

SEVEN DAYS
WITH
TWO
MKs

(missionary kids)

Hi! We're the Hunts.

We've lived in Taiwan (the Republic of China) for eight years. Come visit with us.

Sunday morning:

We have both Chinese and English services at our church. Our dad, Bob Hunt, preaches. Our mother, Rosalie Hunt, plays the organ and directs the English Junior Choir.

Sunday afternoon:
Our Chinese friends enjoy playing on the church playground. They come from Muslim and Buddhist homes but we keep inviting them to Sunday School. They can't speak English so we "play" in Chinese.

8

DISCOVERY

349

Monday morning:
Time for school. The bus picks us up at 8. We go to an American school and study all the subjects you do, plus Bible and Chinese.

Monday afternoon:
Time to practice the piano. We both take piano lessons. Alice plays for Sunday School. Mother is our teacher.

Tuesday afternoon:
It's fun to play with Nixina (honey-colored) and Maylee. (Maylee means beautiful, and she is—right after a bath!)

Wednesday evening:
After school we play basketball in the backyard. Tim Spurgeon, (the teen-age MK next door) helps Jody with his gas-powered airplane. (The building is our Baptist Student Center.)

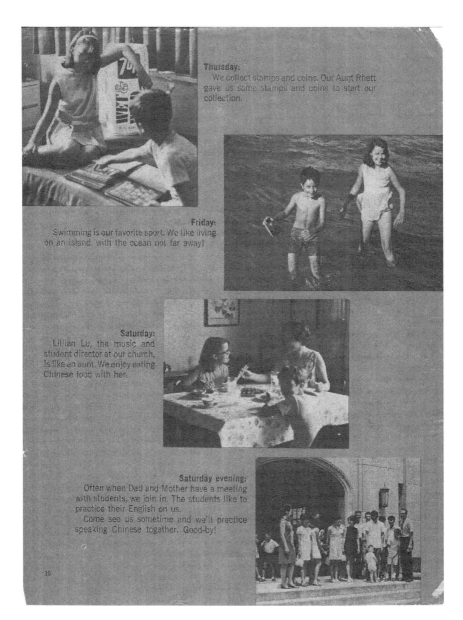

Thursday:
We collect stamps and coins. Our Aunt Rhett gave us some stamps and coins to start our collection.

Friday:
Swimming is our favorite sport. We like living on an island, with the ocean not far away!

Saturday:
Lillian Lu, the music and student director at our church, is like an aunt. We enjoy eating Chinese food with her.

Saturday evening:
Often when Dad and Mother have a meeting with students, we join in. The students like to practice their English on us.
Come see us sometime and we'll practice speaking Chinese together. Good-by!

10